GORE VIDAL'S AMERICA

GORE VIDAL'S AMERICA

DENNIS ALTMAN

polity

The right of Dennis Altman to be identified as Author of this Work has been asserted in accordance with the UK Copyright, Designs and Patents Act 1988.

First published in 2005 by Polity Press

Polity Press
65 Bridge Street
Cambridge CB2 1UR, UK

Polity Press
350 Main Street
Malden, MA 02148, USA

ISBN: 0-7456-3362-5
ISBN: 0-7456-3363-3 (pb)

A catalogue record for this book is available from the British Library.

Typeset in 11 on 13 pt Palatino
by SNP Best-set Typesetter Ltd., Hong Kong
Printed and bound in the United States by the Maple-Vail Book Manufacturing Group

For further information on Polity, visit our website: www.polity.co.uk

CONTENTS

Contents

PREFACE: THE WRITER AS SOCIAL CRITIC

"Writers," said the American novelist Kurt Vonnegut, are "evolutionary cells . . . a means of introducing new ideas into the society, and also a means of responding symbolically to life."[1] As Vonnegut reminds us, novelists, poets, and playwrights foreshadow and imagine political and social trends that may not yet be evident to journalists and researchers. While the current generation of students and activists knows Gore Vidal primarily for his acerbic criticisms of the Bush Administration and its foreign policy, his writings, now stretching back almost 60 years, provide an extraordinary introduction to how we might imagine the United States. Like others outside the mainstream of American politics, Vidal writes as an aggrieved patriot, one who is saddened and angry at the direction his country has moved in over the last half-century. Indeed, his analysis of these shifts has influenced much of the discourse of the left. He sees the United States as caught up in "bloody fantasies . . ." (*Imperial America*: 16), growing out of 60 years of imperial expansion and the destruction of any meaningful choice or genuine information in an electoral process which is increasingly irrelevant to most Americans.

Speaking of his use of the term "the United States of Amnesia," Vidal has said: "We have always had kind of an urgent, hot present – which also means a hopeful future . . . why think of the future if our present looks so good?"[2] Or, indeed, of the past. Vidal's constant preoccupation has been to excavate the past to explain the present and forewarn us of the perils of the future, and to do so by reaching the largest possible audience. His quite calculated creation of himself as a celebrity – author, television pundit, Presidential confidant, movie actor – has given him a significant audience for half a century. Vidal's growing bitterness and resort to what seem extreme political positions may reflect the reality that most Americans appear to have taken little note of his warnings and exhortations.

Many of the celebrities we encounter in popular magazines and television programs are celebrities for no apparent reason, and leave no trace: who now remembers the winner of last year's reality television show who was, for an instant, "a household name"? Those who have achieved celebrity through creating new ways of seeing the world remain influential through their works, and their importance may well outlive their celebrity. Vidal's lasting importance is likely to be as a novelist who mastered several apparently different genres in order to construct a particular vision of the United States, its history and its possible trajectory. It is almost impossible to judge how fiction influences larger social developments. Yet it is likely that across the world hundreds of thousands of people have had their views of American history, politics, sex, and religion challenged or reaffirmed by reading Vidal. Novels as different as *Julian*, *Lincoln* and *Myra Breckinridge* have all shaped popular consciousness and helped develop alternatives to the dominant understandings of American society.

What distinguishes the novels of a writer such as Vidal from the thrillers, romances and fantasies that dominate the best-seller lists is that he challenges, rather than reinforces, what is "taken for granted." His analysis of American history, politics, and imperialism has been taken up by a number of critics in the past decade, and is a clear influence on works such as Michael Moore's film *Fahrenheit 9/11*. He uses both an imagined past, whether pre-Christian Rome or nineteenth-century America, and an imagined alternative present, whether it be Duluth resited on the Mexican border or the Crucifixion imagined as a television spectacular, to illuminate the present and allow him to engage in philosophical and political speculation. Equally, the sexual politics of the past 40 years, especially the emergence of a self-conscious gay literature and queer theory, bears the imprint of Vidal's works. It is not uncommon to meet homosexuals who claim that reading *The City and the Pillar* was important in their coming out, and in 2004 the Queer Collective at Melbourne University told me they still found inspiration in *Myra Breckinridge*.

The novel is dead, Vidal is fond of telling us, meaning that the novelist no longer exercises the sort of cultural power (s)he did in the days before electronic media became dominant. To some extent Vidal represents the last of a generation of writers who aspired to achieve both popular celebrity and critical acclaim, to entertain, yes, but also to instruct and remake their society. In addition to its literary merits, and they are considerable, his writings help explain the apparent contradictions of the contemporary United States. Much of this book provides a background to the social and political events of the past half-century, to allow us, as it were, to engage in an informed reading of Gore Vidal's vision of these events. It is a book about the United States as much as it is a book about one author and his work.

ACKNOWLEDGMENTS

This is always the most enjoyable part of writing a book. Thanks go, first, to Anthony Elliott for proposing the idea, to John Thompson and Andrea Drugan at Polity for pushing ahead with it, and to Marianne Rutter, David Watson and Caroline Richmond for their assistance in the final stages. Jay Parini, himself an expert on and friend of Gore's, was an enthusiastic supporter and helped in a number of ways, as did a number of friends and colleagues in Australia and the United States: Suzi Adams; Premier Bob Carr; Nikolai Endres; Eva Fisch; Dorothy Friendly; Stephen Harris; Thomas Keneally; the Langer family; Michael O'Keefe; Chris Palmer; Peter Rose; Catherine Stimpson and Clara Tuite. Special thanks go to Edmund White for sending me the manuscript of his unpublished play *Terre Haute*, to Gary Conklin for a copy of his film *The Man Who Said No*, and to Tom Seddon for a close reading of the full manuscript. I am grateful for support from the staff and residents of the Rockefeller Foundation Study and Conference Center, Bellagio, during my time there October/November 2004, especially to Daron Aric Hagen and Gilda Lyons. As usual my partner, Anthony Smith, lived through many drafts of the book, and was always willing to discuss my latest enthusiasms. Above all my thanks to Gore Vidal, who both inspired and made possible this book.

INTRODUCTION

In 1994, in the course of a summit of heads of government of the major industrialized nations hosted by Italy, the then first lady Hillary Clinton paid a visit to Gore Vidal at his clifftop house in Ravello. The house, originally built in the 1920s by an English expatriate, overlooks the Bay of Amalfi south of Naples, a coastline familiar to contemporary audiences from the film *The Talented Mr Ripley*. In visiting Vidal Ms Clinton followed many other famous visitors, although her visit was more public and scripted than most. The visit symbolized the importance of Vidal as both a writer and a political figure, and received considerable press coverage, though more of it in the European than the American press.

Vidal's long fascination with the White House would have made him acutely aware that Hillary was far more politically involved than all but a few previous first ladies. Hillary saw Eleanor Roosevelt, the most independent of all first ladies, as something of a role model – in her memoirs she recounts imaginary conversations with her – and Eleanor had also been a mentor for Vidal, helping him in his 1960 run for the House of Representatives from the district on the Hudson River where she lived. Hillary also developed a perhaps surprisingly warm relationship with Jackie Kennedy, with whom Gore shared a stepfather and through whom he had a brief period of friendship with the President. In his novel *The Smithsonian Institution* a number of America's "first ladies" play a central role in what is both a historical fantasy and a personal revelation, and in *Lincoln* he provides a surprisingly warm portrayal of a Presidential wife more often portrayed as a mad harridan.

1

Difficult as it is to assess a writer who still lives, Gore Vidal may well be the most significant American writer of the second half of the twentieth century. Not, necessarily, the best, in literary or aesthetic terms: it is not only politics which awarded the Nobel Prize to Saul Bellow and Toni Morrison. But if one is looking for a writer who has consistently straddled serious writing and political commentary Vidal's only real rival is Norman Mailer, and indeed one could write much of the intellectual history of the post-World War II United States as the constant joust between the two for recognition. Well into writing this book I discovered that a book has already been written which argues that Mailer "more than any other writer of his generation" has made America his subject.[1] As the author of this claim nowhere discusses Vidal, it is impossible to know how he would compare the two.

Vidal's writings taken as a whole touch on almost all the crucial social, cultural, and political changes which have affected the United States over the past 50 years, and he has been remarkably prescient about a number of these changes. Of course his is a partial and partisan view, and one with some major omissions, most strikingly in his treatment of racial conflict. One might want more about, say, sports and music, to name two areas where he has very little to offer. But he straddles many worlds – he has spent much of his life in Washington, New York, and Hollywood, the three centers of American power. In this he resembles the publisher William Randolph Hearst, who is a central character in Vidal's American Chronicles, or, perhaps, the actor/director Orson Welles. "My subject," Vidal has said, "is America," and except for his two "ancient" historical novels, *Julian* and *Creation*, and an early romance about Richard the Lionheart, *A Search for the King*, so it is. In his discussions of politics, American imperialism, gender, and sexuality Vidal prefigured major critiques that in time would become central to national, indeed global, debates.

Like other writers with long and varied careers Vidal is known by different audiences for different works. His first major bestseller, *Julian*, was, after all, his eighth novel (indeed his thirteenth, if one includes those he wrote in the early 1950s under various *noms de plume*), although he had been thinking of him as a subject for at least a decade. His is an extraordinary long career: his first novel was published the same year as the appearance of three staples of American literature: Carson McCullers' *The Member of the Wedding*, Eugene O'Neill's *The Iceman Cometh*, and Robert Penn Warren's *All the King's Men*, while that year's Oscar was awarded to the post-war film classic *The Best Years of Our Lives*. Few people remember Vidal as a dramatist, yet one of his plays, *Visit to a Small Planet*, was a Broadway hit, and probably inspired the television series *My Favorite Martian*.

The United States preoccupies us all, both Americans and non-Americans, for whom America, both real and imagined, looms as a central presence in our lives. Millions of non-Americans make sense of the world from the images of American film and television; one of the early books of the Argentinian novelist Manuel Puig was called *Betrayed by Rita Hayworth* (1968), and is testament to the influence of Hollywood on kids growing up in Latin America in the 1930s. (Puig is better known in the English-speaking world for his novel *Kiss of the Spider Woman*, which was transformed into a musical and film.) In a recent theater work, *Alladeen*, based on international call centers in Bangalore, the operators take their names from the characters in the television series *Friends*.[2] The majority of the world's celebrities are American movie stars, whose images become talismans even in countries where the United States government is hated.

"Love it or loathe it, you can never leave it or lose it," wrote Vidal in the memorable first sentence of *Duluth*, and it is clear he is writing about the country itself, and his own attachment to it. (Vidal fills Duluth, in reality a medium-sized city on the frozen tip of Lake Superior, with palm trees and illegal immigrants from across the Mexican border.) To read Vidal's full set of American historical novels is to be swept up in a coherent narrative which seems modelled in part on Gibbon's *Decline and Fall of the Roman Empire*, and brings to life the powerplays of Washington, not least through his fascination with the changing face of the city itself.

We constantly reinvent what it means to be American, and here Vidal's work is particularly useful in its combination of the rewriting of the American past (in his seven historical novels from *Burr* to *The Golden Age*) and his "post-modern" fantasies of American life, such as *Myra Breckinridge*, *Myron*, and *Duluth*. His 1998 novel *The Smithsonian Institution* crosses genres to create a counter-factual history of America, indeed of Vidal's own life, in the 1940s. Yet in recreating America he can never go further than Americans themselves: Vidal allegedly refused to consider Ronald Reagan for the role of the President in his 1959 play *The Best Man* because "he would hardly be convincing."[3]

Gore Vidal's first novel, *Williwaw*, was published in 1946 and won respectable reviews as one of the more important immediate post-war novels. Over half a century later his attacks on the Bush Administration's war in Iraq were selling well in independent bookshops across the States, thus making for a writing career which has few counterparts in sheer length and diversity. At the same time Vidal's has been a career that has been part of the creation of the writer as celebrity, through television, magazine covers, and membership of the international jet set, helped enormously by his family connection to Jackie Kennedy. As the British journalists Fawcett and Thomas wrote: "It is a safe bet that many more people know Gore Vidal, Truman Capote and Norman Mailer as television showoffs than have ever read their books. All three at their (unfortunately spasmodic) best are in the first rank of contemporary American writing."[4] A kinder assessment comes from the prolific novelist James Michener (*Hawaii*, *Tales of the South Pacific*, etc.), who in his memoirs praised Vidal as both historical novelist and "an important participant in national debates, and a refreshing one."[5] This is interesting praise, given Michener's relentlessly optimistic view of American history as against Vidal's pessimism.[6]

It is true that despite his extraordinary productivity he has won fewer prizes and accolades than might be expected. It is also true that according to the lists provided by *Publisher's Weekly* four of his novels (*Myra Breckinridge*, *Burr*, *1876*, *Lincoln*) were among the ten best-sellers in their years of publication, while others (*The City and the Pillar*, *Julian*) plus several volumes of his collected essays also sold extremely well. As literary critics are deeply suspicious of popular success, he has received far less attention from students of mainstream American literature than he deserves, a matter on which he has himself commented, usually with fairly cutting remarks about the self-absorption of the "lit. crit. industry," and its preoccupation with academic novels.

After 20 years of writing in a remarkable range of genres – romantic and historical novels; television and movie scripts; several successful plays; even three detective stories under the *nom de plume* Edgar Box – Vidal developed a seriousness in his writing which expressed itself through two particular genres, the historical and the satirical. At various points of his life Vidal felt torn between a political and a writing career; more than two decades after his campaign for a New York Congressional seat he ran for the Democrat Senatorial nomination in California, polling 15 percent of the primary vote. As a precocious school student before World War II, Gore Vidal opposed President Roosevelt's pro-British policies. In the early 2000s, after living through the administrations of eleven other Presidents, he was one of the most prominent opponents of George W. Bush's interventions in Afghanistan and Iraq.

By the end of the century Vidal's politics placed him too far to the left of the mainstream for electoral office to be even a fantasy. As the Bush Administration reacted to the assaults of September 11 with two wars and a new doctrine of pre-emptive attack, Vidal articulated a fury with President Bush that grew out of his deep study of American history, and his hatred of the imperial mission. As a young man, Christopher Isherwood tells us, Gore welcomed a fist fight.[7] In later life he certainly welcomed an intellectual one.

——— one ———

VIDAL'S LIFE

Luckily there is no need here to do more than sketch briefly Vidal's life: it has been dealt with exhaustively in a biography by Fred Kaplan, which was written over a period of years during the 1990s, and reflects, perhaps at times too much, Vidal's own perception of his life. Kaplan, an already well-established biographer, tells us on the first page that he prefers his subjects dead, and his book is based on several years' close contact with Vidal, not without some acrimony. Before Kaplan's book was published some of the material was addressed in a less disciplined way by Gore himself in his memoirs, *Palimpsest*, which essentially end with the Kennedy years. The very title of that book – a palimpsest is a paper or parchment that has been written upon more than once – is suggestive: "This is pretty much what my kind of writer does anyway. Starts with life; makes a text; then a *re*-vision – literally, a second seeing, an afterthought, erasing some but not all of the original while writing something new over the first layer of text" (*Palimpsest*: 6). By the end of the book, Vidal muses, he has written "for the first and last time, not the ghost story that I feared but a love story, as circular in shape as desire and its pursuit . . ." (419).

Vidal was born in 1925, a year after the birth of Presidents Carter and Bush Sr. The President at the time was Calvin Coolidge, a man best known for his inaction in office; in Europe Stalin was creating his power base, while a still largely unknown Hitler published *Mein Kampf*, the manifesto which set out the ideology and aims of the Nazi Party. Gore's father was the first aviation instructor at the United States military academy West

Point,* and descended from the Romansch-speakers of the Swiss and Italian Alps, of whom Gore has written in his coffee-table book *Vidal in Venice*. A more significant influence on Gore was through his mother, the daughter of Senator Thomas Pryor Gore, an anti-New Deal Democrat from Oklahoma who lived most of the time in Washington. (Gore reminisces about going barefoot to collect his grandfather from the floor of the Senate.) The Gores had been present in the United States since the end of the seventeenth century, which allows Vidal to claim a particular familial stake in American history. His parents divorced when Gore was ten, and his father went on to become Director of the Bureau for Air Commerce under President Franklin Roosevelt. This connection with early aviation is reflected in the character of Teddy, the female aviator, in *Kalki*, in part modelled on his father's close friend the flyer Amelia Earhart.

"For Gore," writes Kaplan, "childhood was imprisonment, victimization" (1999: 31). These terms refer directly to his mother, Nina Gore, who was by all accounts difficult and alcoholic. She remarried twice, and one of her husbands, Hugh Auchincloss, would later become the stepfather of Jackie Bouvier, later Jackie Kennedy Onassis. Jackie, who was four years younger than Gore, inherited what had been Gore's bedroom in the Auchincloss estate, Merrywood, outside Washington. (Nina and Auchincloss had two children of their own.) But Gore admired his father and particularly his maternal grandfather, whose influence remained through his life. Gore took his grandfather's name for his own, though he had been christened Eugene Luther Vidal. Much of his knowledge of politics, history, and mythology came from reading aloud to his grandfather, who was blinded as a boy.

---

*West Point has produced the leaders of the US military for well over a century. In 1973 Vidal wrote about its role, stressing that his father "was a sort of icon" for the generation of commanders, including Eisenhower, who "created the American world empire [and] gave us the peacetime draft, a garrison state and the current military debacle in Southeast Asia" ("West Point," *United States*: 1,081, originally published in the *New York Review of Books* 1973).

There are echoes of his mother and grandfather in much of his fiction, above all in the semi-autobiographical *Season of Comfort*, where the character, who might be Gore, reflects that "he loved his mother the most, of course, but he liked being with his father more" (*Season of Comfort*: 84). Perhaps not surprisingly the book is dedicated to his father. In writing the novel, Gore confided to Anaïs Nin, his bitterness towards his mother was "almost gone" (Kaplan 1999: 236), but in fact their relationship did not improve, and after a painful visit she made to him and his partner Howard Austen in London for Christmas in 1957, Gore refused to see her again. Nina Olds, as she then was, died in 1978, without being reconciled with her elder son.

Despite a somewhat troubled home life, Gore's schooling, most particularly his final three years at Phillips Exeter Academy in New Hampshire, and his family connections gave him entry to Washington society, and linked him to "ruling-class" families. Before going to Phillips Exeter, he spent several years at St Albans in Washington, where he fell in love with a fellow student, Jimmie Trimble (JT), who was to die in World War II, and who is memorialized in increasingly overt ways in much of Vidal's writings. In both *Palimpsest* and *The Smithsonian Institution*, written in Gore's seventies, the loss of Jimmie, already foreshadowed in his early post-World War II novels, becomes the central theme: "T," the protagonist of *The Smithsonian Institution*, speaks of his best friend, whose "father had something to do with aviation. T often thought about this when the two were belly rubbing and talking of girls" (*The Smithsonian Institution*: 37).

His mother's tempestuous life meant he moved schools rather frequently – including a period at the Los Alamos Ranch School in New Mexico, which was to become the site for the development of the atomic bomb – and his entry to Exeter was facilitated by his Auchincloss stepfather. The Academy was one of the richest and most prestigious private secondary schools in the country, with as clear a mandate to prepare the sons of the ruling class as its counterparts in Britain. (It was founded in 1783, five years after the even more prestigious Phillips Academy at Andover, founded by Phillips' nephew.) At school Gore excelled

at debating and writing – though not at most branches of ortho-
dox schoolwork. Other alumni of the school include members of
the du Pont, Heinz, and Rockefeller families, as well as Arthur
Schlesinger Jr and writers Peter Benchley, John Irving, and John
Knowles, who drew on Vidal for a character in his novel *A Separate Peace*. At Exeter Vidal began seriously to write and debate,
thus setting the contours for the rest of his life.

Despite Vidal's scepticism about the war he accepted that once
one's country was attacked war was inevitable. He entered the
army immediately after graduation, and never went to college,
though one might note that he chose not to go to Harvard, rather
than, say, Oklahoma A & M. On enlisting he was too young for
active service, and he was sent on an intensive training course
in engineering, which gave him an interest in physics to which
he would return, 50 years later, in *The Smithsonian Institution*. As
a "maritime technical specialist" in the army he was posted in
Alaska, and wrote his first novel, *Williwaw*, while serving as first
mate on a freight-supply ship in the Aleutian Islands. The book
relates a possible murder aboard a similar ship in a similar place,
and takes its title from the local word for a strong wind that
sweeps down suddenly from the mountains to the sea. Its publication earned Vidal a place in a cover story in *Life* magazine
hailing a refreshing group of literary newcomers; that Truman
Capote's was the face on the cover marked the beginning of a
bitter rivalry.

Williwaw was published in 1946 by the long-established New
York firm of E. P. Dutton, and after being discharged Vidal
worked briefly in their offices as an editor. It was there he met
the young black writer James Baldwin, an early version of whose
novel *Go Tell it on the Mountain* he sought to publish. When the
book was finally published in 1953 it established Baldwin as one
of the most significant writers of his generation, though he and
Gore were never close.

Before he turned 30, Vidal produced eight novels, plus five
more under *noms de plume*, of which three were the Edgar Box
detective stories. For books he claimed to dash off in a couple of
weeks they remain surprisingly readable, if not as tightly plotted
as one might wish. His early works explore a range of genres

and styles, and only a couple remain of interest, most obviously *The City and the Pillar*, which scandalized the literary world because of its homosexual themes. The *New York Times* refused advertising for the book, and remained unsympathetic to Vidal for some time after, although his claim that they refused to review his next five novels is inaccurate. *The Judgment of Paris* reveals Vidal's satiric gifts (the characters include an eccentric English peer and a writer of detective stories based, one assumes, on Agatha Christie), and *Messiah* is the first of a number of books dealing with religion, and the peculiar American desire to believe in even the most improbable of spiritual claims.

In 1947 Vidal bought a house in the old city of Antigua in Guatemala, and lived there on and off between 1947 and 1949. In retrospect this seems an odd move, in part dictated by the cheapness of living in Central America, in part, one assumes, by a romantic notion of how a writer should live, modelled, perhaps, on Ernest Hemingway. (In *Palimpsest* he points out that living in Europe was not seen as an option in the immediate post-war years.) In the semi-feudal society of Guatemala, a country where wealth was heavily concentrated and the United Fruit Company a major influence, Vidal entered the social elite, which included the future wife of the composer and conductor Leonard Bernstein. Here he wrote prolifically, but the beauty of Antigua was insufficient compensation for the social, sexual, and intellectual attractions of Manhattan. At this time, too, he had a very close relationship with the writer Anaïs Nin, mainly known for her remarkably solipsistic diaries, who was the first of a number of famous women with whom Vidal enjoyed close and flirtatious relationships. Nin was 20 years older than Gore, and already famous for her erotic writings, and her liaisons with writers like Henry Miller and Edmund Wilson. Vidal would savagely caricature Nin in his novel *Two Sisters*, in part in revenge for her assessment of him, particularly her dislike of *The City and the Pillar*, which she described as "ugly" in her *Journals 1944–7*.

While living in Guatemala, Vidal spent some time in Europe, touring Italy with the writer Tennessee Williams, living briefly in Paris, and visiting London, Egypt, and Tangier as a guest of the composer/writer Paul Bowles. Tangier was then under international control, before its return to the newly independent Morocco in 1956, and a regular stopover for the jet set.[1] The time in Europe introduced Gore to a number of people who would be significant in his life, including Christopher Isherwood and his British publisher, John Lehmann. He also met André Gide, E. M. Forster and Princess Margaret's confidante, Judy Montagu, through whom he became a friend of the Princess. Isherwood, almost 20 years older, was already established as a famous writer, largely on the basis of his *Berlin Stories* from the last days of the Weimar Republic in Germany, which would become in turn the basis of the play *I Am a Camera* and the musical and then film *Cabaret*, by which point the narrator of the stories is almost unrecognizable as Isherwood himself. Isherwood had left Britain at the outbreak of war and was to settle in Los Angeles, where he and Vidal would become friends. But despite the glamour of Europe, Vidal was not yet ready to settle outside the United States. He returned home for the publication of *The Season of Comfort*, and lived in and around New York City. In 1950 he met Howard Auster, who would become his lifelong companion. On Gore's suggestion Howard changed his name to Austen to avoid anti-Semitism in the advertising industry.

One of Vidal's characteristics has been a willingness to put into print material that others would rework, although each of his early novels is interesting for the ways in which they foreshadow themes he would return to in later life. When the critic John Aldridge addressed Vidal's work with a chapter in his 1951 book on then contemporary American writing he concluded that: "His writing after *Williwaw* is one long record of stylistic breakdown and spiritual exhaustion. It is confused and fragmentary, pulled in every direction by the shifting winds of impressionism. It is always reacting, always feeling and seeing; but it never signifies because it never believes."[2] Aldridge writes from a deep moral conservatism that grates, but it is also true that little in these first novels foreshadowed the achievements of the somewhat older novelist who would emerge in the 1960s.

While *The City and the Pillar* was a commercial success, novel writing by itself was not sufficient to pay for the sort of lifestyle that Vidal wanted. Despite his family connections he has earned his wealth, and for the first 15 years or so of his writing life money was a constant concern. During the 1950s he turned to the new medium of television, and wrote more than 50 plays, which were produced live, and in turn led him to both Broadway and Hollywood. The biographer of another writer who worked in television drama at the time, Sumner Locke Elliott, lists Vidal as part of a "golden era" of scriptwriting,[3] although of the writers listed only Vidal and Elliott himself were able to establish themselves as novelists.* Television dramas were widely watched through the 1950s: "There they are," wrote Vidal, "your own creations, fleshed out by living people, the symbolic detail isolated by the camera as millions of strangers in their homes watch one's private vision made public" ("Foreword," *Visit to a Small Planet and Other Television Plays*: xiv). Hosting the *General Electric Theater*, from 1954 to 1961, allowed Ronald Reagan to segue from an acting to a political career.

Vidal's favorite teleplay was *The Death of Billy the Kid*, starring Paul Newman in one of his first major roles. It was subsequently filmed as *The Left Handed Gun*. In 1956 Vidal edited an anthology of *Best Television Plays* (New York, Ballantine), in which he included plays by seven other writers, including Paddy Chayefsky and Rod Serling, along with his own *Visit to a Small Planet*.

In 1955 Vidal flew to California to work on his first film, *The Catered Affair*, starring Bette Davis and Debbie Reynolds. Other films which he would help write in the next few years included *Ben-Hur*, and an adaptation of Tennessee Williams' *Suddenly, Last Summer*, in both of which his views on sexuality came up against the limits of what was thought possible to depict on the screen in the 1950s.

Through this period Vidal was moving between Los Angeles and Edgewater, his home on the Hudson, up the river from New York City, where he mixed in both intellectual and "social" circles. His political interests reasserted themselves through contact with John Kennedy, then planning his Presidential race,

---

*Sumner Locke Elliott (1917–91) was an Australian author who lived much of his life in New York, although his best novels, such as *Careful, He Might Hear You*, are based on memories of his Australian childhood.

and Eleanor Roosevelt, and are reflected both in his writing and a concrete desire to become, himself, an elected official. Vidal attended the 1960 Democratic Convention in Los Angeles as a Kennedy delegate, while Eleanor still hoped the nomination would go to former Illinois Governor Adlai Stevenson, who had lost in both 1952 and 1956 to Eisenhower. As Vidal worked on the play *The Best Man*, which revolves around the battle for a Presidential nomination, he mused on the possibility of running for the House of Representatives from the district in upstate New York where he lived.

In 1960, the year Kennedy ran for and won the Presidency, *The Best Man* premiered on Broadway and Vidal ran for the 29th Congressional district in New York. While he lost – though polling better in the district for the Democrats than did Kennedy against Nixon – the play lasted on Broadway for a year and a half. *The Best Man* was filmed in 1964, and revived on Broadway in 2000 in the lead-up to that memorable election. Vidal could content himself with the knowledge that his depiction of American politics was alive long after only the most obsessive collector of political trivia could recall the name of the Congressman whose re-election he failed to prevent in 1960. It is a mark of the times that the press was as silent about the existence of Gore's male partner as they were about John Kennedy's sexual exploits. Forty years later one suspects neither candidacy would have survived a media frenzied to discover any deviation from standards of sexual propriety observed by few of them, and not many of their readers. Had Vidal wanted to run again in 1964, when the Democratic nomination was again available, the Johnson landslide would quite likely have carried him with it, thus giving him the political career he desired.

Television and movies made Vidal financially secure, and in time he would appear on both. But by the age of 40 he had decided that his ambition to write books was unabated, and thus began his huge output of historical novels, polemics, essays, and "inventions." During the 1960s he wrote three successful and very different novels – *Julian*, *Washington, D.C.*, and *Myra Breckinridge* – that together foreshadowed the themes and styles that he would develop for the next three decades. *Julian*, in particular, established him as both a popular and a literary author. Vidal's is the last generation who assumed that a knowledge of "ancient history" was part of the cultural capital of any educated person: someone a generation or two younger than Vidal, even well educated, is far less likely to be familiar with his references to Petronius or Suetonius. (The former wrote the *Satyricon*, the latter *Lives of the Caesars*. Vidal has been compared to both of them.) The success of *Julian* would introduce large numbers of American readers to the ancient world for the first time. His essays also started to make a mark on the larger public, especially after 1967 when he published "The Holy Family" in *Esquire*, a remarkable exploration of his disillusionment with the Kennedys.

Working on the epic *Ben-Hur* had brought Vidal back to Rome in 1958, and by the mid-1960s he and Howard had moved to Italy and established a pattern which would continue for the rest of their lives. They settled first in Rome, later buying the villa La Rondinaia in Ravello, where many of Vidal's books would be written. Howard died in late 2003, after 55 years together, and Gore left the villa at Ravello and moved back to his home in Los Angeles. Though he spent more than half the year in Italy for a period of some four decades, Vidal remained engaged with American politics, and was remarkably informed of current political and intellectual trends through extensive reading and a wide network of gossip. Martin Walker's comment that he "left the country in fastidious distaste"[4] is clever but misses the extent to which Vidal remained consistently immersed in the affairs of his home country.

Over the following 40 years Vidal maintained an extraordinary output of novels, essays, and public appearances, including the series of historical novels which make up "the American Chronicles." As he became more successful as a novelist, with books like *Burr*, *Creation*, and *Lincoln* winning both audiences and critical attention, his political views became darker and more critical of American leaders, and his attacks on American foreign and domestic policy became more caustic. When Tim Robbins cast him in the film *Bob Roberts* (1992) as a liberal Senator, challenged by an opportunistic rightwing folk singer, he provided Vidal with an opportunity to act out his view of the decline of the American political system.

There is an irony in the claim that a patrician, leftist, atheistic, pansexual (his term) writer best captures the contradictions of American society during its rise to unparalleled global pre-eminence. Vidal stands as the almost perfect counterpoint to John Wayne (1907–79), hero of a string of successful westerns, of whom Garry Wills wrote: "He embodied a politics; or his screen image did. It was a politics of large meanings, not of little policies – a politics of gender (masculine), ideology (patriotism), character (self-reliance), and responsibility."[5] The connection between American masculinity and support for a "tough" foreign policy (both Nixon and Reagan liked to invoke Wayne) continues into the present: in a commentary at the end of 2003 the journalist Tina Brown saw Arnold Schwarzenegger, the actor turned Governor of California, as drawing on the archetype of masculinity represented by Wayne, Charles Bronson, and Charlton Heston: "the fantasy figure who clearly represents the strict, punishing father people turn to in time of fear."[6] One might easily argue that George W. Bush is still seeking to inhabit the persona of the tough American man created by Wayne.

An actor can be seen to "embody" ideas more easily than can a writer, though Vidal has been a screen actor as well – on one well-known website devoted to such things he rates two degrees of separation from Kevin Bacon, the hub of this particular site. But Vidal's public persona represents an almost total repudiation of that of Wayne, who supported the election of Richard Nixon, the war in Vietnam (his film *The Green Berets* was a remarkably crude propaganda film for United States involvement in Indo-China), and articulated a particular anti-intellectual individualism that lives on in the rhetoric of the Republican Party.

This book seeks, as Wills did with the career of Wayne, to demonstrate how Vidal "embodies" a particular critique of American society and politics, and, as part of this, seeks to subvert both the triumphalist view of American history and mainstream assumptions of sex and gender. Studying a writer, especially one as prolific and long-lived as Vidal, has the huge advantage that one has a great deal of primary material to work with: we do not have to read Vidal's gestures or body language, as is true in studies of performers; instead we can read his words directly.

Vidal spent much of his life in Italy, yet he never renounced his fascination with America or his role as a gadfly and serious commentator on American politics and mores. Yet if Vidal sees himself as totally American, to Americans he epitomizes a European way of being, an expatriate who denounces the class privilege that he enjoys, and what is worse does so with an air of cynicism. That he has enjoyed considerable access to media coverage in the United States can be read as proof either of American liberalism or of Herbert Marcuse's notion of "repressive tolerance."* At the same time his residence for so long outside the US gives him a particular perspective to comment on American developments, a perspective sometimes more respected abroad. His writings have been translated into at least 35 languages, and his reputation tends to be higher in Europe than it is at home. Perhaps non-Americans see as realism what Americans tend to denounce as a cynical anti-Americanism.

---

*Herbert Marcuse was one of the Frankfurt School of German intellectuals who fled to the United States in the 1930s, and became best known in the 1960s for his analysis of the complex ways in which power is maintained in contemporary western societies, drawing on the theories of both Marx and Freud.

two

CELEBRITY

"a celebrity . . . that means somebody everybody knows"
Roxie in Chicago

"one of the laws of nature is that celebrities adore one another . . .
they are in fact, more impressed by the idea of celebrity than the
average indifferent citizen who never sees a movie star and seldom
bothers to see his Congressman . . ."
Vidal (as Edgar Box): Death before Bedtime: 77

"He is just famous, that's all. There are people like that in public life.
They are there, and no-one ever really knows why."
Lincoln on Edward Everett, Lincoln: 488

"Celebrity! All it means is that you can cash a small cheque in a small
town."
Truman Capote, quoted in Gerald Clarke: Capote, New York, Simon
and Schuster, 1988: 499

The writer as celebrity is not new: Vidal follows the tradition of
Mark Twain and Ernest Hemingway, both of whom also spent
much of their adult lives outside the United States. During the
nineteenth century Twain constantly lectured in public, both in
the United States and abroad, though more perhaps for money
than fame, and was widely recognized as an important literary
and national figure. Hemingway became famous for his image
as a tough guy as much as for his writings: in a widely reproduced advertisement for Ballantine's Ale, which appeared in
Life magazine, he was hailed as an "internationally famous . . .

deep-sea fisherman [and] the greatest living American writer."[1] Hemingway may well be the first author who was as famous for his persona as his writings, although one might argue that honor is Oscar Wilde's.

Nor is the novelist and playwright who makes a career in Hollywood unusual – a list of famous writers for the movies would include William Faulkner, Christopher Isherwood, and Aldous Huxley, none of whom particularly enjoyed the experience. (The same experience was true for many composers, such as Aaron Copland and Erich Korngold, who also turned to film to make money.) Gore Vidal is more exceptional in that he twice ran seriously for mainstream political office, something no other major American author has done. Part of Vidal's fame grew out of highly publicized feuds with other intellectual celebrities, especially Norman Mailer, Truman Capote, and William Buckley. Indeed their generation established a particular script for celebrity, which they have played out for 50 years. Capote died in 1984 and is now remembered as a minor literary figure, who built a major social career out of a series of fey gothic writings. Mailer and Buckley are still alive at the time of writing.

Of course not all writers hanker for celebrity; having published his hit novel *Catcher in the Rye* in 1951, J. D. Salinger became best known as a recluse who avoided media attention. But not uncommonly authors enjoy performance, and recognize it is necessary to attract readers. In 1993 Diane Johnson, herself a distinguished novelist, wrote: "[Vidal] more than most writers is the object of that peculiar form of celebrity desire that allows strangers to feel acquainted, involved, even entitled to their connection to the living man behind his books."[2] Her point is illustrated by the somewhat breathless way in which a leading travel guide to Italy named Vidal as Ravello's "reigning celebrity," following in the footsteps of Richard Wagner, Greta Garbo, and D. H. Lawrence.[3]

By most of the measures available Vidal has been a celebrity for over half a century. Not only has he appeared on television, but a number of television documentaries have been made about him. Not only has he published widely, but he has appeared on the cover of news magazines (both *Time* and *Newsweek*) and contributed to a range of glossy magazines: *Vanity Fair, Esquire, Vogue*. Not only has he written for films, he has become a film actor, whose name is seen as an added attraction in movies boasting more conventional film stars. He is an accomplished public speaker, often combining book promotion tours with political commentary, which took him not just to major cities and campuses but also, as he has remarked, to "conservative audiences in such civilized places as Medford, Oregon; Parkersburg, West Virginia; Longueville, Washington" (*Imperial America*: 5). There is a "Gore Vidal suite" in the plush Oriental Hotel in Bangkok, and in 2005 one could buy his image on a "great authors, great books" calendar, along with that of Dostoevsky, Graham Greene, and Susan Sontag. His name is almost a brand in itself, perhaps the ultimate mark of celebrity.

The word "celebrity" has been used in its contemporary sense since the first half of the nineteenth century, yet it took on a particular form with the development of electronic media, so that film, and then television, made well-known figures instantly recognizable across more and more of the world. Indeed movie stars may well have been the first genuine celebrities in the modern sense, and by the 1930s they were mixing in high society and political circles. Television hastened the process, so that when C. Wright Mills wrote his book *The Power Elite* in 1956, perhaps the single most influential work of post-war American sociology, he devoted a chapter to celebrities. Those he called "the Names that need no further identification"[4] were forged through nationwide means of mass communication, a formulation echoed a few years later by the historian Daniel Boorstin, who suggested that a celebrity is someone who is well known for being well known.[5] More recently, there has been something of a vogue amongst sociologists for discussing "celebrity" as a phenomenon of (post-)modern society.[6]

Through television, and its apparently endless thirst for talking heads, Vidal has become known to millions who have never read his books. "I never miss a chance," he is reported as saying, "to have sex or appear on television," and this may have become the credo of twentieth-century celebrity. In 1968 he quipped that: "My entire life is now devoted to appearing on television: a pleasant alternative to real life" (Kaplan 1999: 593), and he did his best to ensure this continued, proposing, for example, his appearance in six episodes of the popular series *Mary Hartman, Mary Hartman* (in 1976). (The producer of the series, Norman Lear, is a well-known liberal figure in the television industry.) Vidal's comment came in the wake of his clashes with William Buckley, an almost exact contemporary, and a much revered figure on the right.* Vidal's access to television helped establish him as an international celebrity, and British television has presented several laudatory documentaries on his life and work. His 1998 pamphlet *The American Presidency* is based on a three-part series commissioned by Britain's Channel 4, and was severely criticized when it was shown in the United States.

He and Mailer have been constructed as the twin avatars of late twentieth-century American writing, rather as Tennessee Williams and Arthur Miller were juxtaposed as playwrights. As personalities they are remarkably different, the patrician bisexual ironist against the passionate Jewish upholder of patriarchal values. Both of their writing careers began in World War II (Vidal's in Alaska, Mailer's in the Pacific) and straddle the McCarthyite 1950s through the revolutions of the late 1960s, the defeat of the United States in Vietnam, the forced resignation of Richard Nixon, and the gradual triumph of conservatism since. They come together in the flourishing of radicalism at the end of the 1960s and early 1970s; they both continued to write and in some ways to till similar fields, though Vidal's camp irony has no counterpart in Mailer, who is unfailingly serious about his mission as a great American writer. Mailer's writings to date include a long list of novels, plays, and essays, and a number of works that deliberately cross genres. From the publication of his

---

*Buckley founded and edited the influential conservative journal *National Review* and the nationally syndicated television show *Firing Line*, which ran for 33 years. He has published a range of both fiction and non-fiction, worked briefly for the CIA and – like Mailer – run for Mayor of New York City (in 1965). Many see him as the prime architect of the alliance of anti-Communism, support for capitalism, and "traditional" moral values that constitutes contemporary American conservatism.

first novel, *The Naked and the Dead*, in 1948 many, including Mailer himself, saw him as the man who would write "the great American novel."

As Gore mused in 1970: "It is strange how our careers seesaw . . . Whenever I am up, he is down, and the reverse. Currently he is very much up, for this is the age of writer as subject, and Norman is a most appealing subject" (*Two Sisters*: 152). Like Vidal, Mailer wrote a great deal about politics, movies (he too has appeared on screen, even directed a film), and religion, including a retelling of the Christian story, *The Gospel According to the Son*. This appeared in 1998, and is only slightly more modest than *Live from Golgotha: The Gospel According to Gore Vidal* (1992).

Different as some of their values are, they have both been committed activists on the left, even as both have displayed too much independence to have conventional political careers. Mailer ran for Mayor of New York City in 1969 against the liberal Republican John Lindsay, but less seriously than Vidal ran for Congress in 1960 or for the Democratic Senatorial nomination for California in 1982. Age has greatly reduced their feuding: by the 1980s they were willing to appear together in public,[7] and in 2002, as if to cement their role as the odd couple of American letters, they appeared together in a charity reading of *Don Juan in Hell* in Provincetown. This was a major step, given earlier libel suits and a couple of physical fights, one in the greenroom before a taping of *The Dick Cavett Show* in 1971, and one a few years later at a dinner party in New York. In 2003, when both were nearing eighty, they each published pamphlets attacking the war in Iraq.

Like Mailer's, Vidal's work is a half-century meditation on sex, religion, power, and above all the nature of the United States. Nowhere were the two writers further apart than in their views on sex and gender: Mailer, heir to Hemingway, as the defender of "traditional" irrational masculine power, Vidal with his double assault on male and heterosexual privilege. Through his book *The Prisoner of Sex* and his public appearances, most famously at the New York Town Hall with a number of feminists including Germaine Greer in 1971, Mailer created himself as a spokesman for unreconstructed masculinist opposition to women's liberation. Fear, obsession with, and dislike of homosexuality runs through much of Mailer's writing, and stands in stark contrast to Vidal's liberationist view of sexuality. In 1961, reviewing a play by Genet, Mailer had written: "As a civilization dies, it loses its biology. The homosexual, alienated from the biological chain, becomes its center. The core of the city is inhabited by a ghost who senses in the unwinding of his nerves that the only road back to biology is to destroy Being in others."[8]

This sort of metaphysical twaddle suggests Vidal's feuds with Mailer, often depicted as the struggle between two overwhelming egos for supremacy, were also based in very deep differences. Mailer was deeply offended when Vidal's response to *The Prisoner of Sex* was to write an article entitled "Women's Liberation Meets Miller-Mailer-Manson Man,"* but the comparisons are remarkably akin to the sort of rhetoric Mailer himself employed. The reference for both of them was Kate Millett's enormously important book, *Sexual Politics*, which on its publication in 1970 became perhaps the single most important text for the rapidly growing women's movement in the United States. In *Myron* the character of Whittaker Kaiser is clearly modelled on Mailer: "There's still *a few of us*," says Kaiser, "who're fighting to be all-men. To be tough. To kill if we have to. Because that's what it is to be a man . . . That's what the orgasm is all about. Murder is sex, sex is murder" (*Myron*: 88).

As the bitter and public feuds around sex showed, the authors who do become celebrities tend to be known for their non-fiction rather than their fiction, whether as theorists or popularizers. Few novelists are seen as important in the way the immediate post-war generation was, even with the promise of instant fame someone like Oprah Winfrey can provide through her television show. In part this is due to the disappearance of major best-

---

*Henry Miller (1891–1980) was a novelist renowned for his descriptions of (heterosexual) sex – and a lover of Anaïs Nin. Charles Manson was a serial killer primarily famous for his murder of actress Sharon Tate in 1969. In different ways Vidal saw them as symbolizing the aggressive heterosexual masculinity he was critiquing.

sellers which are also "literary" novels, as is true of Vidal's generation; later writers of comparable scope and ambition – say Don DeLillo or Margaret Atwood – now compete with the memoirs of basketball players and former Presidents for attention in publishing houses, while fiction is dominated by formula novels of espionage, romance, and violence. There is no longer a clear line between "highbrow" and "lowbrow" fiction, so a writer like Barbara Taylor Bradford, author of such novels as *Emma's Secret* and *Women in his Life*, can appear on the stamps of several Caribbean nations as a "great writer of the twentieth century." Loren Glass has discussed the collapse of the "literary genius" as a celebrity figure, and concludes that: "Literary celebrity . . . no longer commands the cultural authority it did in the modern era, and it never will again."[9]

Mention of Oprah is in fact the clue: Vidal belongs to the last generation who could establish themselves as celebrities before the widespread introduction of television, which has both reduced the significance of the printed word and increased the need to produce an increasing flood of celebrities. Everyone, said Andy Warhol, will be world famous for quarter of an hour. With the growth of reality television Warhol's quip becomes accurate, but it also reminds us how transitory celebrity is. For everyone who seems to have become a secure part of the celebrity pantheon – Marilyn, Princess Di, Jackie O, *Jesus Christ Superstar!* – there are hundreds who constantly jostle to stay in the public eye, and, if they are sufficiently vain, to establish themselves in the historical record. As Myron/Gore put it: "I am always thrilled when someone entirely without talent is able to become through strenuous and even pathological publicity of himself a part of the nation's consciousness and for a season famous because that is our American way" (*Myron*: 168). In a century's time will the name Gore conjure up memories of a prolific writer or of a Vice President who missed out on the Presidency despite winning a majority of the popular vote – or, most galling of all, neither?

Among intellectuals and writers over the past 50 years Vidal stands out for the sheer virtuosity of his range of interests and interventions. Like most celebrities his greatest success was creating a public persona, and he came close to creating an American legend in the persona of Myra. One might note, of course, that unlike that of some contemporary celebrities, the fame of Vidal, Mailer, and Capote did at least rest on achievement beyond getting on television. Once one becomes a celebrity one is grist for gossip and psychoanalytic speculation, but equally it becomes harder to seriously evaluate a celebrity's ideas and weaknesses. Thus the frequent interviews with Vidal become increasingly reverential, and his responses more and more predictable. Indeed, many of the interviews tend to dwell as much on the beauties and décor of La Rondinaia as on Vidal's writing, and his public persona blends with the self-congratulation of the interviewers for having been invited to sit in the same room as so many of the rich and famous.

Like writers such as Mailer and Susan Sontag, who have also written across genres and remained outside the academy, Vidal defines the role of the writer as exercising influence as a public intellectual, which I define to mean people who use their familiarity with ideas and language to seek to influence debate on a range of major topical issues. It is hard to quantify the role of public intellectuals; probably the most sophisticated attempt to do so in the United States comes from Richard Posner, a rightwing legal scholar and former judge, whose book *Public Intellectuals* (2001) sought to measure mentions of "public intellectuals" in American mainstream and academic media for the last five years of the twentieth century. There are a number of problems with his tabulations – because he does not exclude intellectuals who have also held public office his figures show the top two ranked names in the media as a former Secretary of State, Henry Kissinger, and a New York Senator, Daniel Patrick Moynihan. In his media listings for this period Vidal is outranked by a number of other writers: Arthur Miller, Salman Rushdie, Toni Morrison, Tom Wolfe, Norman Mailer, and Kurt Vonnegut (as well as George Orwell and George Bernard Shaw, who were already dead). Posner excludes "mere" writers from his listing of scholarly citations, the top four of whom are, interestingly, non-American: Michel Foucault, Pierre Bourdieu, Jürgen Habermas, and Jacques Derrida. "Web hits" (calculated by using Google) show a dramatically different picture again – for reasons that are unclear, the poet W. B. Yeats outruns every other name by a huge amount.

All three lists are remarkably male-dominated: Toni Morrison is the *only* woman listed in the top thirty "PIs" by media mention, Carol Gilligan the *only* woman to be listed in the top 30 "scholarly citations."[10] American literary culture has been largely male-dominated, and public intellectual culture yet more so. Indeed, my cursory reading of the texts produced by American critics about post-World War II writing suggests an academic field dominated by men with some anxiety about their masculinity. The great exception in the list of American intellectuals (who is underrated in the particular period surveyed by Posner) is Susan Sontag, who was born eight years after Vidal, and who became an intellectual, if not a popular, star from the early 1960s until her death in 2004. Like Vidal, Sontag was determined to establish herself as a writer; as a middle-class woman without the sort of connections available to Vidal, she had a tougher time, though like Gore's her career was furthered by a charisma based on a mixture of physical presence and intimidating intelligence. Both of them were aware of their striking looks, and used these to their advantage. Vidal and Sontag were never close, but inevitably moved in overlapping circles over the past four decades.[11]

Vidal shared with Mailer, Capote, and Sontag a thirst for fame, and a desire to write books that would be both celebrated by the critics and sell well. "Why should I care for posterity?" he once said. "What did posterity ever do for me?"[12] Yet care he does: Anaïs Nin makes the point that as a child he was already thrown into a world of celebrities, and this affected his later behavior. Vidal himself discusses the thirst of writers for success in the first few pages of *Two Sisters*, a complex novel, part memoir, part mythology, whose title evokes his relationship with Jacqueline Kennedy and her sister Lee Radziwill. Here his desire for fame is at its most naked: "Not since Hemingway was there a young writer so intent on dominance!" (*Two Sisters*: 40) Indeed, the rivalry with Mailer echoes that between Hemingway and Scott Fitzgerald, which some critics have described as sadomasochistic and homoerotic.[13] In *Palimpsest* Vidal declares he "became famous" on at least two separate occasions: from the publication of *The City and the Pillar* and, seven years later, through the television play (later Broadway hit) *Visit to a Small Planet.*

Indeed, as each generation needs to declare its own celebrities, one might add 1968, the year *Myra Breckinridge* was published and Vidal feuded with William Buckley on national television, and perhaps 1976, the year he appeared on the cover of *Time* magazine, ironically for what may be the slightest of his historical novels, *1876*. There must have been a particular satisfaction in this, as his father had appeared on *Time*'s cover back in 1933 for his attempts to expand civil aviation, just as Vidal must have enjoyed the *Time* cover entitled "Monroe meets Mailer" (July 16, 1973) on which Mailer is apparently swamped by the voluptuous actress. (Truman Capote never made the cover of *Time*, although *In Cold Blood* probably generated more attention than any one of Vidal's books.) As late as 2004 – over half a century after his first real moment of celebrity – Vidal's high-profile attacks on the Bush Administration made him both a target for the right and a favorite of some leftists, such as radio station WBAI in New York, which used large advertisements promoting a two-hour "fireside chat" with Vidal as a fundraising promotion for the station. Even so one senses, as is true of so many people who achieve, that there is never enough fame, that there is always someone who steals the spotlight that might otherwise have remained focused on oneself.

All writers mine their own lives for experience, and celebrities have the advantage that they have access to gossip that is of general interest; we all like to name-drop, and Vidal has more names to drop than most. His life became the basis for two of his novels, *The Season of Comfort* and *Two Sisters*, but his own experiences and memories are often central to his essays (for example in his book-length essay *Screening History*), and he is not beyond appearing, like Alfred Hitchcock, as a shadowy figure in his own fictions. He deliberately ends the last of his American Chronicles, *The Golden Age*, by introducing himself into the narrative as Gore Vidal, a distinguished older man of letters whom Peter Sanford, his contemporary, along with his younger cousin

AB (Aaron Burr) comes to interview. In what is clearly meant to be a summary of his life Vidal reminds us not just that he had lived through the great events of the post-World War II era, but that *he had been present at the creation*, as Dean Acheson put it in his memoirs.

Celebrity is in part a matter of mixing with, and being seen to mix with, other celebrities: "In the world of stars," Vidal once said, "no-one is a stranger." His biography and memoirs are full of other famous names, from Princess Margaret through to Hollywood actors and writers such as André Gide and George Santayana, and he, of course, appears increasingly in other biographies and memoirs. Late in life Vidal started appearing in films (*Bob Roberts*, 1992, *Gattaca*, 1997, etc.) where he created characters out of his own persona. As he wrote: "At ten I wanted to be a movie star like Mickey Rooney. At sixty-seven I am one, and not unlike the current Mickey Rooney, in appearance if not in talent" (*Palimpsest*: 143). It is possible that the biologically engineered humans in *Gattaca* are known as "valids" in tribute to Gore. His most recent film appearance was an uncredited appearance in the film *Igby Goes Down* (2002), Howard's death having prevented him from playing the role of the tycoon Huntington Hartford in *Kinsey* (2004), a role which was originally written for him.

There is in Gore Vidal both a monstrous ego and a huge intelligence, which combine to make him one of those figures who become caricatures of themselves. He is also an entertaining writer, an accomplished historian, and, at his best, a man of great wit, and more compassion than he likes to admit. Were this a biography it would be called the *Man Who Would Be President*. In at least one interview he regrets the impossibility of "that golden age, the Vidal Administration," and Gerald Clarke, the biographer of Capote, who spent some time with him in the early 1970s, related him talking of his desire to have been President: "Nobody of my generation was better equipped . . . And I could have made it too, if it hadn't been for this fag thing."[14] As it is, the closest America has come to a Vidal Presidency is the image projected by President Bartlet in the television series *The West Wing*.

Vidal sees the search for fame as almost sexual: he shares with most politicians a love of public speaking; in *Hollywood* he refers to every crowd as "like a lover met and lost, or, more likely, ravished and won" (95). In a very telling line he once wrote that: "The motor drive is the desire not for sex (other briefer fantasies take care of that) but for power . . ." ["Tarzan Revisited," in *United States*: 1,126, originally published in *Esquire* 1963]. One might recall the prescient comments about the Vice Presidential figure in *The Season of Comfort*, for whom "the daydream of the lost Presidency and certain sexual memories were almost the only things he could recall" (*Season of Comfort*: 22).

—— three ——

AMERICA AND ITS HISTORY

"This country isn't like anything that's ever happened before. Oh, maybe your first Romans were like us, but I doubt it . . . We are sui generis . . ."

Sanford in 1876: 63

"As a subject, history attracted him most, largely because there was always something wrong with it."

The Golden Age: 97

"If there is anything an historian hates, it is a fact . . . Henceforth, the story of Rome will be a department of creative writing."

Romulus: 45

In 1946, when Vidal published his first book, the United States bestrode the post-war world, its troops occupying the former enemies of Japan and Germany. With 7 percent of the world's population it produced a majority of the world's steel, oil, and automobiles. There existed considerable areas of poverty, particularly in rural areas and among African-Americans, but unlike almost anywhere else most Americans ate well, drove cars, and had access to consumer goods. The United States was about to be revolutionized by two technological advances, mass air travel and television. Rail was still the common means of travel – President Truman barnstormed the country in the 1948 Presidential election using the train originally built for Franklin Roosevelt – and those ubiquitous symbols of contemporary America, shopping malls, McDonald's, and Holiday Inns, did not yet exist.

Television remained a luxury (only 200,000 homes had television sets in 1948)[1] and radio was still dominant. Within five years there would be television sets in 80 percent of American homes, even as we, in backward Australia, had to wait until the 1956 Melbourne Olympics for its introduction. *Messiah*, published in 1954, was the first of a number of novels in which Vidal would point to the centrality of television in shaping modern consciousness. The dollar was the world's paramount currency, and the generation of writers of which Vidal was part took advantage of this to travel across the Atlantic and live cheaply in Paris, Rome, and Morocco.

The United States remained largely segregated, by law in the south and by custom elsewhere. Two wars had been fought to preserve democracy in which the United States sent its black citizens overseas in segregated units (President Truman ordered the desegregation of the military during the 1948 election campaign). The civil rights movement would make the question of race relations central to American politics for the following three decades, an issue oddly ignored in most of Vidal's writings. The need to mobilize for the war had led to huge shifts in population, with some 15 million young men entering the armed forces and equivalent numbers of women moving into factory production to produce the huge number of planes, ships, and tanks which were to give the United States supremacy on both fronts. The impact of this was to change the geography of American life, as areas like southern California expanded, and as millions of people moved away from small town and rural environments and found themselves able to experiment with new ways of imagining themselves and, by extension, develop new ways of imagining America. (Major population centers like San Diego, Phoenix, and Houston are essentially creatures of the post-war boom.) The new freedom possible in cities was an important element in creating the basis for black, feminist, and gay movements in the post-war world.

Much of Asia and almost all of Africa and the Caribbean remained under European rule, though the Indian subcontinent and the Philippines were clearly on the verge of independence, to be followed by Indonesia and, in the mid-1950s, French

Indo-China. The Cold War was not yet fully in place, although Russian troops occupied most of Eastern Europe, and China was still ruled by the Nationalist government of Chiang-Kai-shek. Winston Churchill used the phrase "Iron Curtain" in 1946, and soon thereafter requested Truman to send troops to Greece and Turkey to prevent alleged Communist insurrections from succeeding. By 1948 the United States was committed to a policy of "containing" any further expansion of Communism, equated with the power of the Soviet Union, and Vidal's generation were to live through a 40-year period in which the battle to contain Communism would become the organizing principle of American foreign policy, and the next generation would find themselves the dominant power in a world where, ironically, the collapse of the red bogey seemed to create more, not less, insecurity and fear of attack.

The works of Vidal reflect the period in which they were written: how could it be otherwise for so political a writer? Unlike most authors, however, he inserts topical references, especially into the plays and "inventions," so they are fixed in time: Richard Nixon not only gives his name to a play – *An Evening with Richard Nixon* is dedicated, "with appreciation," for J. Edgar Hoover and Clyde Tolson* – but is a constant presence in *Myron*. Indeed, other than Vidal's early infatuation with John Kennedy – which ended while Kennedy was in the White House – he has rarely had a good word to say for any President this century, which helps explain the perception that he is anti-American. In his television series *The American Presidency*, he is surprisingly sympathetic to Lyndon Johnson, whom he sees, correctly, as wanting to actually improve the conditions of ordinary Americans, even though he had referred to Johnson in an earlier piece as "the master-criminal" ("President and Mrs. U. S. Grant," in *United States*: 720, originally published in the *New York Review*

---

*J. Edgar Hoover was Director of the FBI (1924–72) and Tolson was his constant "companion." Hoover was noted for his deep anti-Communism, his racism, and his ability to hold power despite being disliked by most of the Presidents he served. He was almost certainly homosexual, although publicly committed to purging homosexuals from government office.

of Books 1975). Like Frank Sinatra he revelled in his brief period in the court of Camelot, and like Sinatra his entrée was abruptly cut off, following, in Vidal's case, an exchange with Robert Kennedy, widely publicized after Truman Capote gloated over the event in *Playgirl*.[2] While Sinatra subsequently moved to the right – and helped organize the celebrations for Reagan's inauguration as he had, twenty years earlier, for Kennedy – Vidal moved resolutely to the left.[3]

Every American writer who wants to be taken seriously faces the challenge of how to match the sheer size and exuberance of the country. Vidal's answer to this challenge has been to rove across genres and subjects, although he did not seem attracted to the solution pioneered by Mailer and Capote, and then carried through by writers such as Tom Wolfe, which was the mixing of journalism with personal experience, as in Capote's account of a brutal murder and the subsequent trial in Kansas (*In Cold Blood* 1966) and Mailer's two books about the politics of 1968 (*Armies of the Night* and *Miami and the Siege of Chicago*). Mailer's subsequent career, which included books on Marilyn Monroe and Lee Harvey Oswald (who shot Kennedy), and Tom Wolfe's own "new journalism," displayed in books such as *The Right Stuff*, showed the viability of this device, although by the end of the 1980s Wolfe turned to writing large political novels such as *The Bonfire of the Vanities*. Vidal has combined a more conventional approach to understanding America, the historical novel based on a close reading of what actually happened, and a series of "inventions," in which he subverts and reimagines reality.

Gore Vidal's American Chronicles

> "History claims everybody, whether they know it or not and whether they like it or not."
> Philip Roth, "The story behind 'The Plot against America'"
> *New York Times Book Review* September 19, 2004: 12

Vidal's most popular works are his extraordinary historical series the American Chronicles. Vidal is unique in writing a series that reaches from the revolutionary wars, which created the United States, to the Kennedy years, thus creating his own chronology of the rise of the United States to world dominance. To this must be added his recent book *Inventing a Nation*, where he returns to the roots of the American republic through a historical sketch of the political philosophies – and intrigues – of the first three Presidents, George Washington, Thomas Jefferson, and, in Vidal's view, the underrated John Adams. Almost 30 years earlier Vidal had revealed his fascination with the Adams family, writing an essay about them in a volume on "great American families,"[4] and *Inventing a Nation* returns to some of the judgments of the early Republic found in *Burr*. Given the veneration with which Americans regard their "founding fathers" – the men who led the war of independence and framed the Constitution for the new United States – the deliberate skepticism with which Vidal regards this generation is itself guaranteed to raise hackles.

Vidal has consistently pointed to the flaws of the first Presidents, and was bitterly attacked, for example, for pointing out that Thomas Jefferson, despite his rhetorical support for equality, was a slave owner who fathered children with his slave mistress, a claim now supported by DNA evidence. Washington is consistently depicted as boring and self-opinionated, and his reputation as a military genius undermined, though "no man was cleverer when it came to business and to the promotion of his commercial interests" (*Burr*: 198). One has to recognize the cloying reverence for the past – and the fudging of such uncomfortable issues as slavery – which typifies much American historical writing to appreciate why Vidal's histories are both widely read and bitterly criticized.

It is the historical saga that is likely to remain Vidal's greatest contribution to American literature; were he to win the Nobel Prize for literature it would be for these, just as Churchill did for his four-volume *History of the English-speaking Peoples*. As a creative writer he is far more worthy of the Prize than Churchill, though his lack of worthiness in its other sense means he is unlikely to receive it. He is a first-rate historian, despite the carping of some academics. Edmund Morgan, himself the author of a number of major books on American history, wrote: "Criticism of Vidal's depiction of Lincoln by my fellow historians seems to me beside the point. When Vidal's novel departs from the historical record, it is only in nonessentials. Everything that matters, everything that affected Lincoln's achievement, is there."[5] In similar vein, the British historian Owen Dudley Edwards praised the book as "much closer to real history than, say, *War and Peace*, provided that we remember Mr. Vidal's history is that of men and Tolstoy's of mankind, and prefer the more old-fashioned approach of Mr. Vidal."[6] If critics like Morgan and Edwards are right, and I think by and large they are, it is surprising how little historians refer to Vidal's novel.

"Carping" is a soft word for some of the vitriol directed at Vidal by historians angered by what they see as distortions of "the truth." In a review of *1876* Harry Barnard, an amateur historian and author of a biography of President Rutherford B. Hayes, called the book "a snide, sneering, soiling thing" which Vidal "with gay zeal" uses to smear Hayes' reputation.[7] Vidal was far more exercised by a review by the historian Richard Current, also a biographer of Lincoln, who claimed Vidal's novel was a "potpourri of his own inventions and bits and pieces he has picked up from other authors."[8] His criticisms are central to a couple of long articles Vidal published in 1988 blasting the "scholar-squirrels" for their attacks on the book ("Lincoln and the Priests of Academe," in *United States*: 669–96, originally published in the *New York Review of Books* 1988).

Other American writers have broached the public and historical spheres – e.g. E. L. Doctorow, Don DeLillo, John Updike – and Doctorow, in particular, has written a series of novels which provides a particular history of twentieth-century America, including the book which would become the musical *Ragtime*.[9] As Vidal's historical novels have often been best-sellers, widely published in paperback and much translated, his view of American history will remain influential for some time. There is an irony in the success of the novels, given Vidal's constant lament that Americans are deeply uninterested in history. Almost against his own complaints, he has demonstrated that there remains a large audience willing to read historical detail if it is well done.

Lincoln, for example, is a book of 650 pages, which concentrates exclusively on Lincoln's Presidency, which lasted four years and a few months. By telling the story from a number of viewpoints, including those of his wife, Mary Todd Lincoln, his personal secretary, John Hay, and his Secretary of the Treasury, Salmon Chase, as well as one of the conspirators who paved the way for the assassination in 1865, he gives possibly the best rounded portrait of Lincoln's Presidency available. Although there are some links to the other historical novels, through the Schuyler/Sanford family whose lives form the pivot of the novels from *Burr* through to *Washington, D.C.*, *Lincoln* stands somewhat apart, and relies less upon imaginary characters than any other of the American Chronicles. It is interesting that a book that was originally conceived as a television program is arguably Vidal's finest piece of historical writing, one that tells the story of Lincoln as both a personal and a national tragedy, which would help determine the future development of the United States.

The Australian author Thomas Keneally, who has himself written a novel, *Confederates*, based on this period of American history, expressed some reservations about the literary consequences of Vidal's concern with the accuracy of the historical record. *Lincoln*, wrote Keneally, "is a strangely dated piece of work lacking in the fantasy, idiosyncrasy and flashes of lightning for which we depend on fiction writers, not least on Gore Vidal."[10] Keneally's review appeared in *The New Republic* under the heading "Bore Vidal," which reflected the animus of the editor rather than Keneally, whose admiration of Gore is clear in the review. I think Keneally is unnecessarily harsh – Walter Clemons saw this as Vidal's "most moving book" – but it is likely that *Lincoln* is the most historically accurate of the Chronicles, though arguably its lack of the imagined characters who underpin the rest of the novels makes it the least entertaining.

More skilfully than most writers, Vidal weaves imagined characters into the narrative, juxtaposing them with real characters whom he recreates, as historians and biographers must. (The most remarkable example in recent times of how the author can reimagine historical characters may be Edmund Morris's biography of Ronald Reagan, *Dutch*, where Morris reinvents himself as an omnipresent observer of Reagan who narrates his life.[11] Like Vidal, Morris was assailed by outraged professional historians, and like Vidal's, his book sold very well.)

In retrospect, national politics was the obvious theme for Vidal, and his 1949 novel *The Season of Comfort* can be read in some ways as a sketch for *Washington, D.C.* In the same way the lures of a political career are one of the central temptations in *The Judgment of Paris*. Vidal wrote *Washington, D.C.* before he had even sketched out the outlines of what would become his ambitious American Chronicles, and it is remarkable how far this novel prefigures the preoccupations of that series. Indeed, *Washington, D.C.* overlaps with what is chronologically the last, namely *The Golden Age*, requiring some dexterity from the author to match the two.

In the terms made common by the feminist movement of the 1970s, Vidal demonstrates that "the personal is political," that domestic and national passions can overlap and that ambition and desire can simultaneously play themselves out within the family and the body politic. The problem is that we may read too much into the novel, for when it was written it is not likely that Vidal had any conscious inkling of the extent to which it would become the final part of a huge historical saga. The critics Susan Baker and Curtis Gibson point to this problem through what they term "an intertextual reading" of the novel; but they fall prey to this themselves in seeing a link between the incarceration of the embarrassing Enid in a mental institution and the forcible relocation of Japanese-Americans in World War II.[12]

The novel is set in the world of Senatorial politics, familiar territory to Vidal and one he had already broached in his Edgar Box mystery *Death before Bedtime* and several of his plays. There is an echo, too, of the world touched on in Hitchcock's movie *Strangers on a Train* (1951), which changed the setting of Patricia Highsmith's original novel from New York to Washington, allowing him to allude to the merging of anti-Communist and homophobic fears of the period. Washington, D.C. covers the period from the second Roosevelt Administration to the beginning of the Eisenhower Presidency, and the three Presidents of the time are shadowy background figures, far less developed than their predecessors would be in later novels. During the first years of the war the city's population grew by 5,000 a month, and the novel is in part a chronicle of the transmogrification of the city from provincial southern town to world capital, symbolized by the building of the Pentagon in the 1940s, the largest office building ever constructed to that point.

The central character, Peter Sanford, who in age and character is to some extent the author himself, is the son of the newspaper proprietor, Blaise, who would reappear as a major character in the later historical novels. Peter's sister, Enid, marries the ambitious Clay Overbury, aide to Senator Burden Day, who is modelled to some extent on Senator Gore. Day, with his bust of Cicero and his romantic view of the Confederacy, for whom his father had fought, is a bridge between pre-World War II America and the global military power that the war would create. Impelled both by ambition and by hatred of Roosevelt, whom he wishes, desperately, to succeed as President, he joins with Blaise to create a political career for Overbury, and in turn is defeated by him.

Vidal uses the novel to sketch the political divisions which were emerging as the end of World War II came closer. Peter, despite his own sardonic view of politics, becomes involved with a new leftwing journal, while Enid's ferocious anti-Communism foreshadows the McCarthyite period. Already he writes with an insider's cynicism about the Washington process, where ruthless ambition overrode human decency in most cases. Enid is locked in an asylum with the complicity of her father and husband, ostensibly because of her alcoholism and mental instability, in reality because she presents a threat to their political careers. (If, as Kaplan suggests, Enid is based upon Vidal's mother, what seems a melodramatic plot device becomes more understandable on a number of levels.) The complicity between the two men makes more sense once we recognize that Senator Day is almost certainly in love with Clay Overbury, a theme which Vidal suggested many years later was also true of George Washington's feelings for his secretary of treasury, Alexander Hamilton (Weise 1999: 269). But while there are various sexual subplots, enough to excite the readers of the time, the true theme of the book is the ambition for power and its corruptions.

Washington, D.C. appeared in 1966, and it was not until 1973 that Vidal produced what is chronologically the first of the series, *Burr*, the story of one of America's more remarkable political mavericks. Aaron Burr was barely defeated by Thomas Jefferson for the Presidency, and became his Vice President (1801–5), under now repealed provisions of the Constitution, which gave the post to the person who came second in the Presidential ballot. In 1804 he killed his political contemporary Alexander Hamilton in a duel; three years later he was suspected of plotting to ally with the Spanish to seize land in the southwest and was tried for treason – and found innocent. Historians remain uncertain as to exactly what Burr intended when he led an expedition of boats towards Spanish lands at the mouth of the Mississippi. The standard historical view has been harsh on Burr, whom Samuel Elliot Morrison, one of the doyens of mid-century American history, termed "a cynical and pliant politician,"[13] and who is regarded in much American mythology as a villain.

Vidal had been long fascinated with Burr – he is already mentioned several times in *Washington, D.C.* – which at one point he attributed to a familial connection through his Auchincloss stepfather (*Views from a Window*: 112) This seems a rather odd link, especially as Burr was a northerner whose election to the Presidency was blocked by the Virginian gentry, who benefited from the built-in southern bias of the pre-Civil War Constitution, where the representation of states in the Electoral College was inflated by including the non-voting slave population. When Vidal speaks of his own family's deep American roots he tends to identify himself as a southerner. The novel laid the foundation for much of his writing over the next 20 years, in part through the creation of a young journalist, Charles Schuyler, who embarks on a biography of Burr – to discover that he is, in fact, Burr's illegitimate son. (Rumor claimed that President Martin Van Buren was the illegitimate son of Aaron Burr, and Schuyler is employed to prove the rumor.) Schuyler's descendents become the central characters of all the following historical novels but for *Lincoln*.

Most Americans have only a vague knowledge of Burr, and in part it was his reputation as a villain, and the animosity he provoked in those two powerful arch rivals, Hamilton and Jefferson, that attracted Vidal to write his novel. Exactly what Burr plotted in the years between 1804 and 1806 in the vast lands around the Mississippi, including what was then Spanish territory along the Gulf of Mexico, is unclear. When President Jefferson ordered his arrest it was on the grounds that he had "received intimations that designs were in agitation in the Western Country unlawful and unfriendly to the peace of the Union,"[14] but various rumors attributed Burr with wishing to lead a western secession from the United States and/or going to war with Spain to conquer either western Florida or parts of what was then Mexico. Even today, there is no clear agreement on what Burr really intended; the author of one of the best available studies, Buckner Melton, concludes we shall never know the full truth.

Prosecuted for treason, but found innocent in part because of Chief Justice Marshall's interpretation of the Constitutional definition of treason, Burr then spent some time in Europe, returning to the United States to live out the last part of his life. He died aged 81, when Americans had already conquered Florida and parts of Texas, continuing the relentless drive across the continent of which he had been accused of plotting. We are reminded of Burr's longevity in the opening of the novel when Burr, then aged 77, marries the rich widow Eliza Jumel. The novel is complex, for it combines Burr's own recollections of the revolutionary wars and the founding of the American Republic, with Charles Schuyler's journalistic ambitions in the New York of the 1830s. This allows Vidal to sketch portraits of both the "founding fathers," about whom Burr is appropriately iconoclastic, and later figures such as Washington Irving and Davy Crockett.

Burr ends in 1840 with Schuyler settled in Naples as American consul; like Vidal, Schuyler sought solace in Europe, though unlike Gore, his interest in politics is largely for patronage rather than born of principle. Three years later Vidal wrote *1876*, which takes up as Schuyler returns to his native country 35 years later, in part to marry off his daughter, Emma, widow of a French prince. As a consummate snob, Gore could wish for no less for one of his favorite characters. Perhaps reminiscent of Henry James' return to the United States in 1904 after a long absence (chronicled in *The American Scene*), Schuyler moves largely in the world of aristocratic and political New York, and becomes a wry commentator on a country grown rich and corrupt. Vidal has written little about the late nineteenth-century Presidents – Cleveland, the only Democrat to be President between the Civil War and Woodrow Wilson in 1912, appears as a good-natured buffoon in *The Smithsonian Institution** – but *Empire*, *Hollywood*, and *The Golden Age* straddle much of the first half of the twentieth century, and continue the saga of the Schuyler family.

The best summary of Vidal's approach to history comes in a note at the end of *The Golden Age*, where he writes: "The lives of such invented characters as Caroline and Blaise and Peter Sanford intersect with those of 'real' people like Roosevelt and Hopkins. What the real people say and do is essentially what they have been recorded as saying and doing, while the invented characters are then able to speculate upon motivation, dangerous territory for the historian" ("Afterword," *The Golden Age*: 466). This statement develops a theme he had mentioned after writing *Burr*, namely that a novelist has "the right – the duty – to speculate on motives, while the biographer is honor-bound to deal only with facts."[15] Or as Don DeLillo has claimed: "Fiction slips into the skin of historical figures. It gives them sweaty

---

*Grover Cleveland was elected President in both 1884 and 1892. He was increasingly at odds with the populist wing of the Democrats, who in 1896 nominated William Jennings Bryan, a major influence on Vidal's grandfather. Bryan in turn lost to the Republican candidate, William McKinley.

palms and head colds and urine-stained underwear and lines
to speak in private and the terror of restless nights. This is
how consciousness is extended and human truth is seen anew."[16]
One might instance the splendid way in which Vidal depicts
the transformation of John Hay, Lincoln's secretary, and one
of the principal narrators of that particular book, into the old,
sickly Secretary of State to President McKinley who appears
in *Empire*.

The historian can – and should be – an artist, and Vidal seems
to follow the precepts of the great English historian George
Trevelyan, who said that history should explain the facts about
the past "in their full emotional and intellectual value to a wide
public by the difficult art of literature."[17] A century and a half
earlier Jane Austen touched on the problems for the historical
novelist, who needs to invent but within the limits imposed by
existing records. "The speeches that are put into their heroes'
mouths," reflects Catherine Morland, "their thoughts and
designs – the chief of all this must be invention, and invention
is what delights me in other books."[18] The real test is whether
the invention is plausible and accords with what is known
through other sources, and here Vidal's record is near impec-
cable. Writing of President Harding, he noted that contemporary
accounts do not necessarily support the popular perception of
Harding as "a sleazy poker-playing, hard-drinking, womanizing
nonentity put in office by cynical Republican bosses . . . In effect
the press invents us all; and the later biographer or historian can
only select from the mass of crude fictions and part-truths, those
'facts' that his contemporaries are willing to agree upon"
("Lincoln and the Priests of Academe," in *United States*: 674, originally published in the *New York Review of Books* 1988).[19]

" 'True history,' said Hearst with a smile that was, for once,
almost charming, 'is the final fiction. I thought even you knew
that' " (*Empire*: 566). Vidal writes history as an intervention in the
present, but with a concern for accuracy: he would not say, as
does one of his characters in *Burr*: "Isn't it better that we make
our own *useful* version of our history and put away . . . the
sadder, less edifying details" (103). Vidal is careful to research

and check his history, and relied upon careful reading by established historians, including Arthur Schlesinger Jr and David Donald (there is something of a Harvard bias here), before his books were published. He creates a strong sense of continuity both through his invented characters, and through deep knowledge of the details of history. Reading the novels, one finds glimpses of the French Prime Minister Clemenceau reminiscing at the 1919 post-World War I Peace Conference about the American Civil War (*Hollywood*: 260), but Vidal is also attentive to shifts in fashion, such as the introduction of the cheeseburger (*The Smithsonian Institution*: 48) or the invention of the phrase "schoolgirl complexion" (*Hollywood*: 382).

Vidal's American novels are written based on copious reading, but also intimate connection to the historical characters whom he conjures up. When several historians criticized him for his less than flattering portrait of Lincoln he was able to reply not just by deflating their scholarship, but also by quoting his grandfather's conversations with Lincoln's son, Robert.[20] As Vidal's grandfather was born in 1870, *his* grandfather could well have conversed with one of the "Founding Fathers," reminding us that while the United States may seem one of the immoveable facts of history, it in fact has existed as a nation for little more than 200 years. (There is a tradition of very long-serving Senators: one of the leading opponents of Bush's intervention in Iraq was Senator Robert Byrd of West Virginia, whose Congressional history spans eleven Presidencies.) Most significantly Vidal's grandfather was born in Mississippi (his father served in the Confederate Army) and Gore has always stressed his southern roots, which help explain his abiding awareness of the toll of war. In 1990 the BBC filmed him attending a Gore family reunion – avoided by then Senator Gore, who was contesting the Democratic nomination for President – in Mississippi.

The care that Vidal takes with the actual historical record imposes a discipline in the historical series, which is not always apparent in his other writings. Vidal seems post-modern in his assumption that there is no one truth, but he might also agree with Thomas Disch, who wrote: "America is a nation of liars, and for that reason science fiction has a special claim to be our national literature, as the art form best adapted to telling the lies we like to hear and pretend to believe."[21] Disch's view of science fiction comes close to Vidal's approach to history in *Duluth* and *The Smithsonian Institution*, where he plays with both the present and the past in ways that must seem deeply savage to American triumphalists.

History can prefigure the present in surprising ways. How could Vidal when he wrote *1876* have anticipated the extent to which the results of that election would foreshadow the 2000 Presidential election? In 1876, where the counting in four states, including Florida, was at stake, a Congressional commission resolved the election in favor of the Republican Rutherford Hayes. As a consequence northern troops were withdrawn from the occupied south, resulting in blacks quickly losing the right to vote, which had been guaranteed by post-Civil War amendment to the Constitution. In 2000, the accuracy of the vote count in Florida, which would determine the outcome of the election, was again at issue. After a number of court challenges, the Supreme Court upheld a decision not to recount votes and effectively gave the election to George W. Bush. The decision was 5–4, thus making Bush the first President of the United States to win on the basis of an election decided by the Court. Crucial in both cases was the fact that US Presidents are chosen via a device known as the Electoral College, whereby each state casts all its votes for the candidate who wins a plurality in that state, each state having a number of votes equivalent to their total Congressional representation. It is therefore possible for a candidate to win with fewer overall votes than his opponent, as happened in both 1876 and 2000. In both cases there were good grounds for believing that the Republicans had "stolen" the election, just as Republicans maintain that voting irregularities in Illinois and Texas gave the 1960 election to John Kennedy.

To understand America through its political history is a long-standing preoccupation of artists and composers. John Philip Sousa, best known for his patriotic marches, wrote a musical, *The Glass Blower*, about the Spanish-American War; George and Ira Gershwin included political satire in their 1920s musicals; Stephen Sondheim's *Pacific Overtures* and *Assassins* explore aspects of the American past.* In *The Golden Age* Vidal quotes liberally from *The Golden Apple*, a now forgotten musical by Jerome Moross and John Latouche, which resets the story of the Trojan Wars in the United States at the end of the nineteenth century. But Vidal's is history from the top down: there is no attempt to look at the Civil War from the slave point of view, as in Leonard Bernstein's musical *1600 Pennsylvania Avenue* (later recast as *A White House Cantata*), which Bernstein once suggested Vidal might rewrite. "I'm touched," Gore claims to have responded, "but you should have gone to Lourdes" (Kaplan 1999: 748). In *A White House Cantata*, for which Alan Jay Lerner wrote the lyrics, black and white voices and experiences are juxtaposed in a way Vidal has never attempted.

At times, as in the discussion of the political maneuvering of Lincoln to control his cabinet or the machinations that gave the 1920 Republican Presidential nomination to Harding, Vidal seems to be a political scientist with a better prose style. Here he echoes Henry Adams, direct descendent of two Presidents and the only American novelist more closely related to Washington power than Vidal (Adams' *Democracy* (1880) is still read for its insight into the American political process). "Continuing Adams' pattern," Todd Gitlin wrote, "Vidal's metier is the comedy of bad manners . . . His public scenes – press conferences, Senate committee hearings and the like – crackle, unlike the stagy melodrama he inserts in private places."[22] Yet this "melodrama" allows Vidal to match the private to the political, so that the historical events and people are echoed and replayed in the lives of the imagined characters.

Vidal's novels display a realist view of politics and a fascination with the intricacies of political deal making. Thus Lincoln is portrayed as the supreme manipulator of factions in a situation

---

*Political themes are remarkably frequent in American opera and musicals. A short list would include Virgil Thompson and Gertrude Stein's *The Mother of Us All* (1947), John Adams' *Nixon in China* (1985), and Scott Wheeler's *Democracy* (2005). Vidal's own preoccupations are echoed in Michael John LaChiusa's *First Lady Suite* (1993) and Michael Daugherty's and Wayne Koestenbaum's opera *Jackie O* (1997).

where he had very few fully loyal supporters, either in his cabinet or among his army commanders. And Vidal's friendship with Eleanor Roosevelt late in her life gave him insight into her quiet ruthlessness as a political operator and into the complexity of her marriage; that Franklin had a series of mistresses, while maintaining the façade of a devoted marriage, is a recurring theme in several of his novels.

Vidal reflects the American fascination with its Presidents, whom he constantly discusses and evaluates, as if to construct his own Mount Rushmore.* His is not a Marxist view of history; he clearly believes individuals can, and do, shape history, and Abraham Lincoln, Woodrow Wilson, and the two Roosevelts, Theodore and Franklin, stand out in his description of the American fall: "'We are Rome indeed,' says the ghost of Thomas Jefferson. 'And the die has been well and truly cast. And our Athens is long dead'" (*The Smithsonian Institution*: 188). Vidal approaches the Presidency with less reverence than is normal, but his concentration on individual Presidents as centerpieces of United States history follows the conventional models. American Presidents combine in the one person ceremonial and real power, as if the British could elect Queen and Prime Minister in one, and hence are both criticized and revered at the same time. Some critics regard Vidal's most significant work as *Lincoln*, whose subject he analyzes in ways that prefigure the view of the "imperial Presidency" of late twentieth-century political science. Thus much of his fascination with Lincoln stems from his expansion of the powers of the executive branch, foreshadowing all future wartime Presidents.

In the popular imagination, Lincoln, "the man who freed the slaves," is surpassed only by Washington as the greatest of American Presidents. Unlike Washington, it is impossible to avoid controversy in writing about Lincoln: too many Americans are descended from slaves and those who died defending

---

*Set in South Dakota this is a huge rock carving of the four "great" Presidents recognized by Congressional authorization in 1925, namely Washington, Jefferson, Lincoln, and Theodore Roosevelt. It is supposedly visible for 60 miles.

slavery to make that possible. In fact Lincoln, while disliking slavery, also believed its existence in the southern states was constitutionally guaranteed, and only proclaimed Emancipation two years after the outbreak of the Civil War, limiting it to the secessionist states. Moreover, like many other northerners, Lincoln spoke of the mass colonization of Central America by former slaves (or their repatriation to Africa); few white Americans in the mid-nineteenth century could envisage any form of integration.

Vidal believes the Civil War was avoidable, that Lincoln could have followed the advice of his Secretary of State, William Seward, to let the southern states secede, though he has never been an apologist for those who supported slavery as the basis of their case. This makes him ultimately a severe critic of Lincoln, whom he regards as a dangerous "titan," who was also tormented by self-doubt. "Nothing that Shakespeare ever invented," wrote Vidal, "was to equal Lincoln's invention of himself – and, in the process, us. What the Trojan War was to the Greeks, the Civil War is to us. What the wily Ulysses was to the Greeks, the wily Lincoln is to us – not plaster saint but towering genius, our haunted and haunting re-creator."[23]

The Civil War involved large-scale butchery, and the total mobilization of resources of a sort not seen before. It gave the United States income tax and "the greenback" (the popular name for the dollar bill),* and enabled Lincoln to assert unparalleled power through his role as Commander in Chief. Lincoln's suspension of habeas corpus (153), to enable the federal government to hold secessionists without trial, paved the way for similar wartime measures by Woodrow Wilson, Franklin Roosevelt, and Bush Jr.

By the time Vidal wrote *The Golden Age* he had become a character in his own telling of history, and the title refers both ironically to the growth of the American Empire and, at another level,

---

*Technically the greenback was a federal banknote not redeemable for gold. Income tax was abandoned after the war, reintroduced in 1884, ruled unconstitutional by the Supreme Court, and adopted through Constitutional amendment in 1913.

to the period of his youth, when he felt part of a new generation of artists and writers who might reimagine America. (It is interesting that historians of science fiction refer to a similar era as that genre's "golden age.") Vidal is not, of course, alone in this view of history: just as his golden age was in the late 1940s, Bill Clinton, and then John Kerry, a generation younger, invoked memories of the Kennedy era when they ran for President in 1992 and 2004. Perhaps Vidal was wiser when he made his character Peter Sanford reflect that: "There never was a golden age. There never will be a golden age and it is sheer romance to think we can ever be other than what we are now" (*Washington, D.C.*: 273–4). Every generation remembers its youth as "golden"; in retrospect, it is harder to believe Vidal's claim that the late 1940s was artistically more flourishing than most.

The growth of American empire

> "Nor was the United States anything more than just another power whose turn at Empire had come . . . by dying, it was suddenly plain . . . that . . . the author of the Four Freedoms [Roosevelt] had managed by force of arms and sly maneuvering to transform an isolationist republic into what no doubt would be the last empire on earth."
>
> *Washington, D.C.*: 197

A great deal of post-World War II American popular culture, from Asimov's *Foundation* novels to films such as *Star Wars* and *Independence Day*, take the growth of empire as their theme, implicitly suggesting the United States acts as the world's redeemer. Vidal not only reverses the triumphalism common to these (and other) works, but has consistently made the ruthless growth of American power central to his history of the American nation. Even in *Lincoln*, set during the Civil War, when the administration in Washington consistently faced the possibility of the city being overrun by southern troops, and the Union's defeat, Vidal stresses the continuing debates about America's future being bound up in continental and then oceanic expansion. Vidal may not have claimed, as Sontag once did, that the United States is founded on genocide – indeed he says relatively little about the wars on and dispossession of the indigenous inhabitants of North America – but to some extent he shares the critique.

Vidal's histories construct a persuasive narrative of the United States as a country that, soon after winning independence in the name of self-government, abandoned the original principles of the Founding Fathers to pursue a policy of imperial expansion. This narrative is based on a particular reading of American history – he was influenced by radical historians such as William Appleman Williams* – and like most narratives that seek to find a coherent pattern in historical events it seems at times overstated. Critics of his views would argue that he both underestimated real threats to the United States and overestimated the degree of calculation and consistency in Washington's responses.

American expansionism is a central theme in *Burr*, with the turn from new state to imperial power within the first two decades of the Republic's life. Much of this Vidal blames on Jefferson, whose purchase of Louisiana from France in 1803 greatly expanded the territory of the United States. The Louisiana Purchase extended north from New Orleans to encompass the entire Mississippi river system as far as Canada, embracing what are now states as far apart as Arkansas and the Dakotas. In Vidal's view the decision to greatly expand the territory of the United States led to a new Jefferson, one who in his second Inaugural Address envisaged a more activist government, and one that must be ready for war ("Homage to Daniel Shays," in *United States*: 907–8, originally published in the *New York Review of Books* 1972).

Through the nineteenth century there were constant moves to expand the boundaries of the United States, most markedly in the war with Mexico (1846–8) which annexed much of what is

---

*Williams (1921–90) was the author of a number of influential books on American foreign policy, including *Empire as a Way of Life* and *The Tragedy of American Diplomacy*, which largely accord with Vidal's view of US expansionism.

now Texas, Arizona, New Mexico, and California. Presidents Polk and Pierce were already interested in acquiring Cuba in the 1850s, but the Civil War slowed down further territorial expansion. It was not until the end of the nineteenth century that an overseas empire was created, first through conquering territory (Hawaii, Puerto Rico, various Pacific islands) and then through the steady expansion of the economic and military power of the United States. There is a long tradition of American historical writing which justifies American expansionism in the name of "manifest destiny," with books such as Bernard De Voto's *Across the Wide Missouri* (1947) and *The Course of Empire* (1952) providing ideological justification for what leftist critics would see as the dispossession and even genocide of Native Americans, and unprovoked wars against anyone who stood in the way of expansionism. As Garry Wills has demonstrated, it was this particular narrative of American history which underlies many of John Wayne's movies, and which Vidal would mock in his depiction of the Smithsonian Institution's dioramas of the "Early Indians" and "the Arctic Eskimos" in the novel of that name.

The United States emerged as a world power in 1898, when it went to war with Spain, and conquered all but a few African outposts of what remained of the Spanish Empire: the Philippines, Puerto Rico, Cuba, and various Pacific islands. Only Cuba was granted independence, partly because of fears in the south, especially Florida, of its large black population and competition from its agricultural and tourist industries, but the United States maintained a base at Guantanamo Bay which was used to detain prisoners a century later in the aftermath of the 2002 Afghan War. President McKinley claimed divine intervention led him to annex the Philippines, and then declare war on an independence movement which had found inspiration in the American "revolutionaries." Bitter debate between the characters in *Empire* over the annexation of the Philippines can be seen as prefiguring divisions over interventions in Vietnam and Iraq a century later.

After McKinley's assassination in 1901 he was succeeded by "the war lover," Theodore Roosevelt, who increased the influence of the United States in Central America, encouraging the rebellion against Colombia, which created the new republic of Panama, and ceded the Canal Zone to the United States. Roosevelt, Vidal has written, was our "first international emperor." Or, as he quotes the then British Ambassador as saying: "We must never forget that the President is seven years old" (*The American President*: 37).

Vidal is very critical of Woodrow Wilson (President 1913–20), whom he blames for dragging the United States into World War I and for arousing unreasonable expectations during the ensuing peace process. It is at this point that the historical and the personal chronicles begin to merge. In 1915 the sinking by German ships of the British liner *Lusitania*, with over 100 Americans on board, and further attacks on shipping by the German fleet, contributed to growing pro-British sentiment in the United States. The following year, Senator Gore introduced a resolution in the Senate in 1916 that would have made it clear the United States would not protect its citizens who sail on belligerent ships. This put Senator Gore in direct opposition to his fellow Democrat Wilson, who had been re-elected in 1916 on the slogan: "He kept us out of war." The following year Wilson led the United States into World War I, which was very unpopular with isolationists centered in the midwest and Americans of German and Irish origin, both of whom claimed it embroiled the United States in a battle that was of no concern to it. The post-war Senate rejected American entry into the League of Nations, which Wilson had seen as an essential part of the peace process. Vidal claims his revenge in *The Smithsonian Institution*, where the schoolboy genius "T" goes back in time to obliterate Wilson from the Presidency in favor of William Jennings Bryan, whom his grandfather had nominated as the Democratic candidate in 1908.

In recent times there has been a flood of commentary on Wilson, who is seen as the progenitor of President George W. Bush's grand designs to remake the world in America's image. In his review of a number of these books Ronald Steel notes: "In finding that the Lord blessed what self-interest dictated, this preacher's son did not break new ground. But he set a high standard to which his predecessors are compared, and his successors aspire."[24] In domestic affairs Wilson was both an activist, who expanded the role of government, and a racist, who cemented the link between white segregationists and the Democratic Party for another generation.

Vidal was seven when Franklin Roosevelt was first elected President; by the time Roosevelt died Vidal had graduated from school, served in the army, and begun work on his first published novel. Moreover, his father and grandfather, the two relatives to whom he was closest, had personal but very different relations with Roosevelt. It is hardly surprising that Vidal is both preoccupied with and ambivalent about him, refusing the reverence of most Democrats and blaming him for America's entry into World War II. Indeed, this is a recurring theme through much of Vidal's writings, first appearing in *Washington, D.C.*, where Senator Burden Day even muses on the possibility of the President being impeached for his failure to forestall Pearl Harbor (123). It is in this book that Vidal gives his most striking description of Roosevelt: "the aging Lucifer ... that haggard glaring face, with the curious dark splotch above the left eyebrow which looked always as if there had been some sort of flaw in the newspaper's system of reproduction, a drop of ink that spread from year to year, edition to edition" (*Washington, D.C.*: 159). Thirty years later he wrote that: "[Roosevelt] was thought to be liberal, but at heart he was a traditional Eastern conservative, with a love of foreign wars inherited from his first employer, Woodrow Wilson, and from his cousin Theodore before that."[25]

During Vidal's adolescence debate about whether or not the United States should enter World War II engendered huge passions in the United States, with former Senator Gore lined up alongside allies such as Senator Gerald Nye and the aviator Charles Lindbergh, who was, coincidentally, a friend of his father's. Lindbergh appears a far more sympathetic character in Vidal's writings than he does in Philip Roth's recent novel, *The Plot against America*, in which Lindbergh is elected President in 1940, allies with Hitler, and supports moves to "absorb" Jews into America. But then Vidal's rewriting of twentieth-century history in *The Smithsonian Institution* avoids World War I, thus allowing Germany to ally with the United States in the war against Japan in the 1940s.

In his discussion of the importance of the movies, *Screening History*, Vidal points to the ways in which Hollywood films such as *Fire over England* and *That Hamilton Woman* prepared us "for a wartime marriage with our English and French cousins, against our Italian and German cousins" (*Screening History*: 41). *Fire over England* referred to the Spanish threat to Protestant England under Elizabeth I, *That Hamilton Woman* to Lord Nelson's victories over Napoleon's fleet. In both films the young Laurence Olivier and Vivien Leigh helped promote what Graham Greene called "the very spirit of an English public schoolmistress's vision of history."[26] The much-publicized state visit of King George VI and Queen Elizabeth in 1939 fits this picture of a deliberate softening up of the American population to convince them to rally to the British side in a coming war. The America Firsters, whose views Vidal seems to be echoing, were remarkably blind to both the totalitarian and the expansionist aims of Nazi Germany. Vidal's insights in this particular essay are interesting, but his political judgment is appalling.

While both isolationists and interventionists were obsessed with the war in Europe, it was the Japanese attack on Hawaii that ended the debate and took the United States into World War II. Vidal has praised Robert Stinnett's *Day of Deceit: The Truth about FDR and Pearl Harbor*, which argues that Roosevelt provoked the Japanese to attack the American fleet at Pearl Harbor, keeping hidden information that predicted the attack. The assertion rests on a belief that Roosevelt saw this as the best way of bringing the United States into the war against Germany: in an exchange with the writer Ian Buruma, Vidal wrote: "Japan looked for a compromise. We looked for war."[27] Yet as John Gaddis has pointed out: "Just because Roosevelt *wanted* the United States to enter the war and to become a world power afterwards does not mean that his actions alone made these things happen."[28] Thomas Fleming, who is very hostile to FDR's maneuvers to bring the United States into the war, also discounts claims that Roosevelt had prior warning of the attack on Pearl Harbor.[29]

Vidal himself, in his novel of the period, *The Golden Age*, is more careful in his claims, which seem far closer to Fleming's than to Stinnett's (*Golden Age*: 209). Not atypically Vidal the novelist is more cautious than Vidal the polemicist. Like Fleming, Vidal draws on an abiding suspicion of Britain in US politics – there are claims that US military leaders were making contingency plans for possible war with the United Kingdom in 1929.[30] He also points to colliding imperial interests of the United States and Japan in the Pacific, and in *The Smithsonian Institution* summons the ghost of George Washington to ask President Roosevelt: "What did your administration do to provoke this attack?" When Roosevelt retorts that all provocation came from Japan, though acknowledging the ban on selling them oil and scrap iron in retaliation for the Japanese attacks on China, Washington responds: "Then, sir, you have made our country the arbiter of war and peace everywhere in the world" (*The Smithsonian Institution*: 195). This is a position that consistently underlies all of Vidal's views of American foreign policy of the past two centuries.

Each generation tends to interpret political crises through the formative myths of their childhood. Like those in the Johnson Administration who defended escalation in Vietnam by reference to a failure to stand up to Hitler, Vidal's analysis of World War II risks being trapped by his views of the First. In his late seventies Vidal became an ardent crusader against the Bush Administration's foreign policy, echoing rhetoric he first used as a precocious teenager in opposing American entry into World War II. In *The Season of Comfort*, he quotes a speech opposing entry into the war which could have come directly from his grandfather (124), and in *The Golden Age* he invokes former President Herbert Hoover, who had overseen relief efforts during World War I, to oppose Roosevelt's desire to enter the War (167). In one of the most constant themes in Vidal's writing, Hoover warns that: "The next war will absolutely transform us. I see more power to the great corporations. More power to the government . . . you can't extend the mastery of the government over the daily life of a people without making government the master of those people's souls and thoughts, the way the fascists and the Bolsheviks have done" (*The Golden Age*: 168).

The most sustained discussion of the causes of World War II comes in his late historical invention, *The Smithsonian Institution*. Following a bequest from an Englishman, James Smithson, the Smithsonian was established by Congress in 1846 as a scientific institute, which now houses a vast array of exhibitions and research institutions. References to the Institution appear in a number of Vidal's earlier writings, as befits one of Washington's oldest grand institutions (Margaret Truman set one of her DC-based detective stories there). *The Smithsonian Institution* is perhaps the most dazzling of Vidal's inventions, in which he plays with time, history, and the laws of physics to create a world in which Jimmie Trimble need not have died. It is, wrote Christopher Hitchens in one of the best appreciations of Vidal, "a cocktail of magical realism, science fiction, and historical realism."[31] *The Smithsonian Institution* manages to be simultaneously entertaining and polemical, to offend almost all the received verities of American history and politically correct views on race and sex, to bring together, in other words, the Vidalian view of the world in a *tour de force* of imagination.

In this novel a fictionalized version of Jimmie Trimble, "T," who is possessed of a mathematical genius which enables him to envisage the manipulation of time and space, is summoned to the Smithsonian, which houses the headquarters of the Manhattan Project, then developing the atomic bomb for use in a possible war. In Vidal's Smithsonian the wax exhibits come to life after the public are sent home, and "T" enters an increasingly complex historical world through the Early Indian Exhibit Room, where he meets "Squaw," the younger wife of President Grover Cleveland: Mrs Cleveland exists in at least three different chronological versions in the book. His capacity to travel both forwards and backwards in time allows him to foresee his own death at Iwo Jima and to alter history to forestall it. With help from Mrs Cleveland, James Smithson, and Charles Lindbergh among others, he intervenes in the course of history to prevent the rise of Hitler, but fails to foresee the Pacific War, thus requiring one version of "T" to die in battle in order to save his facsimile.

Vidal had long been interested in science: in 1965, following the publication of *Julian*, he gave a public lecture at the Library of Congress on "the novel in the age of science." *The Smithsonian Institution* plays havoc with the laws of physics to allow the rewriting of history: "Interesting," Vidal noted, "that three writers as different as Martin Amis (*Time's Arrow*), Tom Stoppard (*Arcadia*) and Gore Vidal should all be writing about physics as history, or vice versa."[32] In some ways the novel is an elaborate series of fantasies upon many of Vidal's favorite themes, invoking his now familiar tropes of historical reconstruction (a brain-damaged Abraham Lincoln is curator of ceramics at the Institution), deliberate bad taste, and his own life to rewrite American history to better fit his ideals.

The novel plays on Vidal's fascination with first ladies, which was first explored in a 1975 article on the (separate) memoirs of Ulysses S. Grant and the posthumous one of his wife, Julia Dent Grant ("President and Mrs. U. S. Grant," in the *New York Review* September 18, 1975). Since the start of the nineteenth century, when Dolley Madison acted as hostess for both Thomas Jefferson and then her husband, the Presidential consort has occupied a particular role in American life, though the term itself did not become widely used until the inauguration of President Hayes, and his wife Lucy, in 1876. With no Constitutional or official sanction she has become a public figure, sometimes largely ceremonial – in recent times it is hard to associate any particular quality other than having married the right man with, say, Bess Truman or Mamie Eisenhower – sometimes, as in the case of Edith Wilson, Eleanor Roosevelt, or Hillary Clinton, with significant political clout. Warren Harding's wife, otherwise known as "the Duchess," is a significant character in *Hollywood*, and in *The Smithsonian Institution* Eleanor Roosevelt acts as intermediary between the dead Presidents in the museum and her own husband, currently occupying the White House.

Some of the rhetoric of the isolationist movement, with its hostility to British imperialism and its belief that the people, if they were not deceived, would opt for peace, reappears 50 years later in Vidal's more recent political writings. But then it is not uncommon for us to recapitulate our adolescent views as we grow older, and there are increasingly echoes of the old Senator Gore in his grandson, less the populist anti-Semitism. Anti-Semitism was remarkably widespread in the United States until after World War II; as Vidal has remarked, both he and John Kennedy had to repudiate the prejudices of their (grand)fathers. How successfully Vidal was able to do this is discussed later in this book.

After World War II, the United States embarked on a new period of global adventure, justified by fear of the Soviet Union and the alleged desire – and ability – of "international Communism" to undermine America and threaten its survival. While the Soviet Union was clearly a brutal dictatorship determined to impose its will on neighboring countries, it is less clear that it posed a real threat to the United States, or that the policy of supporting a string of equally repressive but anti-Soviet dictatorships across the world was necessary for American security. In retrospect it is clear that the United States was paramount in all but nuclear weapons, where the Soviets probably had enough power to deter any American attack. But from the late 1940s on, the United States internalized the apparent threat posed by the Soviets to create a strong fear both of imminent danger of war and of domestic subversion. The two were increasingly connected through allegations of treachery at the highest levels of American society – after all, how else could the most powerful nation on earth be in such danger? – exacerbated by the success of Mao Tse-tung's Communist Party in winning power in China, and forcing America's wartime ally Chiang-Kai-shek into exile in Taiwan. Perceptions of a global threat to the United States were further heightened when in mid-1950 the Communist government of North Korea invaded the South – the country having been divided as a consequence of wartime agreement between the United States and the Soviet Union. The Korean War would involve large numbers of American troops for the following three years, until a ceasefire restored the status quo.

Vidal sees the national security state as a construct of President Truman, under whose Presidency the United States, for the first time in its history, established itself on a permanent wartime footing and introduced loyalty checks on federal employees. He has increasingly argued that the creation of the national security state, and its justification through claims that the very survival of the United States was threatened by the Soviet Union, was essentially a cover for a more sinister intention, namely world dominance. "There it was," thought Peter, after Truman declared American support for "free peoples who are resisting attempted subjugation by armed minorities or by outside pressures," "*droit de seigneur*" (*Golden Age*: 307). Like other critics of American foreign policy Vidal posits a post-colonial imperialism, based on a particular mix of capitalist greed and moral rectitude. This stands in marked contrast to the more conventional view expressed by the British journalist Martin Walker: "The United States, against its instincts and traditions, was forced into a global role. It was bombed into war by Japan in 1941, and lured into remaining in Europe after 1947 . . . Even then the deployment of American power in the Cold War was limited."[33] Vidal would disagree with every one of these assertions.

There is a vast literature on the Cold War and American foreign policy of the past 50 years, and Vidal's view of American foreign policy is now widespread, at least amongst those whom supporters of the Bush Administration might dismiss as wimpish liberal intellectuals. Much of what is now standard criticism of United States foreign policy can be found in Vidal's novels of the post-World War II world, namely *Washington, D.C.* and, particularly, *The Golden Age*. In the latter Vidal has Truman articulate the very arguments which later generations of American political leaders would use to justify the growing involvement in Vietnam, and then reuse many years later in defence of support for the contras in Nicaragua and the invasion of Iraq in 2003: "History taught us all quite a lesson back in the thirties. You can't deal with totalitarian states because they only believe in force . . . Well, we're responding with more force than they ever dreamed of" (*Golden Age*: 402). Very similar language surfaced in the Reagan Administration's distinction between "totalitarian" and "authoritarian" states, and in Bush Jr's attacks on "the axis of evil."

What this criticism ignores is the extent to which Truman, and his advisors, genuinely believed they were threatened by monolithic Communist forces, directed and controlled by the Soviet government. In retrospect we can see that the Greek, Chinese, and Vietnamese Communist parties were as much driven by nationalism as by any direction from Moscow. Whether we can fault the Truman Administration for not understanding this requires a more nuanced analysis than Vidal provides. One could argue that the overthrowing of an elected government in Czechoslovakia in 1948, the attack by North Korea on the South in 1950, and the vast expenditures of the Soviet Union on military forces were real threats demanding a response from the United States for reasons other than a desire to expand American capitalist and military might.

One of Vidal's first published essays was on the Roman Caesars, and before he embarked on the American saga, Vidal was seeking parallels with the Roman Empire. Some of the early exchanges between the Jew, Ben-Hur, and the Roman, Messala, in the film *Ben-Hur* seem to be drawing clear parallels with the contemporary world, but it is risky to quote film scripts, given the number of people involved in writing them. Vidal does not even receive any official credit for the screenplay, half of which he wrote.[34] The comparison is developed in his adaptation of Dürrenmatt's play *Romulus* in 1961, where the Roman eagle stands in for the American, and Rome is threatened by "the international menace of Gothic-ism." Today the play reads like *A Funny Thing Happened on the Way to the Forum* crossed with an unsubtle satire of the Cold War.

Vidal first seriously dealt with the question of United States imperialism in his 1950 novel *Dark Green, Bright Red*, which is based on American interference in Central America, but is largely non-judgmental. *Dark Green, Bright Red* grew out of his own experience of living in Guatemala, and prefigures US action in Guatemala four years later, when the Central Intelligence Agency (CIA) assisted army officers to overthrow the democratically elected President Jacobo Arbenz Guzman, whose actions threatened the interests of the dominant American company, the United Fruit Company. The novel reads as a not very good imitation of Graham Greene, but the book is interesting for the early glimpse of American Cold War perceptions of Central America. Bernard Dick has pointed out that the politics of the book are very muddled, as if a young American is feeling his way in what he knows is US interference abroad,[35] although it is clear that the only real power is the American "company," obviously modelled on the United Fruit Company, which dominated Guatemala through its control of the banana industry. The company's colors were green and red.

Given his concern with both imperialist expansion and secret government, it is perhaps surprising that Vidal did not return in his later works to the critique of the CIA implied in *Dark Green, Bright Red*. For leftists critical of American foreign policy the CIA seemed a constant shadowy force, whose maneuvers explained a series of coups, civil wars, and all that they disliked in the United States' ambitions overseas. But while Mailer wrote a massive novel, *Harlot's Ghost*, on the theme, linking the history of the agency to the assassination of President Kennedy, Vidal returned to his criticism of the agency through satire in *Kalki*, where the CIA is as concerned in peddling drugs as it is in fighting Communists.

Masculinity and empire

"The American *ideal*, then, of sexuality appears to be rooted in the American ideal of masculinity. This ideal has created cowboys and Indians, good guys and bad guys, punks and studs, tough guys and softies, butch and faggot, black and white. It is an ideal so paralytically infantile that it is virtually forbidden – as an unpatriotic act – that the American boy evolve into the complexity of manhood."

James Baldwin: "Freaks and the American Ideal of Manhood", *Playboy*, January 1985; reprinted as "Here Be Dragons" in *The Price of the Ticket*, New York, St Martin's Press/Marek, 1985

Reading Vidal's American Chronicles and political essays, one is struck by the constant theme of war in American history, and the great savagery attendant on the growth of the United States to its current borders and global pre-eminence. Unlike most commentators Vidal sees links between the heroic mythology of settlement and independence (and the constant war on indigenous Americans), the bloodshed of the Civil War, and the semi-constant state of war that has characterized the relations of the United States to the rest of the world for much of the past century. In *Hollywood* Vidal allows one of his least favorite Presidents, Woodrow Wilson, to muse: "You see, I can *imagine* what this war will do to us . . . Because to fight to win, you must be brutal and ruthless, and that spirit of ruthless brutality will enter into the very fiber of our national life . . . But *what* shall we win? How do we help the South – I mean the Central Powers to return to a peace-time basis? How do we help ourselves? We shall have become what we are fighting. We shall be trying to reconstruct a peace-time civilization with war-time standards" (*Hollywood*: 45). Here Vidal allows Wilson, who remembered the Civil War, to sound the alarm that he, Vidal, has been consistently sounding for 40 years.

The preoccupation with empire illuminates both his writings on movies and his attacks on a particular style of American masculinity, which might well be represented by Garry Wills' imagery of John Wayne. Vidal is in some ways a pacifist, but one who can speak from the position of having actually served in war. Wayne did not, and was criticized at the time for avoiding service – unlike Ronald Reagan, whose sight was impaired, he had no physical disability. Wayne's association with military service is largely mythic, through films like *Sands of Iwo Jima* (1949), a film that remained a favorite for rightwing politicians 40 years later.[36] As Vidal tells us, through the voice of Myra Breckinridge: "By arranging so wisely to stay out of the Second World War, John Wayne was able to make not only *Flying Tigers* but *They Were Expendable* and those two pictures did more to defeat Tojo than all of General Chennault's air-raids on the enemy" (*Myra Breckinridge and Myron*: 344).

One of Vidal's great virtues is that, in a country that romanticizes war and violence, he remains clear-sighted in consistently opposing both. The connection between a particular view of masculinity and national expansionism is a consistent theme for Vidal, found in both his historical works and his fantasies. *Myra* and *Kalki* offer a sardonic commentary on masculine pretensions, and the relationship between male insecurities and the need to impose their will through armed force. As Myra reflects: "Thanks to my efforts, the American male now lacks the arrogant sexual thrust to conduct those wars that in the past were so necessary to population control through the playful use of antipersonnel weaponry" (*Myra Breckinridge and Myron*: 293).

In both cases Vidal uses a female narrator to puncture masculine pretensions – and while Myra is a transsexual and Teddy (Theodora Hecht Ottinger) is a bisexual feminist, they are also more than able to deal with male pretensions. Teddy – whose name echoes that most macho of American Presidents – is both a bad mother and a champion aviatrix; Myra, literally, deflowers the athletic Rusty. They stand, equally, against Theodore Roosevelt's admonition that a healthy (white) man should father at least four children; Myra and Teddy, alike, would recognize this as ecological suicide. Theodora recalls Isabella Wing, the independent heroine of Erica Jong's 1973 hit novel *Fear of Flying*, who shared her ability to take the sexual initiative. There is a clear connection in Vidal's writings to the feminist assertion that links masculine dominance and political repression, as when he asks: "Do we want a free society or a patriarchal one?" (*Imperial America*: 81).

In his historical novels the villains are usually those – Theodore Roosevelt is the great example – whose sense of masculinity required them to justify expansionist adventures. Of Roosevelt, Vidal wrote, memorably: "Give a sissy a gun and he will kill everything in sight" ("Theodore Roosevelt: An American Sissy," in *United States*: 733, originally published in the *New York Review of Books* 1981). No President seemed as keen on war as Roosevelt, though few have been reluctant to resort to it.

Vidal's infatuation with John Kennedy meant he was slow in seeing through the militaristic posturing of the President, whose conventionally macho views of foreign policy and sex seemed close to those implicit in the original James Bond movies, the first of which, *Doctor No*, was released in 1962. In a note added to an article on Kennedy, originally written in 1961, Vidal notes: "Secretly, I think he thought war was fun" ("President Kennedy," in *United States*: 803, originally published in the London *Sunday Telegraph* 1961). Many American Presidents might be seen to be acting out their personal insecurities through international posturing: one thinks not only of Kennedy, but also of Johnson, Nixon, and Bush Jr. Of post-war Presidents this analysis is least persuasive in the case of Eisenhower, the former general, and of Truman and Carter, who both served in the military and were consistently attacked for not being sufficiently willing to use maximum American military force. Vidal is hardly alone in pointing to the eagerness of Bush and Cheney to go to war, as against the more cautious positions of those genuine veterans, Secretary of State Colin Powell and the 2004 Democratic Presidential candidate John Kerry.

The constant need for American Presidents to show toughness in the face of small, weak "enemies," whether it was Johnson and Nixon in Vietnam, Reagan in Grenada, or Bush Sr in Panama, makes a psychological explanation attractive, and there have been attempts amongst some recent scholars of international relations to provide such explanations.[37] Yet here Vidal's own skepticism about psychoanalysis should be heeded. Powerful nations resort to force largely because they can, and what seems unique about the United States is not its desire to impose its will upon others, but rather the need to justify it in ideological language of universal virtue. Myra comes close to a psychoanalytic explanation when she points to the collapse of traditional masculinity:

Today there is nothing left for the old-fashioned male to do, no ritual testing of his manhood through initiation or personal contest, no physical struggle to survive or mate ... Marlon Brando was the last of the traditional heroes and significantly, even he was invariably beaten up in the last reel, victim of a society that has no place for the ancient ideal of manhood.

(*Myra Breckinridge and Myron*: 59)

Myra was published in the same year as Norman Mailer's parable *Why Are We in Vietnam?*, the story of a hunting expedition made by an 18-year-old in the wilds of Alaska on the eve of his induction into the army, which some critics have described as a scatological version of *Huckleberry Finn*. Ironically the book suggests that the answer lies in the very constructions of American masculinity that Mailer himself applauded in others of his writings, and that Vidal would satirize in *Myron*.

Myra was, of course, writing in 1968; what, one wonders, would she have made of the caricature of masculinity found in the next generation of stars – Sylvester Stallone, Arnold Schwarzenegger, Jean-Claude van Damme – whose exaggerated masculinity only serves to underline the reality that muscles have become a fashion accessory, acquired more often in the gym than in actual physical labor? Foreigners are struck by the apparently obsessive need of American Presidential candidates to assert their masculinity, which seemed to dominate the contest between George W. Bush and John Kerry in 2004.

Vidal's hostility to war, born of both his own experience and the memories of the defeated south with which he grew up, explains what I have come to see as his greatest blindness, a failure to grasp the full magnitude of the scars left by race on the United States. American imperialism – a word rarely used by Vidal – was deeply racial, and the United States was founded on a double dispossession, that of the original inhabitants and that of the African slaves who were brought to farm the south. Yet there seems more compassion in Vidal's discussion of the savagery with which the United States crushed the Filipino independence movement after wresting that country from Spain than there is when he alludes to slavery and the Afro-American experience.

―――― four ――――

POLITICS

"In politics, as in love, opposites attract, and the misunderstandings
that ensue tend to be as bitter and, as in love, equally terminal."

Lincoln: 106

"People who obtain power do so because it delights them for its own
sake and for no other reason."

Two Sisters: 124

"What were Americans afraid of?"

Hollywood: 361

For Vidal politics is sexier than love. He sees himself as born to
politics: reminiscences of his grandfather anchor his increasingly
autobiographical reflections on public life, and his sometimes
bizarre mix of snobbery, populism, and abiding suspicion of
Franklin Roosevelt. Senator Thomas Pryor Gore had been a
populist who moved from Mississippi to help establish the state
of Oklahoma, joined the Democrats at the age of 29, and was
elected Senator for Oklahoma for three terms (1907–21; 1931–7),
living in Washington until his death in 1949. However, he
became increasingly conservative, a shift reflected in his falling
out with both Presidents Wilson and Roosevelt, and his opposition to the New Deal. His influence on Vidal is striking. His
grandfather is an explicit presence in *Hollywood* and *Washington,
D.C.*, but he also inspires much else: it is not accidental that the
narrator of *Creation* is an old blind statesman. From Senator Gore
came a lifelong preoccupation with politics, and the desire for a

political career. Even Vidal's pseudonymous detective novels show a fascination with contemporary politics rarely found in that genre.

Combine this with his (twice removed) family link to the Kennedys (via Jackie) and a southern connection to Vice President (1993–2001) Al Gore, who is either a first cousin once removed or a fifth cousin, depending on which source one consults, and there exists a burden as great as that borne by hereditary peers in Britain renouncing their titles. (At times Vidal also claims a relationship to former President Carter, though it does not restrain his contempt for him.) Recently Vidal has spoken of "the Gore blood" in ways that recall the haughtiest of the Bourbons.[1] In an interview in 1992 he exclaimed: "I have a general view that this is *my* country. My family helped start it, and we've been in political life of one kind or another since the 1690s" (interview with Larry Kramer in Weise 1999: 259). Some of the pull of a political career is explored in his early picaresque novel *The Judgment of Paris*, whose protagonist is tempted to choose between pleasure, making money, and the possibility of a political career. Senator Gore hoped that his grandson might establish himself in New Mexico, which he saw as providing the basis for a political career, but the Senator died in 1949, a decade before Vidal's first real attempt to enter political life.

Vidal inherited his Democratic allegiance from his grandfather, who brought together two of the main streams of the twentieth-century Democrats: a white southern base, reflected in the settlement of Oklahoma, and agrarian populism. Unlike Wilson and Roosevelt, Senator Gore had little to do with the big city bosses of the northeast or the liberal intellectuals who would play an increasing role in the party, and whose support was so crucial for John Kennedy. But until his break with the Kennedys, Vidal seemed to envisage politics as an enterprise, not a matter of principles, which might explain the ferocity of his latter denunciations of political expediency. The closest he came to continuing the family business, as he referred to it, was the race for a House of Representatives seat in 1960 in Dutchess County, north of New York City, where Harry Truman, Jack Kennedy, and Eleanor Roosevelt all campaigned for him. Although he lost he did outpoll

Kennedy in a traditionally Republican area. Forty years later, Dutchess County also voted strongly against Hillary Clinton in her (successful) bid for the Senate representing New York.

Two decades later Vidal ran for the Democrat Senatorial nomination in California in 1982, which he lost to former Governor Jerry Brown, who in turn lost to Pete Wilson. Unlikely as it was that he could beat Brown, who had the support of the party machine, Vidal was prepared to use his celebrity and own money to run a plausible campaign (in a sixway contest he polled 15 percent against 51 percent for Brown). Vidal drew large crowds, particularly on university campuses, and had some support from intellectual, leftist and gay Democrats, but was without any real political connections to major groups within the party, especially racial minorities and unions. In an interview a few years later with the British *New Left Review* Vidal briefly discussed the campaign, claiming he was hated by "the wine-and-cheese liberals," and claiming support from "blacks, from Jewish women, from some Hispanics,"[2] but I have not been able to find a reliable analysis of the Democratic vote. His policies put him to the left of Brown and allowed him to propose measures such as a nuclear freeze and tax on corporations, which would otherwise not have been voiced. In 1992 Brown approached Vidal for help in his campaign for the Democratic presidential nomination, which was subsequently won by Bill Clinton.

Had Vidal won the primary it is almost inconceivable that he could have been elected Senator by a state that at the time was largely conservative. In retrospect it is difficult to understand his decision to enter the race, and he has been surprisingly reticent about it: in a long interview about his life in 1989 he discussed his earlier race for Congress, and his role in the People's Party, while saying virtually nothing about the California campaign.[3] Asked whether he would ever run again after his defeat, Vidal commented that: "All politicians are recidivists."

At one point he even mused with several Labor politicians about moving to Australia to enter politics. While this was almost certainly idle speculation, he has had warm relations with some Australian Labor politicians, particularly Gough

Whitlam, Prime Minister from 1972 to 1975, and Bob Carr, Premier of the largest state, New South Wales, since 1995. Vidal met Whitlam on his first visit to Australia in 1974, and was delighted by a head of government who was not only a social democrat but also knew enough ancient history to discuss the Emperor Julian with him. In some ways the two men resemble each other: "Difficult," reflected Vidal, in speaking of Whitlam, "to distinguish between vanity and overweening vanity."

The ambivalence Vidal demonstrated about entering a serious political career, in particular his rejection of what was almost certainly his best opportunity to do so in 1964, reveals a certain recognition of the near impossibility of combining creative writing and mainstream politics. It is difficult to imagine a Congressman Gore Vidal immersing himself in the concerns of the upstate New York dairy industry, or the state of the roads in Poughkeepsie, which are the sort of concerns that demand the most constant attention from elected representatives. A writer can create the world in his own image, and then master it. A politician is constantly required to serve the whims of others, and while both careers demand largescale ego and ambition, one wonders whether Vidal ever had the ability to suffer fools graciously to the extent required by the democratic process.

Between his two widely separated forays into electoral politics, Vidal became a regular commentator on American politics; commencing in 1972 he delivered an annual "state of the union" address for some years on David Susskind's television show, sometimes using it as the basis for public speeches and publishing it in major magazines. The title is both homage to and an ironic echo of the President's annual address to Congress. In his role as a Pennsylvania Senator in *Bob Roberts* (1992) he also gets to address the camera on the faults of the American system.

From a standard Democratic liberalism, under which banner he ran for Congress, Vidal has moved to a position in which left and right populism merge: even though he is seen as on the left, his views are strangely sympathetic to some rightwingers on some issues, especially isolationism. He is praised by some libertarians,* and his books can be found on one website devoted to "survivalist books," along with more predictable works on self-sufficiency, home schooling and protection of firearms. Despite their political differences Vidal regarded Barry Goldwater, the Republican candidate for President in 1964 and the precursor to the rightwing shift of the Republicans under Reagan and Bush Jr, as one of the few honest men in politics ("Introduction," *An Evening with Richard Nixon*: x).

Vidal's move to the left during the past 30 years has some echoes in a few sections of the Democratic Party, although he defies the standard assumptions, more often inaccurate than one might think, that age makes one more conservative. He stands, then, in marked contrast to the greater number of Democrats whose response to the social and cultural upheavals of the 1960s was to move to the right, many of them becoming neo-conservative supporters of Reagan in the 1980s. He stands in even more marked contrast to Reagan himself, who at the time Vidal was publishing his first books was a strong New Deal Democrat, and campaigned against Richard Nixon when he ran for the Senate in California.

Vidal first started questioning the conservative populism of his grandfather in the 1950s, a time when seeming content and consensus, presided over by President Eisenhower, whom Vidal liked to call "the great Golfer," concealed unspoken inequalities of race and sex. Economic affluence produced a huge growth of suburbia, of white-collar jobs (symbolized in Sloan Wilson's "man in the grey flannel suit"), of women socialized to believe that all happiness was to be found in the right home, husband, and children. This was an image of social arrangements parodied in *The Stepford Wives*, and one that would be critiqued in Betty Friedan's feminist work *The Feminine Mystique* (1964), probably the founding text of contemporary American femi-

---

*Libertarians believe in absolute individual freedom, and might be regarded as anarchists who believe that the market will create order. Generally thought of as on the right, they are bitterly opposed to the moral and legal agendas of the Reagan or Bush Administrations. Those libertarians who praise Vidal carefully avoid mentioning his support for social democratic policies of redistribution.

nism. In fact there was more resistance to the apparent political harmony in the 1950s than is often acknowledged, in particular through the growth of the civil rights movement and the emergence of a teenage culture, symbolized in the films of James Dean and the music of Elvis Presley, which foreshadowed the cultural and political upheavals of the 1960s. Todd Haynes' film *Far from Heaven* (2002) captures very well the gap between the respectable surface and the deep frustrations and repressions hidden beneath.

Much of the political landscape of the period was overshadowed by fear of what was widely believed to be the inexorable threat of Communist expansion and possible nuclear war. That events abroad seemed to threaten the United States in ways unknown since Pearl Harbor was fodder for the demagoguery of Senator Joe McCarthy. Through his highly publicized Senatorial hearings into "un-American activities," McCarthy's allegations about Communist influence in Hollywood, the universities, and the State Department effectively destroyed large numbers of careers, until McCarthy himself was brought down by increasingly wild allegations directed even at figures such as General George Marshall, former Secretary of State and a hero of World War II.

"McCarthyism" has come to stand for a tendency during the late 1940s and early 1950s for patriotism to justify increasing demands for ideological conformity, when any signs of dissent were dismissed as pro-Communist and hence anti-American. In 1948 President Truman established the Attorney General's list of subversive organizations and a system of government security clearances, helping to create a mood of fear and suspicion. It is a mood that Richard Nixon profited from to build his political career, and one that is now remembered through Arthur Miller's allegorical play *The Crucible* and two powerful novels based on the Rosenberg trial, Robert Coover's *The Public Burning* and E. L. Doctorow's *The Book of Daniel.** In the 1990s Tony Kushner

*Julius and Ethel Rosenberg were among a small group of American Communists accused of passing atomic secrets to the Soviet Union. As the only ones of the accused who refused to cooperate with the government they were finally executed for treason in 1953.

made one of McCarthy's key lieutenants, Roy Cohn, a central character in his allegorical play *Angels in America.*

Such moods are not unprecedented in American history: there is a long tradition of a search for internal enemies being used as a justification to limit the freedoms guaranteed by the United States Constitution. McCarthyism built on a similar "Red Scare" at the end of World War I, and in some ways prefigured the special powers assumed by the Bush Administration to fight terrorism after the events of September 11, 2001. As Vidal wrote in *Messiah*, a book published in the wake of McCarthy's downfall: "The body politic was more than unusually upset by signs of nonconformity . . . I have often thought that much of our national irritability was closely related to the unexpected and reluctant custody of the world the second war had pressed upon the confused grandchildren of a proud, isolated people, both indifferent and strange to the ways of other cultures" (13). In later years he would restate these views somewhat more stridently.

Vidal was too young to have been involved in any of the organizations targeted by McCarthy, but he opposed McCarthyism in a number of his writings, including one of his television plays, *A Sense of Justice*, where he posed the question of when is it moral to kill a tyrant. His first detective story, *Death in the Fifth Position* (1952), satirizes McCarthyism in a way unusual for a genre novel, and allegations of Communism become crucial to the plot. There are also considerable references to homosexuality, which is handled in a way that was both brave and unusual for the period. Indeed political references run through all three of his detective novels; *Death before Bedtime* (1954) is his first Washington novel and includes a cutting satire of President Truman's daughter, Margaret, whose father publicly supported her ambitions as a singer.

The Kennedy Presidency was formative for Vidal's political shifts, and it is instructive that he begins his memoirs by stressing his links, familial and for a time political, with that period of American life. Through his half-half-sister, Jackie, he had established an entrée to the White House, although President Kennedy, while seemingly enjoying his company, ignored Gore's offer to serve in his administration. When Vidal ran for Congress in 1960 he was seemingly untroubled by Kennedy's Cold War rhetoric, although he did advocate the recognition of Communist China, a policy that was both obvious and deeply divisive. It was not until 1972 that President Nixon abandoned the myth that the exiled government of Chiang-Kai-shek in Taiwan spoke for China, thus allowing the Beijing government to assume China's seat in the United Nations. Nixon had previously attacked such a position as being "soft on Communism."

Vidal was attracted by Kennedy's charm, ruthlessness, and successful promiscuity – indeed he has compared his own sexual exploits with Kennedy's. His break with the President had nothing to do with policies, but followed a bitter dispute at a White House party with Kennedy's brother and Attorney General, Robert, whom he distrusted and who he suspected, probably rightly, resented Gore's claims to a family relationship with Jackie.[4] In 1964, when Robert ran as a Democrat for the Senate seat from New York, Vidal actively campaigned for the incumbent Republican, Kenneth Keating. Robert Kennedy won the election and remained in the Senate until his assassination while seeking the Presidential nomination in 1968.

Robert Kennedy almost certainly did Vidal a service in ending, abruptly, the illusion that he might be part of a mainstream administration. By the mid-1960s, when Vidal wrote *Washington, D.C.*, he sought to come to terms with his own disillusionment with Kennedy through the creation of the ambitious Clay Overbury, a false war hero who rises to become a conservative Democrat star: *"the* young man on the rise" (366). (Overbury dies in a mysterious plane crash in *The Golden Age* to allow his similitude, JFK, who was not a character in *Washington, D.C.*, to become President.) Vidal stresses Overbury's good looks, echoing Tennessee Williams' comment that Kennedy was too good-looking to become President (and to explain the attraction Overbury holds for his patron, Senator Burden Day). But Kennedy remains a presence through Vidal's subsequent political writings, and it is revealing that he ends his 2003 meditation on the Presidency, *Inventing a Nation*, with a reference to

Kennedy's musing on the greatness of the eighteenth-century Founding Fathers. In his widely read article *The Holy Family*, first published in *Esquire* in 1967, Vidal concluded that the administration, despite drawing on "the best and the brightest" of American minds, was a failure: "He was reluctant to rock the boat, and it is significant that he often quoted Hotspur on summoning spirits from the deep; any man can summon, but will the spirits come? JFK never found out; he would not take the chance" ("The Holy Family," in *United States*: 821, originally published in *Esquire* 1967).

In retrospect Vidal blamed Kennedy for the escalation of the war in Vietnam, an escalation inherited and expanded by Presidents Johnson and Nixon, though interestingly Indo-China is not mentioned in his 1967 article on the Kennedys. The men who planned the escalation of United States commitment to South Vietnam were men whose worldview was shaped by the memories of World War II, the failure to stand up to German and Japanese aggression, and the invasion of South Korea by the North. But these situations were strikingly different. Vietnam, along with Cambodia and Laos, was part of the former French Indo-Chinese colonies that had been conquered by the Japanese in World War II. After the war the French sought to restore their colonial rule and were opposed by a nationalist movement led by the Communist Party under the leadership of Ho Chi Minh. President Eisenhower refused military support to the French, who finally agreed to leave Indo-China in 1955. In the peace settlement Vietnam was divided into two, but the partition was supposed to be ended within two years with national elections. As the Communists would almost have certainly won free elections, the United States decided to support the then South Vietnamese government in seeking to make the division of the country permanent. When the North responded by military support for Communist guerrillas in the South (the National Liberation Front), successive American Presidents sent increasing military aid, and under President Johnson effectively went to war with North Vietnam. While many Americans drew parallels with Hitler's aggression in the 1930s, the more appropriate comparison may well be Lincoln's determination to hold the Union together, with Ho Chi Minh the national unifier in the case of Vietnam.

Like many other Americans, Vietnam led Vidal to question increasingly the assumptions which underlay the Cold War: "Thanks to Vietnam," he wrote in a 1993 preface to *Empire*, "we came to realize that, like everyone else, we are simply at sea in history, and that somehow our republic had got lost along the way." By the 1970s this had become a constant theme in most of his writings.

Vidal was clearly marked by the widespread radicalization of the 1960s and his subsequent political writings echo much of the critique expressed by the New Left. In its defining statement, drafted largely by Tom Hayden, the newly formed Students for a Democratic Society (SDS) proclaimed:

> We are people of this generation, bred in at least modest comfort, housed now in universities, looking uncomfortably at the world we inherit . . . Freedom and equality for each individual, government of, by, and for the people – these American values we found good, principles by which we could live as men [sic] . . . (Port Huron Statement 1962)

But Vidal was a generation older than the baby boomers, for whom the civil rights and anti-war movements were defining experiences, and the New Left's emphasis on the generational divide must have been a sharp reminder that time had already made him and the Kennedy brothers politically middle-aged. Even so, his sympathy for the New Left meant his politics started to diverge from those of many of the intellectual and heavily Jewish New York literati with whom he had been associated, leading to future public feuds with such neo-conservative figures as that redoubtable New York intellectual couple Norman Podhoretz and Midge Decter.

1968 was the crucial year for many leftists. It was the year in which the growing anti-war movement forced Lyndon Johnson to withdraw from recontesting the Presidency; the assassination of Martin Luther King was followed several months later by that of Robert Kennedy; black riots and student demonstrations erupted across the country. In some ways this seemed too much for an overstretched nation to bear, and the year ended with the election of Richard Nixon, the man who had claimed to have run his last political race six years earlier. Vidal was a media commentator at both the Miami Republican and the Chicago Democratic Convention, paired by ABC television with the rightwing commentator William F. Buckley, with whom he had already publicly feuded. By the time of the Chicago Convention the internal debates within and around the Democrats, bitterly divided between their eventual nominee, Vice President Hubert Humphrey, and anti-war Senator Eugene McCarthy, seemed to duplicate the divisions within America at large.[5] The Chicago police clashed with anti-war demonstrators in scenes of considerable violence, which at times threatened to extend to the floor of the Convention itself.

Both Vidal and Buckley were angry and upset by the events in Chicago, but they saw them in radically different ways. For Vidal there was unmistakeable evidence of police brutality directed at the large numbers of protestors who gathered in the streets and parks of Chicago. For Buckley the crowds threatened the democratic process, and encouraged the enemy against whom American soldiers were fighting in Vietnam. Out of mutual anger, frustration, and dislike came a televised exchange in which Vidal called Buckley a "crypto Nazi" and Buckley responded by addressing Vidal as "you queer."[6] In retrospect – perhaps even then – Vidal's comment seems the more offensive, and he has acknowledged that he should have used the term "fascist-minded" instead. But neither used language as offensive as that heard within the halls of the Convention itself: Governor Ribicoff of Connecticut referred to Gestapo tactics on the streets of Chicago, to which Mayor Daley responded by addressing him as "you Jew son of a bitch, you lousy motherfucker" (Kaplan 1999: 599).

The early 1970s saw a polarization in American politics not to be matched until the Presidency of George W. Bush, 30 years later. Richard Nixon had been elected in 1968 promising he would end the war in Vietnam; instead he escalated it. The expansion of the war saw a corresponding growth in the anti-war movement, and a significant shift to the left within the Democratic Party. By the 1970s Vidal was clearly identifying with a left critique of the US: in his play *An Evening with Richard Nixon* the ghost of George Washington has the following exchange with former President Kennedy:

WASHINGTON: You were murdered, your brother was murdered, more citizens are murdered in the streets of the United States than in all the other western countries put together. And of course your armies specialize in murdering civilians by the million . . .

KENNEDY: The United States has six percent of the world's population. Yet America uses forty percent of the world's raw resources. That is why we are in Vietnam. (*An Evening with Richard Nixon*: 94)

This was a period when many of America's best-known writers were expressing their opposition to the administration, which reciprocated by including some of them on its infamous "enemies lists." In addition to Norman Mailer's novel *Why Are We in Vietnam?*, Philip Roth wrote a scathing satire of Nixon, *Our Gang* (1971), which, unlike Vidal's device of largely quoting Nixon's own words, takes those words and parodies them in a savage indictment of the President. At one point Vidal claimed that, just as Virgil wrote a history of Rome for the Emperor Augustus, so he wrote *Burr* for "the Emperor Nixon."[7]

Vidal became co-chairman of the People's Party (1970–2), an attempt to create an electoral alternative to the two major parties. Neither the party, nor Vidal's interest, lasted much beyond the 1972 election, where the Democrats did, after all, nominate their most radical candidate of the century, George McGovern, allowing Richard Nixon to win an even greater victory than had Franklin Roosevelt in the Depression election of 1936, which had established the Democrats as the majority party for the next half-century. The People's Party's nomination of Benjamin Spock in 1972 for the Presidency took a few votes away from McGovern, who at the time Vidal dismissed as "noble but futile,"[8] though they made no difference to the ultimate result. While the forced resignation of Nixon is often argued as showing the ultimate success of the American system, it seemed to lead to a growing pessimism in Vidal's perceptions of the United States, and gloomy forecasts of its inevitable fall from military and economic power. The growing pessimism apparent in Vidal's writings from the 1970s reflected the national mood, influenced as it was by the defeat in Vietnam and the shock to the economy of major oil price hikes in 1974. But Vidal's position was in no way shaken by Reagan's promise of "morning in America," or even by the hopes which lasted for a few years after the fall of the Berlin Wall, and the end of the Cold War, for the possibility of "a new world order."

After 1972 Vidal seemed unexcited by the prospects of a Democratic President, and in his campaign for the Senate nomination in 1982 he had no connection to any potential national Democrat leader. Of the 1984 election Vidal acknowledged there were marginal differences between President Reagan and former Vice President Mondale, allowing Mondale only one substantial advantage, when, in typically hubristic mode, he wrote:

> Mondale has said corporations ought to pay tax. In fact he picked up something from my '82 Senate campaign; corporations no longer pay any tax, and I was going around giving this speech saying they should pay a flat 15% on profits, and no fiddling. Mondale made the mistake of saying that, and now there is not a chance in the world that he will be accepted as President.[9]

In the afterword to *1876* he observed: "[this] year was probably the low point in our republic's history" (363), and in *Kalki* (1978) he refers to "that majority of the electorate who were not apathetic yet never vote because there was no point" (137). Because Vidal has often refused to draw distinctions between politicians who might actually be elected, he increasingly irritates those who work within the mainstream. Writing in 1980, he claimed that there was no real choice between Carter and Reagan, and he gave money to the Independent campaign of John Anderson, a liberal Republican. The possibility that Carter tried to reduce American triumphalism, indeed to develop a foreign policy in which respect for human rights was not simply defined in terms of dominant American ideology, is not even considered by Vidal. Indeed, other than Ford, the most accidental of all American Presidents, Carter seemed to have interested Vidal least of all his contemporaries, although a more nuanced analysis would actually find much in Carter to admire. "He was ill-suited for the Presidency," wrote Vidal almost twenty years later, "because his virtues – an engineer's convergent mind – were of no use in a job that requires almost surreal divergency . . . Happily, he was born to be a *former* President, a phantom office that he has since enhanced" ("Candid in Camera," in *The Nation,* September 27, 1999).

During the Presidencies of Carter, Reagan, and Bush Sr, Vidal positioned himself as the voice of permanent opposition. As he was to say of his contemporary President George Bush Sr, "I know exactly how Bush of Mesopotamia sees the world because I see it as he does, but Bush has never questioned any of it as he scrambled up the conventional ladder, while I pushed the ladder away and drifted off into the vision thing" (*Screening History*: 80). A more accurate way of putting this might be to have pointed out that Vidal's trajectory was leading in largely the opposite direction to that of the country at large: as the mainstream seemed to shift to a more conservative position, Vidal's own politics became more clearly leftist. Vidal never had any illusions about the Soviet Union, or indeed any other alternative to the American model; his leftism is a deeply American one, born of a deep belief in the liberal ideals of the eighteenth-century rebels against British rule.

The conservative alliance that Nixon foreshadowed, and that Reagan built from support for free market economics, a staunchly anti-community foreign policy and moral conservatism, has persisted sufficiently to divide the country almost exactly between conservative Republicans and somewhat more liberal conservative Democrats, represented by President Clinton and the two successive Democratic candidates, Al Gore and John Kerry. In such an America Vidal found himself increasingly marginalized, and the election of Bush Jr in 2000, and the terrorist attacks the following year, increased both his marginality and the urgency of his appeals for Americans to reverse course. One should also note that while Vidal, at least in some moods, likes to suggest his links to ruling-class families such as the Bushes and the Kennedys, he also stresses, rightly, that his family is not wealthy, and despite Senator Gore's support for the oil industry in Oklahoma there is no suggestion of the sort of major financial benefits that have linked the Bushes to both domestic and foreign oil interests.

Despite his cordial meeting with Hillary, Vidal had little time for Bill Clinton through most of his Presidency, and as late as 1998 was referring to the "protofascist program" of "lots more prisons, death penalties, harassment of the poor, cries of terrorism, and, implicitly control by government over the citizenry" (*The Last Empire*: 146). The attempt to impeach Clinton in that year did, however, lead him to turn his full bile against the Republican right for their attempt to, as he saw it, undermine the Constitution by promoting impeachment on spurious grounds. Here the majority of Americans appeared to agree with Vidal, and while the Republican majority in the House of Representatives voted to impeach, the Senate found him not guilty of perjury and split evenly on the question of obstruction of justice. Five Republican Senators – all from the northeast, and the rump of what used to be called moderate or Rockefeller Republicans – supported the President on both votes.

But if Vidal had sympathy for Clinton once he ran foul of rightwing venom masquerading as a defence of morality, he was far less sympathetic to Clinton's overall policies, either domestic or foreign. Of the terrors in Rwanda, Kosovo, and Bosnia – and Clinton's reluctance to use American force to intervene – Vidal has little to say, although he clearly saw Clinton as continuing a bipartisan policy of American expansion.

Vidal's opposition to American expansionism grows out of a genuine American tradition, but it has put him increasingly at odds with the dominant mood, and leads to accusations of his being "anti-American." As he wrote in 2003:

the great combine of military, media, religious mania, and lust for oil has overthrown those safeguards that the first three Presidents, for all their disagreements, were as one in wishing to preserve, protect and defend. (*Inventing a Nation*: 127)

Post-War America has been both triumphalist and uneasy, simultaneously proclaiming the superiority of American achievements and fearing attacks and infiltration (by Communists, drug dealers, terrorists). Vidal has made himself deeply unpopular with defenders of American hegemony by pointing to the absurdities of many American actions, such as "Operation Urgent Fury," when President Reagan sent marines to Grenada, a country with the population of Fargo, North Dakota, to overthrow a government which he claimed threatened regional peace. In response Vidal might well quote the South African satirist Pieter-Dirk Uys, who said that a patriot is someone who protects his country from its government.[10]

Vidal is fond of invoking the second law of thermodynamics, which states that everything must inevitably decline. This view seems to underlie his analysis of the American polity, thus setting him firmly against the dominant belief in progress and the inevitable march towards an American world. Rereading his political essays from the past 30 years, one is struck by his increasing gloom about the United States, and the predictions of disaster and disintegration that have essentially not occurred: the United States under Bush Jr may be more loathed and feared in many countries than before, but it remains demonstrably the world's dominant military, economic, and cultural power. Perhaps Vidal's pessimism is his greatest affront to mainstream American pundits, both liberal and conservative: even smart conservatives, like Anders Lewis, use it to argue that: "Vidal does not like America,"[11] an absurd statement given Vidal's lifelong commitment to restoring what he sees as the true strengths of America. His tone may have got shriller, but his belief in restoring what he claims is the true American political heritage has not diminished. He may not like America but he clearly loves it. In his defence of isolationism, *America First*, Bill Kauffman devotes a chapter to "Patriotic Gore Vidal."[12]

Already in 1982 the acerbic English writer Martin Amis was presenting Vidal as "incorrigibly anti-American": "My, is Gore unpatriotic! No pomaded Hanoverian swaggerer could have such natural contempt for that coarse and greedy colony . . ."[13] It is not surprising that by the time Vidal published his 2003 book on the first three Presidents he was seen as "anti-American," and attacked for "his antipathy toward the 'American Empire' and contempt for the American public" (*Publisher's Weekly*) and "contempt for contemporary America" (*Booklist*). Yet as Daniel Lazare has pointed out: "the more anti-American he becomes, the more American he reveals himself to be. In politico-taxonomical terms, he is an 'Old Whig,' a premodern Anglo-American type that our eighteenth-century Constitution has preserved as if in amber. The Old Whigs were angry patriots, furious over their country's slide into imperialist decadence and filled with nostalgia for the rustic old Republic, when ways were simpler and people were braver, more courageous and more honest."[14] The note of nostalgia to which Lazare points is important, and not uncommon amongst leftists: in Vidal's case it is combined with a particular snobbery that recalls Oscar Wilde's famous quip about dining with Tories while voting with Whigs. Despite Vidal's scathing criticisms of him, John Kennedy was the last of the aristocratic Presidents, and shared a set of values with Vidal that are missing in his cruder successors.

The United States has enormous tolerance for self-criticism, but only when it ultimately reaffirms the American Dream. A writer like Tom Wolfe is also preoccupied with the "ruling class," those men (and they appear to be all men) whom he termed "masters of the universe" in his novel *The Bonfire of the Vanities*, and he appears more aware than Vidal of the huge divides of race and class, which are central in his 1998 novel *A Man in Full*. But while his novels could be read as a searing indictment of the failures of the United States, Wolfe retains a strong faith in the success of the American Dream. No one would call Wolfe anti-American. But the term itself is largely nonsense, usually applied not against those who would destroy the United States but rather against those who are motivated by patriotism to remake it.

Vidal and America in the twenty-first century

"I am no less a historian than those who are paid to keep the two
essential facts of our condition from the people at large: the American class system (there is no such thing, we are flatly told) and the
nature of the U. S. empire (no such thing, either)." (*Dreaming War*:
159)

By the turn of the century Vidal's political analysis was so critical of mainstream American politics as to place him outside the
conventional divide between liberals and conservatives, or, as
the current language has it, between "blue" (Democrat) and
"red" (Republican) America. (I am not sure why American usage
has reversed the long established link of "red" to the parties of
the left, which must sound ironic to a generation who grew up
in fear of "the red menace.") In 2002 Vidal published his pamphlet *Perpetual War for Perpetual Peace* (*PWPP*; the title comes
from a phrase of Charles Beard's, the radical American historian), but only after sections of the manuscript had been rejected
for publication in the United States, and had first appeared in
France and Italy. Published in the United States by the Nation
Press, it did remarkably well, 50,000 copies selling out in the first
few weeks, despite an absence of reviews and advertising. His
subsequent pamphlet, *Dreaming War: Blood for Oil and the Cheney-
Bush Junta*, was listed by Amazon Books (one of the best guides
around to how books are selling) as particularly popular in
Californian college towns, in Jamaica, New York, and Croatia.
The essays have been translated into over half a dozen languages, and, attending the Adelaide Festival of Ideas in 2003, I
noticed both books selling well to the largely middle-class and
middle-aged Australian audience. Yet Todd Gitlin, a former SDS
leader, and a man still identified with the left, excoriated Vidal
for his views in these pamphlets, referring to him as a former
great wit, now "a witless crank."[15]

The lead essay in *Dreaming War* first appeared as a cover story
in the London *Observer*, whose cover proclaimed "a shocking
new view of 9/11." While Vidal suggested that warnings of a
terror attack had been ignored (a charge subsequently made by

Richard Clarke, head of counter-intelligence within the White House),[16] his main concern was to argue that the Bush Administration used the attacks as a pretext for war with Afghanistan, and then Iraq, because of a desire to control oil resources in the Middle East, a less "shocking," though not necessarily accurate, view than it might have seemed at the time.[17] Yet if the major aim of the United States was to ensure access to oil resources, which Saddam's government was keen to sell, then embarking on a war to overthrow the government – and possibly increase political instability in the country and the wider region – was hardly a rational means to achieve this end.

This is not to negate some of the criticisms Vidal makes of the Bush Administration. Vidal did not claim, as has sometimes been alleged, that the administration had specific warnings of the September 11 attacks. Equally his assertion that "the awesome physical damage Osama and company did to us on Dark Tuesday is as nothing compared to the knockout blow to our vanishing liberties" (*PWPP*: 18–19) seems less provocative now, in the wake of the Iraq War and the 2004 campaign, than it did in the immediate aftermath of the September 11 attacks. And his assertion that the "war on terror" is as absurd as a "war on dandruff," because one cannot go to war against an abstract noun, is more than a clever grammatical point. Even the more outrageous of Vidal's pronouncements are based on careful assessment of political realities, and are supported by many mainstream commentators and analysts.

Since his radicalization during "the sixties" Vidal has fairly consistently maintained that there is "only one party, which I call the Property Party . . . It makes no difference whether a Democrat's elected or a Republican's elected" (Stanton and Vidal 1980: 256). He elaborated on this theme in his essay "Homage to Daniel Shays," where he argues:

> Whether he knows it or not, the middle-income American is taxed as though he were living in a socialist society. But for the money he gives the government he gets nothing back. He does pay for a lot of military hardware, and his congressman will point to all the jobs "defense" (that happy euphemism) contracts bring to his

district, as if the same federal money could not create even more jobs doing things that needed doing as well as benefiting directly the man who paid the taxes in the first place. (*United States*: 909)

This is essentially a restatement of John Kenneth Galbraith's famous quip that America has socialism for the rich and capitalism for the poor, and 30 years later the taxation policies of the Bush Administration make that judgment all the more accurate. Daniel Shays led a revolt of small farmers against land taxes in the early years of the Republic, and his spirit lives on in the frequent populist moves to restrict taxes. Vidal has consistently said he is willing to pay taxes, but they should be spent on social programs, not bolstering "defense" and the incomes of huge corporations. Vidal might have shown how deep-rooted are these practices by citing evidence uncovered by Harry Truman's Senatorial investigations before World War II, which demonstrated the way in which certain major American-based corporations colluded with German companies to maintain supplies and profits.[18] To do so would, however, undermine his own claims that Truman's "national security state" acted at the behest of these same corporations.

His is a tempting analysis, but one that on reflection seems flawed. The reduction of power in the United States to a simple equation of wealth to political power is to miss the sheer messiness and accidental nature of politics on the one hand, and the real importance of mass movements and political pressure on the other. The civil rights movement, and the changes it wrought in the whole fabric of American life, is not easily explained in Vidal's picture of the world. Vidal's view of the "ruling class" is a fairly simple one: back in 1973 he was explaining to a British readership that "the owners of the United States" are "a loose consortium that includes the editors of the *New York Times* and the *Washington Post*, the television magnates, the Rockefellers, Kennedys, ITT, IBM, etc." ("Political Melodramas," in *United States*: 854, originally published in *New Statesman* 1973). A couple of years later he drew attention to the persistence of certain families, "the names that are now every bit as awesome as titles."[19] More recently he relates lecturing Mrs (now Senator) Clinton on

"who actually owns and is rather idly ruling the United States –
a very small class into which Bush [Sr] had been born and
trained and they had not" ("Bubba Rules: Clinton-Gore II," in
Virgin Islands: 153, originally published in *GQ* 1996). As his
example was the destruction of the health insurance scheme,
which Mrs Clinton had tried, and failed, to steer through during
her husband's first term in office, this was presumably listened
to with interest, though Vidal's analysis failed to explain why
Clinton had been able to beat Bush in the 1992 election – or,
indeed, why the right would be unable to stop Hillary's election
to the Senate in 2000.

Although Vidal maintained a consistent lack of apparent interest in the 2000 election, despite the candidacy of his cousin,
he has subsequently acknowledged that "[the Bush Administra-
tion] is unlike any other administration in our history" (*Dreaming War*: 51). In 2004 he did express a clear preference for Kerry
over Bush, seeing Kerry as an imperialist but one less likely to
"start wars like bushfires just to distract attention."[20] His preferred Democratic candidate in 2004 was Ohio Congressman
Dennis Kucinich, who rarely held more than 2 percent support
among Democratic voters.

There is a logical problem with Vidal's position: if there is no
real difference between Republicans and Democrats, as critics
like Vidal claim, then why is so much money spent on elections?
Ambition may explain the vanity of very rich men who seek to
buy office, but although they are often successful – the United
States Senate now contains as many millionaires who are popu-
larly elected as it did when it was chosen by corrupt state
legislatures – money is not enough. Rich candidates, like Steve
Forbes, who spent vast sums seeking the Republican nomination
in 2000, or securities trader Blair Hull, who failed to win the
Democratic nomination for Illinois Senator in 2004 after spending $29 million, do not necessarily poll well – although poor can-
didates, one might note, do even worse. That all candidates need
to raise huge sums of money does not mean that they all serve
the same interests: the 2004 contest between the very wealthy
John Kerry (who had married the widow of the even wealthier
Senator Heinz) and George W. Bush clearly pitted two starkly

different views of America. At the same time it was clear that a change in control of the Presidency or Congress would not mean any radical restructuring of economic arrangements. Kerry's proposals were for readjustments, not for major change. But Kerry lost because he failed to persuade enough Americans to go to the polls to vote for those readjustments, not because of lack of resources.

There is an arrogance in the sort of leftism that dismisses such readjustments in favor of some idealized view of a radical politics that, in practice, aids the most conservative forces to maintain their hold. This was the arrogance that led Ralph Nader to run for President in both 2000 and 2004, probably taking votes away from the Democratic candidate, an echo of the earlier moves of the People's Party to take votes off George McGovern in the 1972 election. In his novels, above all in *Lincoln*, Vidal shows a keen appreciation of the need to compromise in order to achieve the best possible outcome in any given situation. There is room for utopianism in political life, but it should not lead to a position where real differences between parties and candidates are dismissed because they can never measure up to what is ideal.

"Part of the not-so endearing folklore of my native land," Vidal wrote in 1993, "is that we have no class system; this means that any mention of it by a novelist will provoke deep, often quite irrational, anger" ("Introduction," *Empire*: vi). The reality is more complex: many American novels are infused with a clear sense of class, but it is not necessarily spelt out. The same might be said of Vidal's own work, which provokes anger for apparently questioning the moral worth of the revered figures of American history, not for suggesting class differences. Vidal places himself on the left, but his novels rarely deal with the world as seen by those who are at all underprivileged. His characters are largely those people who take servants for granted, not those who serve. His own early encounters with poverty and dispossession were viewed from a position of privilege; in an essay on the film *Sullivan's Travels* (Preston Sturges 1941), he writes of his early memories of war veterans who came to Washington to demand a war bonus – which his grandfather opposed – and of the lasting impact on him of "the hoboes and convicts" in Sturges' film.[21]

A constant theme in both his fiction and commentary is the ambition of "ruling-class" families to maintain economic and political control, not least through marriage alliances – one of Vidal's favorite terms is "hypergamy," meaning marrying above one's social class. In *Lincoln* one of the sub-themes is the determination of Kate Chase to see her father, Salmon Chase, nominated by the Republicans for the Presidency: she seeks to further this by marrying the odious Governor Sprague of Rhode Island for his money. Chase failed to win the nomination, but did become Lincoln's Secretary of Treasury and then Chief Justice. Kate is one of a number of women in Vidal's historical novels who is compelled to live out her political ambitions through a male relative.

The return of the Bush family to the White House in 2000 seemed to reinforce Vidal's argument that the United States is controlled not just by the rich, but by dynastic families from both sides of politics. Kevin Phillips, who first became prominent as a Republican Party apologist, published a bitter attack on President Bush and his family in 2004, which echoed many of Vidal's earlier claims about the growth of dynastic politics.[22] Yet of the eleven Presidents since Franklin Roosevelt (himself the nephew of a former President) only three – Kennedy and the two Bushes – could be said to come in any real sense from a "ruling class." The others are, in Vidal's own phrase, "plebes for sale" ("Reflections on Glory Reflected," in *United States*: 1,257, originally published in *Threepenny Review* 1991), and the cynic might note the apparently unlimited supply of men from poor backgrounds – Nixon, Carter, Reagan, Clinton – available to be recruited into running the Republic. In *Palimpsest* Vidal identifies Nixon and Truman as "Protestants of the American ruling establishment" (396), but this seems to stretch the definition of establishment beyond mere elasticity. An American booster would argue that the "humble" backgrounds of most twentieth-century Presidents proves the essential openness of the American political system, indeed the reality of the myth of "log cabin to White House."

In some ways Vidal reflects a particularly American leftism shared by men such as Noam Chomsky, Michael Moore, and Oliver Stone, which their critics perceive as bearing out Hofstadter's analysis of the "paranoid style" of American politics. (When Moore used his 2003 Oscar award for *Bowling for Columbine* to attack President Bush it was rumored inaccurately that Vidal had helped write his acceptance speech.) In Vidal's political analysis left and right populism merge: even though he is seen as on the left, some rightwingers are strangely sympathetic to his views on the influence of big money and isolationism. As Vidal acknowledges with some surprise in his *State of the Union* (1980), his view of the central importance of the Trilateral Commission, as a mouthpiece for the monied controllers of the United States, won some acclaim from the American right, "a group of zanies who ought to love the bank and all its works" ("The State of the Union: 1980," in *United States*: 939, originally published in *Esquire* 1980).

Radicals on both the left and right are attracted to conspiracy theories in which the villains are remarkably similar, though the leftist script of corporate criminals is less likely to be conflated with the anti-Semitic and racist fears of the right. Thus Oliver Stone's film on the Kennedy assassination, *JFK* (1991), can fit both left and right theories that see Kennedy's assassination as a de facto coup by the Mafia, the CIA, the Cubans, and anyone else convenient. Vidal did raise some doubts about the Warren Commission's findings about Oswald's sole responsibility for the assassination in an article published in 1976 ("The Art and Arts of E. Howard Hunt," in *United States*: 876), but he has been far less preoccupied by the Kennedy assassination than have either Mailer or Don DeLillo, both of whom have written major novels around the theme.

Vidal's view of American politics as being controlled by a small cabal of the very wealthy is one widely shared on both left and right, and is reflected in a series of American movies, some of them made by Oliver Stone. The election of George Bush Jr in 2000 saw a marked rise in claims that the United States was in the grip of an oligarchy closely linked to the oil interests that were amongst Bush's biggest backers. By 2000 the majority of those in Vidal's earlier list of the "owners of the U.S." (the *Washington Post*, the Kennedys) were amongst the most severe critics of President Bush, which seems to undermine any illusions about the solidarity of the "ruling class." It is worth remembering that had President Clinton had one more chance to replace a Republican-nominated Supreme Court Justice with one of his own, the results of the 2000 election would most likely have seen Al Gore elected.

As Vidal's critique of contemporary administrations of both parties sharpened, so he came to echo both left- and rightwing allegations of government bureaucrats trampling on the basic Constitutional rights of Americans. Vidal saw in Clinton's Anti-Terrorism Act of 1996 the same assault on basic American values that many more Americans have seen in the various pieces of legislation enacted under President George W. Bush. Clinton's legislation was largely a response to the blowing-up of a federal building in Oklahoma City in 1995, which was characterized in the media as the product of rightwing vigilantism. Timothy McVeigh, the man who admitted to the bombing, wrote Vidal that he "would be surprised at how much . . . I agree with [you]" and after a correspondence between the two asked him to be one of the witnesses at his execution. Vidal was in Italy, and says he did not have enough time to get to the execution.

McVeigh first wrote to Vidal after reading an article by him in 1998, where he argued that the freedoms guaranteed all Americans through the Bill of Rights was under attack, and gave as one of his central examples the attack by the FBI on David Koresh's Branch Davidian religious settlement in Waco, Texas, in 1993. Vidal's commentary is particularly interesting, as most of the available literature on Waco is written by people who are concerned to defend alternative religions against what they see as the threat of secular trends in the United States.* Accused of possession of illegal weapons and drugs, and of sexual molesta-

---

*Novelist John Updike, with whom Vidal has half-heartedly feuded, also draws on the Waco incident in his novel of twentieth-century America, *In the Beauty of the Lilies*. See Vidal's excoriating review in the *Times Literary Supplement* April 26, 1996 ("Rabbit's Own Burrow," in *Virgin Islands*: 68–94).

tion of children, Koresh's compound was stormed by large numbers of federal agents, leading to a major fire and the death of 82 Branch Davidians, including 25 children. Subsequent inquiries by various levels of government have failed to find any threat posed by the Davidians that could justify in any way the severity of the government's response.[23] President Clinton accepted responsibility for the raid, but seemed to contradict this by indicating his gut instinct was to avoid the raid. McVeigh, a veteran of the first Iraqi War, seemed motivated to blow up the federal building by the raid on Waco.

"Nothing," Vidal wrote, "could justify the murder of those 168 men, women and children [in Oklahoma], none of whom had, as far as we know, anything at all to do with the federal slaughter at Waco, the ostensible reason for McVeigh's fury" (*PWPP*: 78–9). But Vidal was sufficiently intrigued by McVeigh's actions to seek some explanation that went beyond merely characterizing him as either mad or evil. In the course of a number of years researching and writing he seems to have concluded that McVeigh deliberately confessed to the crime, which he was unlikely to have perpetrated by himself, because he believed that the attack on the Murrah Building was, in McVeigh's words, "no different than what Americans rain on the heads of others all the time" (letter from McVeigh, quoted in *PWPP*: 110). Most commentators read Vidal's interest in McVeigh, in particular the extent to which he appears to consider seriously his rationale for the bombings, as further proof of Vidal's own deep anti-Americanism. Yet Vidal's suggestion that there is little moral distinction between the government-sanctioned raids which led to considerable loss of life in Waco and the individual (and therefore criminalized) attack on the Oklahoma City federal building is an argument which deserves reasoned scrutiny. The distinction, which has become central to contemporary politics, between "terrorism" and "pre-emptive defense" is foreshadowed to a remarkable degree in Vidal's earlier discussions of Waco and Oklahoma City.

Vidal's relationship with McVeigh seems to echo, in a later period, Capote's relationship with the two murderers whose story makes up *In Cold Blood*, and Mailer's long involvement with the murderer Gary Gilmore, which produced the very long book *The Executioner's Song* (1979). It is impossible for anyone, Vidal included, to know to what extent there was an element of wanting to match his old adversaries. Yet McVeigh's crime was rather different, in that it was motivated by political aims, and Vidal is less interested in the psychology of a killer (especially as he grew less certain that McVeigh's confession should have been believed) than in arguing that a response such as McVeigh's is the logical consequence of terror practiced by the United States government itself. Not surprisingly this attempt to raise a set of moral problems around the accepted script of the Oklahoma City bombings was deeply unpopular with almost all parts of the American establishment, and won Vidal unwanted kudos from a set of kooks and rightwing crazies. At a speech at the 2001 Edinburgh book festival Vidal appeared to be actually praising McVeigh, comparing him to Paul Revere, the American patriot whom Longfellow turned into a folk hero through his poem "Paul Revere's Ride."[24]

Increasingly Vidal is dismissed by many, even on the left, as too prone to overstatements and simplification, an impression not helped by his tendency to publish prolifically and in small presses that seek controversy through hyperbole. Like Noam Chomsky, with whom he seems often paired, and Michael Moore, his polemics – though not his historical novels – pile up damning fact after fact in the manner of a clever prosecutor, who will skip inconsistencies or contradictions that might weaken the case. Moore, in particular, seems to have taken some of his analysis of American foreign policy from Vidal, and his anti-Bush documentary, *Fahrenheit 9/11*, shares the same reductionist desire to move from the undoubted links of Bush and his inner circle to both the domestic and Saudi oil industry to insinuations that these links provided the primary motive for decisions about war and security. Yet what works in satirical fiction becomes a real problem in political analysis, where actions are far less intentional than hindsight might suggest. The historian Gordon Wood, by no means unsympathetic to Vidal, wrote that we can say of him what Franklin said of Adams: "He means well for his country, is always an honest man, often a wise one, but some-times and in some things absolutely out of his senses."[25]

Perhaps the gay author and AIDS activist Larry Kramer was right in characterizing Vidal as both sad and angry. When Kramer interviewed Gore in 1992, an interview that is both revealing and maudlin, he wrote that: "His list of wrongs that provoke this anger because they are wrong is by now too familiar to him . . . Who has listened to him? What has his wrath made right? The world is further away than ever from his dream."[26]

Vidal's political pronouncements of the past few years have combined his two consistent themes: the persistence of the American Empire and the centrality of money in controlling gov-ernment decisions. As overstated as his attacks on American imperialism might seem, many experts in international relations, within and outside the United States, are in close agreement with Vidal's prognosis, if not his language. Thus Andrew Bacevich, to cite one recent study almost at random, concludes: "Those who chart America's course do so with a clearly defined purpose . . . to preserve and, where both feasible and conducive to United States interests, to expand an American imperium."[27] Bacevich is Professor of International Relations at Boston University, hardly a hotbed of radicalism. Equally Chalmers Johnson, one of the most respected American scholars of East Asia and its rela-tions with the United States, has come to speak of American foreign policy in terms which are remarkably close to those used by Vidal, though without acknowledging this. In his 2004 book *The Sorrows of Empire* Johnson speaks of four ongoing conse-quences of American imperialism: a state of perpetual war; a loss of democracy and constitutional rights; a system of propaganda and glorification of war and the military; and bankruptcy at home.[28] Vidal is neither as radical nor as isolated in his views as he sometimes likes to paint himself.

Indeed in the twenty-first century to speak of American Empire is neither as oppositional nor even as leftist as it once seemed. The British historian Niall Ferguson, who has become something of a media celebrity for his defense of President

Bush's policies, acknowledges Vidal's hostility to American imperialism but rather snidely attributes this to a view that " 'the national security state' [is] relentlessly encroaching on the prerogatives of the patrician elite to which Vidal himself belongs."[29] As Vidal has consistently argued that United States military expenditure has limited domestic programs that would benefit the less well off, this is either a deliberate or a careless misreading of his position by Ferguson, who in contrast would increase American expenditure on maintaining its imperial position.

Increasingly Vidal seeks to document the rise of American Empire directly, relying less on satire and the recreation of history in favor of what he terms "the oldest form of American political discourse, the pamphlet" (*Dreaming War*: ix). Pamphleteering is a fine tradition, which demands both simplification and exaggeration to make its points. The problem comes from a failure of balance, so that, to take one example, being asked to produce photo identification at airports becomes for Vidal a breach of civil liberties equivalent to indefinite detention without trial (the fate of those confined at Guantanamo Bay after the war in Afghanistan). Thus he argues that the Patriot Act of 2002 is a linear descendent of Harry Truman's National Security oaths, and in both cases that the ultimate reason is to increase control over the citizenry in the interests of a small elite.

Vidal works hard at documenting his claims – both his collection of essays *The Last Empire* and his pamphlet *Perpetual War for Perpetual Peace* contain a long list of military, political, and counter-drug operations derived from the Federation of American Scientists. The source is a respectable one, but because the list makes no distinction between interventions generally regarded as peacekeeping, or supported by United Nations mandates, and those generally regarded, at least outside the United States, as representing big power interference, it seems to suggest that all use of military power is equally illegitimate, a position only a total pacifist would argue. Occasionally Vidal makes silly mistakes that betray gaps in his knowledge, such as a confusion of ASEAN with SEATO (*Last Empire*: 115) or calling 1948 South Africa "a totalitarian state" (*Golden Age*: 309), at a time when South Africa's racial laws were actually less draconian and oppressive than those exercised in the southern states of the United States. And can we take seriously the suggestion that, were Osama bin Laden alive, he would be "in a comfortable mansion in Osama-loving Jakarta, two thousand miles to the east and easily accessible by Flying Carpet One" (*Dreaming War*: 44)?

Such lists and misstatements express a characteristic of many American leftists, a bleak view of their own country that attributes more power and influence to the United States than it does, in fact, exercise, and a corresponding lack of interest in the internal dynamics of other societies. Thus Michael Moore's *Fahrenheit 9/11* was criticized, correctly in my view, for recognizing neither the awfulness of Saddam Hussein nor the support for the United States from elected governments in countries such as Britain, Poland, Australia, Spain, and South Korea. One suspects that American left and right are united in a perception of the rest of the world almost exclusively through an American lens, and both are equally offended by an analysis that places the emphasis on political, social, and cultural factors over which the United States may have relatively little influence. Thus American leftists, including Vidal, like to refer to allegations that the CIA was involved in the dismissal from office of the Australian Labor government of Gough Whitlam in 1975, but even if the CIA *did* support the actions involved, there is little reason to believe their involvement was of much consequence beside the purely internal political maneuvers of Australian politicians.

Despite the evident interest in non-western religion and history displayed in *Creation*, Vidal remains as America-centric as any of the neo-conservative ideologues he despises. Even though his novels have occasionally commented on the contemporary world outside the United States – as in *Dark Green, Bright Red* or, much later, *Kalki* – there is none of the loving attention to detail that characterizes his descriptions of American society in the Chronicles. Even though the subtitle of *Perpetual War for Perpetual Peace* is *How We Got to Be So Hated*, the pamphlet does not, in fact, address this question. Nor do his consistent attacks on American foreign policy ever suggest much of an alternative, short of a return to eighteenth-century isolationism.

When the polemicist takes over, Vidal, like Chomsky, though in more elegant prose, ignores the mix of ideological self-serving and genuine idealism that underlies much of American foreign policy. Here, for example, is the contemporary novelist Henry Bromell (b. 1947) reflecting on American foreign policy in his novel *Little America*, which explores United States involvement in the politics of the Middle East during the Eisenhower Presidency:

> The cold war was not simply a geopolitical extension of national hubris, though hubris did indeed rule the day. Rheumy Episcopalians and flinty Presbyterians from Yale and Wall Street held sway, projecting onto the world their own vision of churchly virtue versus the godless unwashed hordes. It was not imperialism, exactly, though American businessmen clamoured for more markets and felt it their right and obligation to seize them when and where they could.[30]

What is most frightening to foreigners about the United States is the apparently unlimited capacity of Americans to believe that serving the interest of capitalism is pure altruism. Yet having said this, one has also to acknowledge that Theodore Roosevelt's peacemaking between Russia and Japan (for which he received the Nobel Peace Prize); Wilson's establishment of the League of Nations; Franklin Roosevelt's and Truman's support for the United Nations; Kennedy's "alliance for progress" in Latin America; Carter's willingness to relinquish the Panama Canal; and certainly Bush Sr's and Clinton's military interventions in Somalia, Haiti, and the former Yugoslavia were motivated as much by idealism as they were by a desire to expand American control. Opponents of American foreign policy from both left and right find it hard to fit interventions like that in Kosovo into their overall framework. Indeed, one needs to be more careful than is Vidal in distinguishing between Bush Sr's war on Iraq – which followed the invasion of a sovereign state, Kuwait, and was backed by the United Nations Security Council – and the war of his son, which rested on largely unsubstantiated claims and was clearly not supported either by the United Nations or by some of the United States' most significant allies.

Idealism can be naïve, and its consequences can be horrific: it is easy to demonstrate the damage done by American idealism in the redrawing of post-World War I boundaries in Europe, the long unsuccessful military intervention in Vietnam, and the overthrow of Saddam Hussein in Iraq. In all of these cases realists and isolationists would both argue that a less interventionist United States policy would have caused less human suffering, and they may well be right. Vidal has at least been consistent in his isolationism: the English critic Christopher Hitchens, a friend until they split bitterly over Hitchens' support for the invasion of Iraq, wrote of being brought "almost to tears" by his failure to persuade Gore of the need to support intervention by the United States to stop Serbian massacres in Bosnia.[31]

A more interesting critique will, however, take the ideological framework of American policy makers seriously, rather than dismissing it as mere cover-up, as seems to be the case with critics such as Chomsky and Michael Moore.[32] As Vidal himself wrote as far back as 1967: "Beneath a genuine high-mindedness (puzzling to foreigners who find the American nonparanoid style either hypocritical or unrealistic), American leaders have unconsciously accepted the 'English-speaking Teutonic' role of world conquerors for the world's good" ("Paranoid Politics," in *United States*: 772, originally published in *New Statesman* 1967).

Yet it is too easy to dismiss Vidal's critique as "paranoia." As the once neo-liberal economist Paul Krugman wrote: "Journalists . . . don't want to sound like crazy conspiracy theorists. But there's nothing crazy about ferreting out the real goals of the right wing; on the contrary, it's unrealistic to pretend there *isn't* a sort of conspiracy here, albeit one whose organization and goals are pretty much out in the open."[33] In the same tone, the Asian expert Bruce Cummings, in reflecting on United States government activities during the Cold War, had reason to chide himself for "the fallacy of insufficient cynicism."[34] Unfortunately what may have seemed wild and unsubstantiated allegations when Vidal first made them often turn out to be truer than the critics wanted to believe. In 1968 William Buckley considered Vidal's suggestion that the United States should back Ho Chi Minh on the grounds that Vietnam and China were natural enemies as a sign of his *Realpolitik* gone mad. (He also used the statement to quote an alleged comment from Robert Kennedy to the effect that he should change the slogan "Let's give blood to the Vietcong" to "Let's give Gore Vidal to the Vietcong.")[35] Yet shortly after the American withdrawal from Vietnam, China and Vietnam did, indeed, go to war, suggesting that Vidal was, in fact, far more prescient than successive American administrations.

Vidal's critique of power and foreign policy in the United States is a powerful counter to the dominant ideology, echoing not only a certain amount of radical scholarship (e.g. William Domhoff, C. Wright Mills),[36] but also the famous warning delivered by President Eisenhower in his farewell address against the power of the "military industrial complex." By the standards of virtually all other contemporary liberal democracies, except perhaps Italy under Berlusconi, the unchecked role of money and influence in American politics seems extraordinary. The huge sums of money required to run for office, the access of lobbyists to policy makers in Washington, the political nature of the senior bureaucracy, the dominance of unelected and unaccountable White House advisers, the fact that control of elections and apportionment of Congressional districts is in the hands of politicians rather than impartial authorities – all these are serious blots on the American claim that theirs is a model of democracy.

In 1999 Vidal wrote an introduction to a study of money and elections, in which he quoted John Jay, one of the "Founding Fathers," who said: "The people who own the country ought to run it." (One might be somewhat cynical about this sentiment, given that at the establishment of the United States only white men with a certain amount of property could vote.) Vidal ends his introduction with the comment that while Americans assert that theirs is a government of, by, and for the many, "it is so notoriously the exclusive preserve of the few."[37] As he had previously written: "Persuading the people to vote against their own best interests has been the awesome genius of the American political elite from the beginning" ("Homage to Daniel Shays," in *United States*: 918).

There is the idealist Vidal, who weights the present against an updated eighteenth-century liberalism, and finds it wanting, and there is the practical Vidal, who can suggest changes to the political system of the United States such as restricting the time and money spent on elections, while doing away with the Electoral College. He has consistently called for an elected Convention to reassess the United States Constitution, a provision envisaged in the Constitution itself (e.g. "Time for a People's Convention," in *Inventing a Nation*: 32, originally published in *The Nation*, January 22, 1992). In *The Best Man*, Vidal used his knowledge of the American political system to write one of the first realistic plays about the workings of government. Vidal has summarized the play as "about a contest for the presidency between a man with a virtuous public life and a messy private life, and a man with a vicious public life and a private life beyond reproach" (*Screening History*: 83). The "messy private life" refers to treatment for a nervous breakdown, which is countered by allegations against the other candidate of homosexuality, which, as Vidal later pointed out, were made of Adlai Stevenson, the Democratic Presidential nominee in 1952 and 1956 ("Political Melodramas," in *United States*, originally published in *New Statesman* 1973), just as Thomas Eagleton's history of depression led to his withdrawing as Vice Presidential candidate in 1972. There are some similarities to *The Best Man* in the more melodramatic novel by Allen Drury *Advise and Consent*, which was published at about the same time, and the genre of political intrigues has recently become very popular on both film and television.

When he is not inveighing against the ongoing collapse of American virtue, Vidal is one of the best guides available to how politics actually work, to the constant balance between ambition, ideology, self-interest, and altruism that characterizes politicians. In *Washington, D.C.* he observed that Senator Day "had learned very early that to do any good thing in the Senate, one must first present it as an act of self-interest since to do good for its own sake aroused suspicion" (221). Vidal has recounted his shock on learning from his grandfather that his old ally Senator William Borah had been paid in exchange for his support of isolationist views ("Political Melodramas," in *United States*: 854).

Both the idealist and the pragmatic are likely to be drowned out by the satirical Gore, and it is very difficult to combine satire with analysis. Satire, by its very nature, takes reality and pushes it to a logical – and hence absurd – conclusion. This works better in fiction, as in *Kalki*, where he claims that the Bureau of Narcotics has "the single, nay, unique objective . . . the increased sale of every kind of drug all over the world" (*Kalki*: 191). This is less removed from the reality of successive administrations' "war on drugs" than apologists for the United States might like. But when satire ceases to stand aside and becomes either polemical or patronizing, it loses its impact, and the satirist seems either silly or ranting. Vidal has walked this line for 50 years, and the mood of twenty-first century America is not one that takes kindly to suggestions that it has betrayed its ideals.

Vidal's critique of American politics and foreign policy is important because over a long period of time he has been able to bring leftist analysis into arenas, such as primetime television, where it is rarely heard. The idea of a "ruling class," of the dominance of money, of the largely symbolic nature of party differences, is rarely discussed in the mainstream media or the civics texts that are used to instil a particular version of American government. What is striking about mainstream American discourse is its capacity to embrace considerable controversy and apparent dissent within a set of taken-for-granted assumptions, which normalize extraordinary inequalities, poor government services, and huge boondoggles for the corporate sector while excluding any realistic alternatives from the political agenda. In the same way, Vidal's analysis of American foreign policy from Truman on has tended to foreshadow an analysis of United States foreign policy that has become increasingly common during the Bush Administration. Vidal liked to complain that he and Chomsky were lone voices in their attacks on American imperialism. This is hardly a complaint he can make with much credibility after the second Iraq War.

Even in the few years since Vidal published *Dreaming War*, with its inflammatory subtitle, *Blood for Oil and the Cheney-Bush Junta*, his views seem far less outrageous. In the lead-up to the 2004 election Luke Mitchell, a senior editor of *Harper's Magazine*, hardly a particularly radical publication, argued that no other explanation could account for the Bush Administration's policies. In a piece which used Vidal's phrase (without acknowledgment) he wrote: "Although our desire for Iraqi oil may seem a distasteful explanation for war, it is the only explanation by which we may continue to believe we live in a rational universe. Put another way: if this war is *not* about oil, then truly we stand poised at the abyss."[38]

By the time of President George W. Bush's second inauguration, Vidal's pessimism about the future of the United States seemed to have led him to that abyss. "They," he said, speaking of the current administration, "are now beyond motivation, and that is insanity."[39] If this seems extreme it echoed the feelings of many Americans at the beginning of the second Bush term. Indeed, as *Publisher's Weekly* rather grudgingly acknowledged in reviewing his most recent collection, *Imperial America*: "Vidal may be in tune with the zeitgeist again because his polemical writing resembles the new blogger punditry: conversational, tart, fervent, digressive, susceptible to idiosyncratic theories but capable of worthwhile provocations."[40] A leading religious conservative once said you can be an advisor or a prophet, but not both. After his several forays into electoral politics, Vidal has clearly opted for the latter role. His voice remains a significant one to the left of mainstream Democratic opposition to the current administration.

Gore Vidal and "political correctness"

Commentators on Vidal often point to his extraordinary erudition, and he is remarkably well read in history, literature, and religion. There is less sign in his writings or interviews of any particular interest in the social sciences, or of an understanding of social structures and interconnections that C. Wright Mills termed "the sociological imagination." In his book of that title, published in 1959, Mills spoke, in rather overblown prose, of understanding "the larger historical scene ... [taking] into account how individuals, in the welter of their daily experience, often become falsely conscious of their social positions . . . the capacity to range from the most impersonal and remote trans-formations to the most intimate features of the human self – and to see the relations between the two."[41]

At one level Mills is describing the accomplishments of good novelists, particularly those with the ambition to encompass larger social issues. His words would be certainly applicable to Vidal's achievements in conjuring up the ancient worlds of *Julian* or *Creation*, indeed to some extent of his entire American saga. Yet in a more prosaic sense, where sociology involves untangling the interconnection between larger social factors and individual experiences, there is a gap in perceptions, which reveals itself in Vidal's apparent insensitivity to race; in his rather simplistic approaches to power within the United States; and in his scorn for identity politics, which is taken up in the later discussion of sexuality.

To be ignorant of social theory is not a problem for a novelist, where Vidal's sense of specificity and his ability to read widely and carefully in the existing literature stands him in good stead. But as an essayist Vidal makes grand claims in fields of interna-tional relations, politics, economics and public policy, and here his ignorance of "the field" is more disturbing. One might argue that a polemicist should not be bound by the limits of academic discourse, with its tendency to equivocation and pretentious lan-guage. But (to equivocate academically) one feels that his po-litical polemics are far more careless in their claims than anything he would write as a novelist. The care with which he discusses history in, say, *Burr* or *Lincoln* is unfortunately absent from a project such as his television series, and subsequent booklet, *The American Presidency*.

While Vidal writes and speaks constantly of power, he fails to recognize sufficiently the ways in which individual choices are limited and conditioned by social conditions. This is perhaps most apparent in much of his writings about sex, where his general defence of prostitution and pornography eschews the difficult questions of power and choice. There is little sign in Vidal's impassioned defence of sexual freedom, the great bulk of which I would endorse, of any recognition of how those who work in the sex industry are coerced or manipulated into the job. The very features of Vidal's work which make him attractive to libertarians of both the left and the right are those that limit his appreciation of how inequality and inferiority are maintained through complex social and psychological factors.

Critics of Vidal accuse him of snobbery, anti-Americanism, racism, and anti-Semitism. Indeed the perception of Vidal as anti-Semitic has entered a certain amount of popular mythology; by the sort of serendipity that occurs when researching a book, I came across this comment in a cult counterfactual historical novel which rewrites the history of post-World War I: "trust the anti-semites at Gore Vidal's People's National Radio to call Arpad a Hungarian but omit the fact that he was a Jew."[42] The comment is gratuitous, but it is nonetheless revealing of a widespread attitude towards Vidal held by many Jews, and one that goes back to his famous comment in 1959 that: "Each year there is a short List of the O.K. Writers. Today's list consists of two Jews, two Negroes and a safe floating *goy* of the old American Establishment just to show there is no prejudice in our Loving world; only the poor old homosexualists are out" ("Love, Love, Love," in *United States*: 60, originally published in *Partisan Review* 1959). The critic Leslie Fiedler acutely pointed out that the comment was written "in mock horror (but with an undertone of real bitterness too)."[43]

More recently, the prominent neo-conservative Norman Podhoretz, former editor of *Commentary*, has claimed Vidal is clearly anti-Semitic: he identified a piece written by Vidal for *The Nation* in 1986 as "the most blatantly and egregiously anti-Semitic outburst to have appeared in a respectable American periodical since World War II." In the piece Podhoretz claims Vidal declared that "the Jews were impoverishing the United States and bringing the world closer and closer to a nuclear war" and warning "that the Jews (never mind if they were born here or were naturalized citizens) had better watch out if they wished 'to stay on among us.'"[44]

This would be damning, if indeed Vidal had written it. Checking the original article, to which Podhoretz himself referred me, I cannot find these alleged quotes. What Vidal does say is: "He

and Midge [his wife] stay on among us, in order to make propaganda and raise money for Israel – a country they don't seem
eager to live in . . . Although there is nothing wrong with being
a lobbyist for a foreign power, one is supposed to register with
the Justice Department" ("The Empire Lovers Strike Back," in
The Nation, March 22, 1986). No mention of the warning to Jews
watching out "if they want to stay on among us." Several years
later the literary critic Edward Alexander echoed Podhoretz,
writing that Vidal had claimed: "Since Jews are guests in
America, they ought to remember that *'tact . . . requires a certain
forbearance when it comes to the politics of the host country' . . ."*[45]
Vidal *did* write the piece in italics. But it is clear he was referring
not to "Jews" but to those Jews whose primary identification is
with Israel. For men who pride themselves on their role as
writers and commentators, Podhoretz and Alexander seem
remarkably casual in the way they quote others. It is clear that
in the original article Vidal's complaint was with American Jews
who act primarily as lobbyists for Israel, and to do this "make
common cause with our lunatic right."

On balance, this seems a legitimate political comment,
although Vidal is far too single-minded about the complexities
of national allegiance, and Alexander is right to point to the
extent to which apparently divided loyalties are common
amongst many groups in the United States – Irish-, Greek- and
Cuban-Americans have all, at various times, exhibited a similar
preoccupation with the fate of their ethnic patria to that of which
Vidal complains. It is unfortunate that even to discuss the power
of the pro-Israeli lobby in the United States – which includes a
number of fundamentalist Christians and excludes a number of
Jews – is often read as anti-Semitism. The central problem,
namely that, for people like Podhoretz and Alexander, American
and Israeli interests are self-evidently identical, and therefore to
attack Israel is to attack America, is one that resounds still in
debates on the Middle East policies of the United States. One
might further point out that Vidal's preoccupation with pro-
Israeli lobbyists led him to underrate the enormous influence
of Saudi pressures on successive American administrations,
although he did start talking about this after September 11. But

one might also note that Arthur Schlesinger Jr, who had previously disagreed strongly with Vidal's pessimistic views of the United States (and whom Vidal mocks as the court chronicler of the Kennedys), has recently pointed to the problems caused to the United States by its close identification with Israeli governments.[46]

What is missed in those attacks on Vidal for anti-Semitism is any recognition of his sense of betrayal when some New York Jewish intellectuals, with whom he had mixed as a young writer, enthusiastically denounced the new gay movement. In 1981 he published the influential essay "Pink Triangle and Yellow Star," in which he first argued for the alliance between "Jews, blacks and homosexualists" that would become central in his feud with Podhoretz at the end of the decade. (In 1970, in his very funny review of David Reuben's book *Everything You Always Wanted to Know about* Sex,[47] Vidal had already pointed to the similarity between anti-Semitic and homophobic language.) Rather than a work of anti-Semitism, I read "Pink Triangle and Yellow Star" as an expression of surprise and regret that Jews, who had so often been persecuted in the name of Christian morality, would so enthusiastically echo the language of homophobia. Midge Decter, in particular, became a leading exponent of homophobia, as both a writer (her piece "The Boys on the Beach," published in *Commentary*, which her husband edited, provoked this particular article) and a publisher. One of the first gay liberation activities in New York was a sit-in at *Harper's Magazine*, where Decter was an editor, which had published an article by Joseph Epstein in which he wrote: "If I had the power to do so, I would wish homosexuality off the face of the earth."[48] It was Vidal, not the Jewish Decter, who saw the striking parallel in this language to that used by Hitler.

But then Midge Decter, 30 years later, would publish a book on Secretary of Defense Donald Rumsfeld, in which she extolled Rumsfeld's "manliness." Even Vidal's ironic best may not be sufficient to explain the strange mix of patriotism and old-fashioned gender ideology that could produce a book that even *Publisher's Weekly* called an "overwrought hagiography." In the same way, there is a sneering homophobia in both Podhoretz's and Alexan-

der's attacks, and a determination to depict AIDS as a consequence of homosexual promiscuity, which, given the realities of
the epidemic, already clear to those who looked outside the
United States in the late 1980s, is just wrong.

At one level to call Vidal anti-Semitic is an absurd allegation,
as Vidal has spent much of his life surrounded by Jews, and
when Howard encountered anti-Semitism Vidal was clearly
angered. In his earlier novels, particularly *Washington, D.C.*,
there is an unmistakeable satire of the prevalent anti-Semitism
in government circles. But it is too simplistic to claim that his
personal history exempts him from the charge. My sense is that
while Vidal has been savage in his criticism of both Judaism and
Israel he has never, at least in public, crossed the line which
distinguishes legitimate criticism from prejudice. Yes, he has
stressed the power of organized Jewish and pro-Israeli groups
in the United States (which are less identical than he suggests).
In the 1960s he spoke of the centrality of Jews in American literature and criticism, though without the venom Truman Capote
used in attacking "the Jewish mafia." One might feel uncomfortable when he draws attention to the number of Jews in the
movie industry (in *Hollywood*), or prominent in second-wave
feminism (in *Kalki*). Effectively Vidal is pointing to the huge shift
in the social and political position of Jews in the United States,
a legitimate point that he makes less offensively than those who
speak carelessly of the power of the Jewish lobby. In a country
where ethnic identity is so much spoken of, is it prejudice to call
attention to the achievements of a particular group?

At least one observer has postulated that the shift of a number
of prominent Jews to the right during the 1980s was due to an
anxiety of illegitimacy "that did not haunt the all-American
intellectuals . . . Did more principle and less angst infuse the
radicalism of non-Jewish intellectuals? Did the radicalism
steeped in anxiety slide into conservatism, while the Texan,
Puritan or Scottish identities of [Wright] Mills or [Edmund]
Wilson or Vidal or [John Kenneth] Galbraith give rise to a bony
radicalism more resistant to economic and social blandish-
ments?"[49] Quite apart from the oddity of naming Vidal as a
"puritan," and the denial of such prominent Jewish intellectuals

as Chomsky, Sontag, and Mailer, who did not move to the right there is a strange essentialism to this judgment.

None of Vidal's writings suggest anti-Semitism in the real sense, which implies a dislike of all Jews qua Jews. His review of the book *America in Black and White* appears to hint at Judaism as the source of racism, though the accusation is confused and historically specious. Vidal writes: "Judaism's two dreary spin-offs, Christianity and Islam, have given even wider range to the notion of true godless folk as 'white man's burden', 'cursed infidels' and 'lesser breeds' so much less human than those whipped up in the true God's bookish image" ("Bad History," in *Last Empire*: 156, originally published in *The Nation*, April 1998). While there are certainly historical links between some sections of the Christian Church and white racism, the inclusion of Islam seems particularly nonsensical in this context, and the overall argument unconvincing. On the other hand his recognition of the common fate of Jews and homosexuals under the Nazis, in the essay "Pink Triangle and Yellow Star," which so enraged Jewish neo-conservatives, shows a genuine concern about anti-Semitism, and also allows him to quote Christopher Isherwood's comeback to the young man who counterposed the alleged 600,000 homosexuals killed by Hitler to the six million Jews: "What are you?" asked Isherwood, "in real estate?" The figure of 600,000 is probably exaggerated, but does not change the basic point Isherwood was making.

Vidal is determined not to be politically correct: in one interview, during the mid-1980s, he compared himself to the tennis player John McEnroe, who was renowned for his temper on and off the court.[50] There is a certain glee with which he spares no one, showing off his capacity to offend like an adolescent proving his contempt for good manners. Deliberate offensiveness is a delicate weapon, as likely to cut the satirist as his target. It is also true that his particular leftism is not one which has a great deal of empathy for those oppressed due to race or ethnicity, and there is an almost total absence of non-Europeans from his vision of America. Thus his historical novels refer often to Washington as an "African city," without ever giving us a sense of how it might have seemed to the "Africans." The only major black characters in any of his writings are found in his 1968 play *Weekend*, a success in Washington but a flop on Broadway, in which a Republican contender for the Presidential election faces the prospect of a black daughter-in-law. The play could not have been helped by appearing shortly after the film *Guess Who's Coming to Dinner*, which is based on the same premise; while *Weekend* clearly intended to make fun of the current preoccupation with race, it also has a jarringly superficial tone at a time when the United States was deeply divided by responses to racial injustice. After the upheavals of the time, and the literary responses of Baldwin and Malcolm X, a comedy of manners seemed old-fashioned and insensitive.

Vidal's patrician satirical tone strikes a wrong chord when it comes to racial issues. The attempts to satirize American racism in *Myron* or *Duluth* leaves the reader uneasy: the language of satire deployed to skewer old movies and television doesn't transfer well to racial injustice. The *deus ex machina* who seems to control events in *Myron* is black, but Vidal's intention here is hardly clear, although a reference to the "golden bowl" has led several critics to see "Mr. Williams" as Henry James, already regarded in his lifetime as "the master" of all American novelists.[51] In *Duluth* Vidal appears torn between satirizing white racism and making fun of symbolic attempts to rectify it: "the news team at *Six O'Clock News* consists of one Oriental female, one Occidental male and one paraplegic Polynesian" (*Duluth*: 8), while the city is constantly threatened by riots in black and Hispanic areas. Yet beneath the irony is a real attempt to capture the extent of racism in Reagan's America:

> She has just observed . . . a number of white men slowly hoist from the frozen ground a black man with a rope that has been slung over the branch of a tree. As the white men all pull together, the black man slowly leaves the ground for whatever afterlife the Supreme Author may be writing for him.
> "I believe, Edna, that a Negro is being lynched."
> "You'll love Duluth. I can tell." Edna revs up her jalopy's motor. "We have excellent race relations here, as you can see. And numerous *nouvelle cuisine* restaurants." (*Duluth*: 4)

This was written in the aftermath of the case which acquitted four police officers charged with the assault of Rodney King, a black man stopped while driving, whose beating was recorded on videotape. The verdict led to rioting in south central Los Angeles, and a subsequent conviction of two of the officers for civil rights violations. The Los Angeles Police Department had a long history of brutality and racism; Vidal's reference here would have been clear to readers at the time.

Vidal has consistently denounced racism, if without the passion and specificity of his other critiques of American life. One might note how little interest Vidal shows in African-American writing, even though he was a contemporary of Baldwin's and, more loosely, Toni Morrison and Ralph Ellison. He tried belatedly to deal with racial issues in a review article in *The Nation* in 1998, in which he attacked Stephen and Abigail Thernstrom for their book *America in Black and White*, which Vidal reads as an attack on affirmative action and the civil rights movement (republished as "Bad History" in *The Last Empire*). There is lots of clever indignation here, reminiscent of his attacks on that other neo-conservative couple the Podhoretzes, but little specificity: other reviewers, such as Nicholas Lemann in the *New York Times* and Martin Duberman in the *Los Angeles Times*, also refuted the Thernstroms' claims, but with less vitriol and more substance. The book provoked considerable controversy, and was generally seen as a neo-conservative attack on "affirmative action," but Vidal's characterization of it as a "curiously insistent racist tract" suggests more indignation than analysis. There seems no evidence that the Thernstroms are in a real sense racist, although their book was certainly seized upon by many people who were, and to argue against it requires more than cleverness interspersed with asides about Vidal himself and his one encounter with the Thernstroms at Harvard, where she, "an adorable elfin minx," allegedly defended the Los Angeles police beatings of Rodney King (ibid.: 155).[52]

While contemptuous of racist rhetoric, he is not immune from using it himself, as in the offensive – and historically dubious – appeal in a 1986 article in *The Nation* for "the white race" to join together or else become "farmers – or, worse, mere entertainment – for the more than one billion grimly efficient Asiatics" ("A Cheerful Response," in *United States*: 1,017, originally published in *The Nation* 1986). A perception of Japan and/or China replacing the United States as the world's dominant power was a major preoccupation of the 1990s, and is echoed in some of Vidal's writings, as in the takeover of American media by Japanese companies implied in *Live from Golgotha*. In the current decade that fear is less openly expressed – Muslim fundamentalists now fill the space available in the popular imaginary for overseas threats to the United States – but it is a preoccupation that runs through much of his writing.

Of course, the lack of a sociological imagination is in one sense an expression of the dominant individualism in American political life, the entrenched ideology that assumes all individuals have equal opportunity to make something of themselves. What, after all, is the American Dream if not the power to reimagine and remake oneself? While Vidal can mock the pretensions that the political system is other than elitist, to some extent he buys into the perception of society as composed of autonomous individuals, and where he does seek to go beyond this, to some sort of structural analysis, he falls back on easy rhetoric. Certainly untangling the systems of class, power, gender, and race that determine the division of resources in the United States is enormously complex, and not something one usually demands of a novelist.

While Vidal writes often of the significance of class in America, and refers to the "ruling class," there is a lack of any coherent analysis of what class means and how it affects political behavior. He seems to suggest that an analysis of class means a concentration on the behavior of the "ruling class," which only he and Louis Auchincloss amongst "quality" novelists practice, and ignores the ways in which there is a very clear sense of class from a somewhat different perspective in novels as different as Roth's *Portnoy's Complaint* or Ellison's *Invisible Man* or Joyce Carol Oates' or Raymond Carver's stories of working-class trouble and violence. Indeed it becomes difficult to think of any significant contemporary American writer who does *not* address class, and many do so in ways that are at least as nuanced as Vidal's. While

he likes to quote Mary McCarthy's complaint that among the
many things not found in the serious novel is a cabinet meeting
("Lincoln and the Priests of Academe," in *United States*: 671), one
might respond that this is a narrow view of the political, and that
post-war fiction in the United States has been more likely to
address politics than has, for example, that of Britain.* Vidal
seems to stress too much the personal knowledge that he and
Auchincloss have of the "ruling class" as if that, by itself, defined
the political. One exception is his shrewd discussion in *Inventing a Nation* of how changing class allegiances determined the
shift in Britain to New Labour under Tony Blair (44).

From the late 1960s Vidal accepted the ecological critique of
overpopulation, which is a major theme of both *Myra* and *Kalki*,
indeed is already foreshadowed in *Messiah*. Kalki destroys the
world in order to save it from pollution and nuclear destruction:
beneath the froth of prose there is a Swiftian satire and bleakness about the future of the planet. When Vidal visited Australia
in 1974 he advocated licensing women to have children, with the
possibility of them selling their license to others who wanted
more than one child,[53] an ironic foreshadowing of suggestions
for trading the right to pollute, which has now become common.
An underlying fear of the total obliteration of human life is
remarkably frequent in much of Vidal's writings, and found in
almost all of his inventions, so that in *Duluth*, which stands as
the ultimate expression of this fear, the world is inherited by
extra-terrestrial insects who create some unknown future out of
the ruins of Duluth, just as Kalki wished to recreate the world
with his descendents.

But then common to all of Vidal's writings is a sense of the fall
from grace, with the early American Republic cast, rather
improbably, as some lost Garden of Eden. In one recent interview he has actually spoken of the foundation of the United
States in these terms:

*Mary McCarthy (1912–89) was a significant novelist and critic, best
remembered for her novel *The Group*. On her death Vidal wrote: "She was
our most brilliant literary critic because she was uncorrupted by compassion" (Carol Brightman: *Writing Dangerously: Mary McCarthy and Her
World*, NY, Harcourt Brace, 1994: 493).

That was something special on Earth and Jefferson was something special on Earth when he said that life, liberty and the pursuit of happiness – nobody had ever used that phrase in the constitution before or set that out as a political goal for everyone. So out of that came the energies of the United States to have made it the number one country in the world and the most inventive and the most creative, and then the Devil entered Eden and we ended up with an Asiatic empire, and a European empire, and a South American dependency and we are not what we were.[54]

But perhaps the United States never was "what we were." Clearly Vidal does not support slavery, the dispossession of Native Americans, or the exclusion from public life of all women. Yet his constant invocation of the decline of the United States seems to leave no room to recognize that in some ways it has become more rather than less inclusive, that the flaws of contemporary democracy, while huge, are not necessarily greater than the rather different flaws of the past. In other moods, after all, Vidal blames Jefferson, both for his defense of slavery and for his expansion of United States territory. One ends wondering just where Vidal does find the golden age whose loss he seems so constantly to bemoan.

——— five ———

VIDAL AS WRITER

" 'Ultimately how would you like to be remembered?'
'I suppose as the person who wrote the best sentences in his time.' "
Interview with Michael Lasky 1975,
quoted in Starton and Vidal 1980: 53

"Unhappily the novelist, by the very nature of his coarse art, is greedy and immodest; unless he is read by everyone, he cannot delight, instruct, reform, destroy a world he wants, at the least, to be different for his having lived in it."
"French Letters: Theories of the New Novel"
Encounter December 1967

Vidal has always taken his vocation as a writer extremely seriously, and had already determined upon making it his career while a schoolboy. He is equally concerned for his reputation, and perhaps too willing to answer his critics, some of whom have been extraordinarily vituperative. Writers rarely reflect on why it is we feel a need to write: in Vidal's case it seems to combine a need for fame, power, and money with a deep political commitment, and over a period of perhaps 30 years Vidal developed a mastery of several genres – the historical novel, the post-modern satire, the polemical essay – which have become lasting platforms from which to address/redress the American people. Writing allows him a freedom to shape the political discourse that is denied to actual politicians, but it is also deeply frustrating in that it provides no easy means to translate critique into action.

Vidal places himself in the tradition of Henry Adams (1838–1918) and Henry James (1843–1916), both of whom appear as characters in *Empire*. "I cannot remember," writes Vidal, "when I was not fascinated by Henry Adams" ("The Four Generations of the Adams Family," in *United States*: 661, originally published in the *New York Review of Books* 1976). Adams, a descendent of the Massachusetts political dynasty, was a historian who also wrote what might well be regarded as the model for American political fiction, *Democracy* (1880). He was a central figure of Washington life over many decades, and Vidal was told stories of him by Eleanor Roosevelt which he draws on in his novels. Indeed, *Washington, D.C.* and *The Best Man* are in part tributes to Adams' political fictions. Vidal would not echo Adams in describing himself as a "conservative Christian anarchist," but there are frequent echoes of Adams' patrician republicanism in much of his writing.

In Vidal's youth Henry James was widely regarded as the most significant of all American novelists, and Vidal duly read all of his considerable output, which includes a number of novels usually regarded as central to the American canon. The Library of Congress catalog lists over 700 publications for James, who remains the most analyzed and discussed American novelist. Kaplan tells us that Jack Kerouac, the Beat writer with whom Gore had a brief sexual encounter, dismissed Vidal's early novels as "sophomoric imitations of Henry James" (Kaplan 1999: 368). Given Kerouac's disdain for structure in his own writings, this is hardly a surprising comment. Thirty years later Vidal was still rereading James – no other canonical writer is as much referred to in *Palimpsest* – and wrote several essays about him for the *New York Review of Books*. In some ways his interest is surprising, given James' emphasis on maintaining the novel as aesthetic and detached from political controversy, although one sees echoes of James in Vidal's emphasis on elegance in writing, and, perhaps, in his creation of the strong-willed Caroline Sanford, who recalls Isabel Archer in *The Portrait of a Lady*.

In some ways Vidal seems more in the tradition of Mark Twain (1835–1910), and Fred Kaplan, who has written biographies of both, has pointed to some of the similarities: "self-projection,

celebrity, political gadflys, humor mixed with deep seriousness."[1] Vidal admires Twain, who in addition to producing two
famous novels, *Tom Sawyer* and *Huckleberry Finn*, was a prolific
satirist and a passionate anti-imperialist. Twain was responsible
for the publication of the memoirs of Ulysses S. Grant , the vic-
torious Civil War General, and later President (1869–77), and
Vidal often cites Grant's opposition to the Mexican War, which
he saw as a major cause of the Civil War a decade later. In his
old age Twain was a critic of the imperialist policies of Theodore
Roosevelt, but, notes Vidal, "As he was only a writer who said
funny things, he was ignored" ("The Day the American Empire
Ran out of Gas," in *United States*: 1,012, originally published in
The Nation 1986). Indeed, one senses some degree of identification in Vidal's comment that: "Oddly for someone who had
made his fortune out of being the American writer, as he once
described himself, Twain spent more than a decade in Europe
. . . He was admired on the Continent in a way that he never was,
or so he felt, by the Eastern seaboard gentry, who were offended
by his jokes, his profanity, his irreligion, and all those Scotch
sours he drank."[2]

Vidal's style varied enormously during his early writings, and
reveals the influence of wide reading: he has acknowledged
influences as diverse as Voltaire and Somerset Maugham, whom
he met while he was still a teenager. Most commentators agree
that Vidal experimented with a number of literary models in his
first books, and he acknowledges the influence of the nineteenth-
century realist novelist Stephen Crane on *Williwaw*. (The book
may well have been influenced, as well, by Malcolm Lowry's
1933 novel *Ultramarine*, based on Lowry's own experience as a
deckhand.) More recently Vidal acknowledged that he was con-
siderably influenced by the writings of Thomas Mann, especially
The Magic Mountain, and appears delighted that Mann apparently read and much appreciated *The City and the Pillar* (Introduction to the Vintage edition, New York, 2003). Since the 1960s
he appears to have settled for a combination of the elegant and
the ironic in almost everything he writes.

Kaplan's biography also mentions the influence of several
books read while Gore was at school: most interesting is Sholem

Asch's *The Nazarene* (first published 1939), which presented the story of Jesus through three witnesses, including Judas Iscariot and the governor of Jerusalem. Vidal himself acknowledged that both *Julian* and *Burr* were influenced by Asch, an emigrant to the United States, and later Israel, who was a central figure in American Yiddish writing. Given some of the subsequent attacks on Vidal for alleged anti-Semitism, it is interesting that some of his views of Christianity came in fact from a prominent Jewish writer. Kaplan has also written of the lasting influence of the now forgotten book *The Spartan*, by Caroline Snedeker, first published as *The Coward of Thermopylae* in 1911, which introduced him to themes of culture versus militarism, of love between men, of patriotism and the search for home (some of the book is set just south of Amalfi).[3]

As with all writers of fiction there is a certain amount of disguised autobiography, and his claim in the afterword to *The City and the Pillar* to be "the least autobiographical of novelists" (revised edition: 156) is somewhat misleading. The book is dedicated "for the memory of J.T.," whose presence haunts a number of his novels, above all *The Smithsonian Institution*, *The Season of Comfort*, and *Two Sisters*, which is described as "a memoir in the form of a novel." In *Season* there is a chapter titled "the parallel construction" in which the thoughts of a son and mother appear on opposite pages, as close to revealing Vidal's own turmoil in dealing with his mother as he has ever come. In *Palimpsest* he tells us that his mother "went on a bender" when she read it (235). But these books stand out as exceptions amongst his fiction, and he has been most successful in imagining lives and times completely outside his own experience, unlike a writer such as Philip Roth, most of whose fiction seems an increasingly inventive set of variations on his own life.

Unlike, say, mathematicians and tennis players, most writers improve with age. As Vidal wrote in his forties: "By themselves, the early drafts are simply glum reminders that at any given moment in one's youth unripeness was all . . . though the basic text varies little from youth to age, the means of execution shift and change" (*Two Sisters*: 19). The seeds of his later accomplishments can be found in the early works, although it was not until mid-career that he hit upon the two genres, the fiction of political history and the satirical novel, in which fantasy bends time and space, which represent his best writing. Vidal's writing is inspired by huge confidence and ambition, and he works very hard: the sheer amount of reading and synthesis found in, say, *Lincoln* or *Creation* exceeds that of the average doctoral thesis. His satire can reveal prejudice – usually racial – but is also corrosive, if sometimes less than subtle. No other contemporary author combines so deep a knowledge of history with an easy irony about the pretensions of both the political and the rich. In books like *Myron* and *Duluth* the satire first essayed in the detective stories and *The Judgment of Paris* is by now more honed if more savage.

His novels are often quite complex in structure, using multiple narrators. *Julian* is framed by an exchange of letters between two of his former teachers; in *Burr* Charles Schuyler is writing a pamphlet about Burr, which comes to incorporate sections of Burr's own memoirs; *Two Sisters* is a narrative by "V" (clearly Vidal), incorporating a notebook written by Eric but addressed to his twin sister, Erika, which in turn includes a movie script also written by Eric. By the time Vidal wrote *Duluth* this complexity becomes less a device than central to the satire itself, although at times one wonders if even the author is always certain which voice is currently dominant.

His inventions, such as *Myra Breckinridge*, *Duluth*, and *The Smithsonian Institution*, display a knowledge of post-modern tropes which should dispel the claims that he is an old-fashioned or non-literary author. Indeed the inventions seem to illustrate perfectly Ihab Hassan's comment that "fiction now . . . explodes in ludic, parodic, ironic forms."[4] The 1954 novel *Messiah* is seen by some as science fiction, a genre with which he flirts in most of his inventions. Indeed it was published as one of Ballantine's science fiction paperbacks, along with such classic works as Ray Bradbury's *Fahrenheit 451* and Arthur Clarke's *Childhood's End*. In ways that would be worth exploring there are similarities with the writings of his contemporary Kurt Vonnegut, whose books, such as *Cat's Cradle* and *Slaughterhouse Five*, also play with time and genres to depict an America for which much of the time he seems to despair. Vidal is probably more highly regarded as a writer in Europe than in the United States, winning consistently good reviews in Britain and high praise from international literary figures such as Gabriel García Márquez and Italo Calvino, whose work he helped introduce to American readers.

Through the inventions Vidal uses deliberate offensiveness to subvert and sabotage: here, he walks a fine line which doesn't always work, but when it does it is brilliant. Indeed, as Richard Poirier pointed out, the inventions are "comic-nightmare versions of Vidal's more realistic historical novels" ("Vidal's Empire," in Parini 1992: 237). The inventions echo his preoccupations: sex and procreation (*Myra*); television and the movies (*Myron, Duluth*); the Cold War (*Kalki*); American politics and media (*Duluth*); World War II (*The Smithsonian Institution*); religion (*Kalki, Golgotha*) – and in all cases Vidal delights in taking bad taste as far as he can. The famous anal rape in *Myra Breckinridge* is repeated in *Golgotha*, where the Emperor Nero fantasizes marrying a powerful young man and turning him into a gorgeous girl: "once altered, all-boy becomes part-girl and the two-in-one are all mine" (*Live from Golgotha*: 173). Together the inventions make up an imaginative and sardonic commentary on the preoccupations of the post-World War II United States. They also reveal a bleakness in which human greed and aggression consistently threaten to end human life itself.

American satirists face the problem that reality constantly exceeds what can be invented. In *Duluth* Vidal invokes Dan White's "twinkie defence," which is as bizarre as anything a writer could invent.* There is a serious purpose to Vidal's inventions that is often overlooked in commentaries, yet they are among the most imaginative and perceptive images of certain aspects of American reality available. There are few better introductions to the contradictions and ambitions of American mass culture than reading, say, *Myra/Myron* and *Duluth*.

*Dan White was a San Francisco City Councillor who, after resigning in dudgeon from the Council, assassinated Mayor George Moscone and openly gay Councillor Harry Milk in 1978. In his subsequent trial he pleaded that he was unhinged by eating too much sugar. He was sentenced to seven years' jail, for manslaughter rather than murder.

By the time he wrote *Duluth* Vidal was clearly ready to take great risks, to create a novel that would be satirical, in bad taste, and able to straddle academic debate and popular culture. James Tatum claims it is his angriest book, and concludes it has "the sharp bite of a satirist like Juvenal: not pleasant, often not even funny, and thoroughly Roman" ("The *Romanitas* of Gore Vidal," in Parini 1992: 218–19). Not for nothing does Duluth, Vidal's transplanted city which manages to simultaneously abut the Mexican border, the Great Lakes and Louisiana, start with a "D," invoking those memorable television series of the 1980s, *Dallas* and *Dynasty*. For *Duluth* is simultaneously the place and a television program set in Duluth, and the novel is at once a satire on pop culture and on literary fashion, in which the fate of Betty Grable, a Hollywood actress who achieved fame as a leggy pin-up during World War II, or the romance paperbacks written by Barbara Cartland and her followers, are as relevant as the latest literary fashions, such as "Pynchon's lesser corollary to the law of gravity" (a reference to the novel *Gravity's Rainbow*). The characters move in and out of Duluth the city, *Duluth* the television program – a device foreshadowed in *Myron* – and a Regency-Hyatt novel by the famed plagiarist – novelist – Rosemary Klein Kantor, who will, in her final appearance, deconstruct deconstructionism. In Duluth, the city, Lt Darlene Ecks, a clear descendent of Myra Breckinridge, although indisputably, as she would put it, *all woman*, seeks out illegal aliens and drug dealers, and sexually humiliates them.

Duluth is as divided by racial hatreds as any city in the United States, and the portrayal of Hispanic Americans, in "little Yucatan," is as savage as any in satirical literature. It is also a precarious balancing act, for here Vidal plays off sexual stereotypes that risk being misunderstood as racist. Meanwhile the mayor and police chief are contesting an election, in a campaign that clearly reflects contemporary southern Californian politics, just as President Reagan has mysteriously divided into a multiple set of Presidents in Washington. An alien spaceship, whose movements are seemingly controlled by a red thumbtack wielded by the police chief, sits somewhere in or outside the city, and will, in the end, take over Duluth. Or *Duluth*.

Duluth is Vidal's most successful and mordant black comedy. The Italian writer Italo Calvino caught the spirit of the novel when speaking at the presentation to Vidal of honorary citizenship by the town of Ravello:

> I must ask myself if we are indeed in Ravello, or in a Ravello reconstructed in a Hollywood studio, with an actor playing Gore Vidal, or if we are in the TV documentary on Vidal in Ravello . . . Or since there is a spaceship in Duluth manned by centipedes who can take on any appearance, even becoming dead ringers for U.S. political figures, perhaps we could be aboard that spaceship, which left Duluth for Ravello, and the E.T.s aboard could have taken on the appearance of the American writer we are here to celebrate . . .[5]

While Mailer and Baldwin also wrote powerful novels and essays, of the next generation of writers perhaps only Joyce Carol Oates has the same range. Neither Vidal nor Mailer were included in a review in 2003 by Joseph O'Neill, which listed the "big three" novelists of his generation as Bellow, Updike, and Roth.[6] The jockeying for position in the American literary world can be harsh: after Mailer and Updike criticized Tom Wolfe's *Bonfire of the Vanities*, Wolfe retorted by naming them, along with the novelist John Irving, as "the three stooges."[7]

Even in literary terms I would dispute O'Neill's categorization: both Joyce Carol Oates and Toni Morrison have equal claims to inclusion, and Mailer and Vidal have had a larger impact upon the direction of American writing. Vidal has never felt he has had appropriate recognition as a writer: he has not been lauded by critics and academics (of whom he is unforgivingly harsh), or included in many literature courses, as are, say, Updike, Bellow, Morrison, or Roth. I have been surprised in working on this book how many critics ignore Vidal, even where he would illuminate their theses – but then, most literary criticism has a remarkably small readership. One exception was the very laudatory review the influential literary critic Harold Bloom wrote of *Lincoln*:

Vidal's imagination of American politics, then and now, is so powerful as to compel awe. Lincoln is to our national mythology what Whitman is to our literary mythology, the figure that Emerson prophesied as the Central Man . . . No biographer, and until now no novelist, has had the precision of imagination to show us a plausible and human Lincoln . . . Vidal . . . gives us the tragedy of American political history, with its most authentic tragic hero at the center, which is to say, at our center. ("The Central Man: On Gore Vidal's *Lincoln*," in Parini 1992: 223)

It is true that Henry James, whose putative approval seems to hover above critics of American literature with remarkable constancy, saw historical novels as "tainted by a fatal cheapness," but novels which draw on historical events and (re-)create historical characters have become very fashionable over the past decade: one thinks of the works of William Styron, of E. L. Doctorow, of Don DeLillo, indeed of Colm Tóibín's *The Master*, which dutifully quotes James' judgment.[8] In some ways, turning to historical and satirical novels allowed Vidal to avoid the central problem he faced as a popular novelist, namely that he never created a convincing heterosexual romance. Yet it is difficult to think of a greater demand on the novelist than the ability to write good historical fiction – which the literary critic Daniel Aaron defines as "the power to reconstruct and inhabit as space in time past, to identify with it almost viscerally, feel it in their bones, and extract its essence."[9]

The success of *Julian* and *Creation* placed Vidal in a small but important tradition, of serious literary attempts to retell the stories of what used to be called "the ancient world." Critics have compared him to Robert Graves, whose *I Claudius* was published in 1934, to Mary Renault (*The Charioteer* 1959), to the French Marguerite Yourcenar (*Mémoires d'Hadrien* 1951, published in English 1954). It is perhaps not accidental that both Yourcenar and Renault were lesbians, who were able to explore homoeroticism through the safety of the "historical novel." Vidal himself drew attention to this parallel in a 1973 essay where he compared Renault's later novel *The Persian Boy* to *The City and the Pillar*, observing that "the only true love story on the best-seller list is about two homosexualists" ("The Top Ten Best Sellers," in *United States*: 80, originally published in the *New York Review of Books* 1973). Yet it is the resolutely heterosexual Graves who most resembles Vidal, having been shaped by World War I much as Vidal was by World War II, and having something of an equivalent range of concerns and interests in a very long literary life.

Despite his extraordinary productivity Vidal has never won a Pulitzer Prize, the best-known American award for writing – though he claims *Lincoln* missed out when the custodians of the Prize overruled the fiction judges (*A View from the Diners Club*: viii). The best novel in the year of *Burr* was Eudora Welty's *The Optimist's Daughter*, and in the year of *Lincoln* the Prize was awarded to Alison Lurie for her novel *Foreign Affairs*. In retrospect both decisions seem to support the argument that Vidal's fiction has been systematically underrated. Vidal fell foul of literary critics for his choice of genres, his often expressed contempt for the "LitCrit" industry, his cynicism about personal relationships and his views on sexuality, perhaps for his refusal to identify with a particular minority, other than "the ruling class," which was unlikely to win critical approval. He *was* awarded the National Book Award for non-fiction for his collected essays in 1993, which strikes one as equivalent to the lifetime achievement award presented at the Oscars to those who have unaccountably never won a specific prize.

Vidal is usually rated as one of the top essayists of the Cold War era, and together with a number of prominent American and British authors, including Mailer and Sontag, he was a contributor to the first issue in 1963 of the *New York Review of Books*.[10] The *New York Review* was founded to allow for lengthier consideration of current books than was possible in the mainstream media, and has become arguably the most influential "intellectual" journal in the United States. Its circulation of 100,000 plus ranks it with other "journals of opinion" such as *The Nation*, *New Republic*, *American Spectator*, and *National Review*, though it is puny beside that of, say, the *New Yorker*, a far glossier but not always less intellectually interesting publication. Over the following decades Vidal continued to contribute to the *New York*

Review, although its editors have also rejected some of his pieces, particularly those seen as too strident in their criticism of Israel. Since the early 1960s, Vidal's essays have been collected in a number of anthologies – not always with the same titles or content on both sides of the Atlantic – sometimes with deliberately ironic titles, such as *A View from the Diners Club* and *Virgin Islands: A Dependency of the United States*. In explaining the first of these titles, Vidal likes to relate the story that he turned down an offer of membership in the National Institute of Arts and Letters on the grounds that he was already a member of the Diners Club.

Becoming an established author involves a complicated interaction between artistic creativity and the business of publishing, promotion, and marketing. Vidal had no inherited wealth, but expensive tastes: he had to earn his income from writing and was willing to try almost all types. Thus in the early 1950s Vidal published five books under pseudonyms, one of which, *A Star's Progress* by Katherine Everard (also available as *Cry Shame!*), is now sold by second-hand dealers for more than 400 times its original 25 cent cover price. His Edgar Box mysteries sold well on both sides of the Atlantic; when they were republished in 1964 Vidal wrote a blurb for them as himself, in which he claimed: "The work that Dr. Kinsey began with statistics, Edgar Box has completed with wit in the mystery novel."[11]

An author as well known as Vidal – and with a track record in film and television writing – is a valuable commodity, requiring both agents and accountants as well as the resources of major publishing houses. Some very high-profile agents have represented Vidal, but none seems to have been a formative influence in the way that is true of some agent/author relationships. (At different times separate agents have represented Vidal as a writer of books, screenwriter, actor, and public speaker.) Although Vidal's own career in publishing was short, Dutton remained his publisher until the late 1950s, when he moved to the Boston firm of Little, Brown, leaving them in turn for Random House, through the influence of his friendship with their editor Jason Epstein. Epstein, however, became increasingly uncomfortable with the direction of Vidal's political and sexual writings, and their relationship deteriorated, especially after *Live from Golgotha*, which Epstein hated. Kaplan, who also seems uncomfortable with the book, claims Epstein saw it as "contemptible" (Kaplan 1999: 772–4). Vidal's first British publisher, John Lehmann, had begun his publishing career at the Hogarth Press, founded by Virginia and Leonard Woolf.

Over the past decade or so Vidal has turned to several small leftwing presses to produce his pamphlets, and has also published with both Harvard and Yale University presses. That mainstream publishers, most of which are owned by multinational conglomerates, are unwilling to publish his political writings could be seen as evidence of the conservative bias of American publishing, just as the ability of small presses to reach a considerable audience with pamphlets such as *Perpetual War for Perpetual Peace* or *Imperial America* can be read as showing the strength of political dissent within the United States.

Few authors are satisfied with their publishers; most of us feel that with more and better efforts they could have attracted more reviews, better sales. Some of Vidal's books were clearly very successful on all counts, others (e.g. *Two Sisters, Live from Golgotha*) did not achieve either the reception or the sales that the author had hoped. Best-seller lists are notoriously unreliable, tending as they do to overstate sales in certain sorts of shops – the most significant omission in the United States is probably of "Christian" publishers, hardly likely to have any impact on figures quoted for Vidal – but few serious authors have been able to make these lists over as protracted a period as Vidal. Literary critics may not see him as sufficiently serious for major consideration, but half a dozen or so of his novels have done surprisingly well, given their critique of mainstream American values. Many of his books have been republished a number of times, and there is increasing interest in his earlier or forgotten works, as in a staged reading at Duke University in 2005 of an expanded version of his 1959 play *On the March to the Sea*.

It is not accidental that the only university course of which I am aware that is dedicated to the works of Vidal is taught outside the United States, at the University of Vienna, although there is a website offering to provide "Gore Vidal essays and research papers." His books have been translated into over 30 languages, with the most editions appearing in French and Italian. There are a few books of criticism and many interviews available; indeed, some strange mix of vanity and courtesy means Vidal has made himself available to a strange range of interlocutors, some of whom have hardly served his reputation. Typical of the critical assessment of Vidal is the comment from Robert Kiernan, in one of the first books written about Vidal, that he is "an artist of the middle rank."[12] There exist a small number of critical studies of Vidal, of which Jay Parini's collection *Gore Vidal: Writer against the Grain* stands out; it is interesting that he is also included in a series on "popular contemporary writers" along with V. C. Andrews, Tom Clancy, and Stephen King.

Newsweek critic Walter Clemons referred to Vidal as "the best all-round American man of letters since Edmund Wilson,"[13] who died in 1972, and who dominated American criticism for much of the mid-twentieth century. His biographer, Fred Kaplan, suggests that the failure of the literary establishment to take Vidal sufficiently seriously as a creative writer is related to the fact that "intellect drives his artistry," unlike authors such as Bellow, Mailer, or Updike for whom "the heart is the defining organ, both for life and for literature."[14] In some ways Vidal's very celebrity, and his frequent appearances on television and, later, film, have detracted from a proper appreciation of his seriousness as a novelist, most serious, perhaps, when he is most apparently sardonic. Reflecting on one of his earlier novels, *Messiah*, the novelist Dawn Powell wrote: "More impressed by the writer than the book, which was engaging enough, but the trouble with being a clear, sharply cut, extraordinary individual with a rich articulate gift is that no characters can equal the author himself . . ." Yet Powell was prescient in seeing that he would "not to be fit in any fashion, but will outlive them all, like the great ones."[15]

Vidal's range is greater than that of any of his contemporaries, and the views that he is not a first-class writer – or is a far better essayist than he is a novelist – are standard clichés that I would dispute. Both the English poet Stephen Spender and Norman Mailer made the claim for his essays in the early part of Vidal's career,[16] and it is one often repeated. In similar vein Martin Amis praises Vidal as "the cleverest book-reviewer in the world . . . Essays are what he is good at: you can't be too clever for them."[17] Similar claims were made about James Baldwin, and in both cases by critics who found their homosexuality distasteful. In Baldwin's case his non-fiction burnt with a passion and intensity that is less concentrated in his novels. The case of Vidal is more complex, and seems to stem from the fact that his best novels are written in genres that are not regarded as totally serious. Harold Bloom has made the point that because much of Vidal's best writing is found in his historical novels, his reputation has suffered because this genre is no longer regarded as "available for canonization."[18] Amis is at least honest, and admits he has read very little of Vidal's fiction.

Vidal's pugnacity, cynicism, and dark irony discomforts most critics. The theatre critic John Lahr wrote: "No-one pisses from quite the height that Vidal does. In his detachment, he is too clear-eyed to hate and too knowing to be grave. His goal, it seems to me, is to teach, which is why he so often writes in epigrams. He doesn't want to be remembered; he wants to be memorized."[19] Vidal once wrote of his plays: "I use the theatre as a place to criticize society, to satirize folly, to question presuppositions" (Foreword to *The Best Man*: ix). In an interview in 1972 he reputedly said of himself: "[I am] . . . complacently positive that there is no human problem which could not be solved if people would simply do as I advise" (cited by Harry Kloman: *The Gore Vidal Index*). His wit is sometimes reminiscent of Oscar Wilde's, though he is not sufficiently cynical to escape the polemical. As Christopher Hitchens, the British journalist and writer who was a favorite of the American left until he enthusiastically backed the war in Iraq in 2003, wrote: "Rather like Gore Vidal in our time, Wilde was able to be mordant and witty, because he was deep down and on the surface, *un homme sérieux*."[20] More to the point he was both homosexual and socialist, as well as sharing Vidal's enjoyment of mixing with high society.

Vidal's writing can be both caustic and bitchy, as in the many public feuds which are scattered through his life, and which provided the sort of frisson for the literary world the rest of us get from reading *People* magazine at the hairdresser. His most famous line may be the quip that "Whenever a friend succeeds, a little something in me dies." In his inventions he calls on the devices and references of popular culture ranging from the latest television series through to computer games, and by combining them with classical and literary allusions subverts the divide between high- and lowbrow – the narrator of *Kalki* is given to quoting in the original French, if occasionally inaccurately. Most of Vidal is fun to read, though his polemics do sometimes slip from irony to indignation and to that extent miss their mark. His reinventing of himself, most obviously in *Palimpsest*, shows wit, erudition, and a taste for gossip that makes it particularly entertaining to read.

His essays on literature reveal a wide reading and a few recurring themes, above all a dislike of "English teachers," whom he sees as increasingly writing novels meant only to be read by each other. One suspects that, despite all his effort to keep up with the latest French fashions of the 1950s and 1960s, his literary essays will be remembered mainly for their praise of writers who would otherwise be totally forgotten, writers such as Dawn Powell and John Horne Burns. Following Vidal's long article praising Powell's forgotten novels in the *New York Review* her books started to be brought back into print.[21]

Vidal has consistently criticized the limited scope of the "literary novel," revolving, as he likes to say, around the crises of divorce and tenure in a college town. Unlike writers such as Bellow, Oates, and Morrison he has always stayed away from universities, except for short appearances, usually in connection with book promotions or political campaigns. His view of contemporary American writing deliberately downplays the scope and ambition of writers such as Joyce Carol Oates, E. L. Doctorow, and Don DeLillo, all of whom have written books which go far beyond the confines of "the university novel." Nor has Vidal paid much attention to recent works of science fiction, by writers such as Neal Stephenson and William Gibson, which clearly stretch the boundaries of "literary" writing, although he did display a passing interest in Doris Lessing's forays into the genre. One suspects he has too much of a vested interest when insisting, as he wrote in 1970, that: "Literature . . . has no relevance to the young who were brought up on television and movies, and though they are doubtless happier for the whole experience, they are quite unable to comprehend the doubleness of things, the unexpected paradox, the sense of yes-no . . . [the] means of examining life as opposed to letting it wash over one" (*Two Sisters*: 40).

six

SEX

"It is no accident that in the United States the phrase 'sex and violence' is used as one word to describe acts of equal wickedness, equal fun, equal danger to that law and order our masters would impose upon us."

"Women's Liberation: Feminism and Its Discontents,"
in *United States*: 583–94, originally published in the
New York Review of Books, 1971

"Since those who believe in romantic love suffer so much anyway, I would not dream of adding to their suffering."

Views from a Window: 301

In 1948 Vidal published his third novel, *The City and the Pillar*, which immediately established him as a "homosexual writer," creating a whole set of expectations and assumptions that have affected both him and his critics ever since. Vidal claimed he wrote the book "to examine the homosexual underworld (which I knew rather less well than I pretended), and in the process show the 'naturalness' of homosexual relations, as well as making the point that there is of course no such thing as a homosexual. Despite current usage, the word is an adjective describing a sexual action, not a noun describing a recognizable type" (Afterword, rev. edn: 155).

Probably the sanest commentary on the book comes from a French scholar, George-Michel Sarotte, who ironically wrote the first full-length study of male homosexuality in American literature. As Sarotte writes:

> Vidal's novel is a confession: it is the confession of failure. "Normal" homosexuality cannot exist in American reality, despite all the examples one can cite, despite all the defenses of the "bisexuality" natural to all human beings that fill the works of the author of *The Season of Comfort*.[1]

Sarotte was writing in 1976, about a book already almost 30 years old: another 30 years on, his claim that American homophobia is so all-pervasive that it was impossible to imagine a realistic homosexual character who is "normal" seems less convincing. Sarotte seems at times to be overly judgmental, too prone, perhaps, to echo French stereotypes of America's shortcomings. Another French scholar of Vidal's works, Nicole Bensoussan, concentrates on his depiction of American "decadence."[2]

The central character of *The City and the Pillar*, Jim Willard, is an athletic tennis player who falls in love with a childhood friend, Bob – note the schoolbook-type Anglo names preferred by Vidal – and spends the rest of his life trying to recapture their brief sexual encounter. (At the time Vidal was writing the book the famous tennis player Bill Tilden was arrested and sentenced for homosexual acts with minors.) Jim is clearly *not* bisexual, and when, after a long absence, Bob rejects him, he resorts to force: murder in the first draft, rape in the second. Vidal strenuously denied anything autobiographical about the book, but it clearly represented a wish, shared perhaps by a majority of men of his generation who felt homosexual desire, to proclaim their "normality." As the critic Leslie Fiedler, who was one of the first to try to write seriously about homosexuality in American writing, suggested: "The existence of overt homosexuality threatens to compromise an essential aspect of American sentimental life: the camaraderie of the locker room and the ball park, the good fellowship of the poker game and fishing trip . . . a kind of passionless passion, at once gross and delicate, homoerotic in the boy's sense, possessing an innocence above suspicion."[3] Jim Willard was a far greater threat to assumptions of sexual and gender normality than the fey creatures who waltzed through the pages of Truman Capote or Carson McCullers at the time.

Within the confines of the period, the novel rejected the stereo-type of the homosexual as sissy, or the homosexual as victim, to foreshadow the sort of homosexual men whom the next gen-eration of writers (Edmund White, Christopher Bram, etc.) would create. Some stereotyping remains: not only is the ending melodramatic – as Vidal acknowledges in his own afterword to the revised edition – but Jim does seem to foreshadow another common trope, the homosexual as narcissist, which is true of the writings of both Yukio Mishima and John Rechy.

By publishing *The City and the Pillar*, Vidal became a "gay hero" even while denying the identity, and insisting on a uni-versal bisexuality, which seemed justified by a particularly misogynist version of psychoanalysis. In a set piece at a party two characters dispute whether homosexuality is to be under-stood as "a return to the natural state where it was possible to openly love and desire an image similar to one's own as well as one's opposite," or perhaps "a hatred of women, a repugnance, a revolt against their authority" (*The City and the Pillar*: original paperback version 1950: 144). Much of this discussion disap-pears from the revised version. Vidal's attempt to break out of the dominant stereotypes which surrounded homosexuality led to the creation of a central character who is clearly "masculine," as Americans understand that term, and thus quite unlike the "pansies" and "sissies" who had dominated previous literary references to homosexuality.

As Sarotte argues, Vidal also fell back on dominant stereotypes in the melodramatic ending, in which Jim turns on his former lover and kills him when he is rejected, although the reverse would have been more stereotypical. Vidal rewrote the ending in 1965 to become one of rape, but remains true to the script whereby all homosexual stories needed to have an unhappy ending. In James Cain's *Serenade* (1937) the protagonist, a singer, risks losing his voice when he has sex with men, but gets it back when he turns to women, thus turning a plot device into a lesson in morality. In the 1941 novel by R. H. Newman, *Fling Out the Banners*, which Kaplan tells us had a considerable impact on Vidal, not least as it was set in a very similar school environment to his own, the homosexual schoolboy commits suicide, and the predatory teacher is forced from the school in disgrace. The mandatory tragic ending changed somewhat with the overtly gay novels of the 1970s and 1980s – although for a period death from AIDS became a new theme – but has not disappeared. In the 2003 play by Richard Greenberg *Take Me Out,* a redneck baseball player kills another player with a deliberate pitch after his own sexuality is questioned.

When *The City and the Pillar* was first written Christopher Isherwood agreed to write a blurb for the book, but criticized it privately for suggesting homosexuality leads inevitably to "tragedy, defeat and death." While Isherwood lectured Vidal on his failure to present an image of homosexuality that would help promote legal and social change, he did acknowledge that the same criticism could be made of his own writings. It was not until 1964, with the novel *A Single Man,* that Isherwood directly wrote about homosexuality in the way he had advocated to Vidal.[4] Tellingly, the book is dedicated to Vidal, just as Vidal later dedicated *Myra Breckinridge* to Isherwood.

The City and the Pillar was attacked by mainstream critics, but it sold a million copies in paper, one of the first "literary" US paperbacks – but also part of the boom in "daring" novels which the paperback made possible. While Vidal has consistently claimed it set back his career as a novelist, it established him as a literary hero to a whole generation of homosexual men, and remains one of the pioneering works in the development of gay literature in the United States. In 2003 a special symposium was organized at Yale University to commemorate the 55th anniversary of the book's publication.

Twenty years later Vidal won similar notoriety with the publication of *Myra Breckinridge. Myra Breckinridge* is the first of Vidal's novels to deliberately mix popular culture, academic theory, and gratuitous offensiveness to create an alternate universe, an America which appears more uniquely American than the real. The book relates the story of Myra Breckinridge, she "whom no man will ever possess," who comes to Hollywood after the death of her husband, Myron, to claim her inheritance, a half share in Myron's Uncle Buck's Academy of Drama and Modelling. Her real objective, however, is to destroy the supremacy of male heterosexuality, focused as it is on the person, and increasingly the arsehole, of her student Rusty Godowski, then to win the attractions of his former girl friend, Mary-Ann. Myra is, of course, Myron, having been surgically modified in Copenhagen, and a car accident undoes her apparent femininity, thus allowing her to marry Mary-Ann, settle down in the San Fernando Valley and re-emerge six years later in Myron.

Vidal claimed he named Myra after a drag queen, but the name "Myra" may be an anagram of "Mary," a common word for an effeminate homosexual. She was inspired by the huge statue of a buxom woman who stood, revolving slowly, on Sunset Boulevard outside the hotel, the Chateau Marmont, where Vidal spent much of his scriptwriting days in the 1950s. Myra

> is a creature of fantasy, a day-dream revealing the feminist principle's need to regain once more the primacy she lost at the time of the Bronze Age when the cock-worshipping Dorians enslaved the West, imperiously replacing the Goddess with a god. Happily his days are nearly over; the phallus cracks; the uterus opens; and I am at last ready to begin my mission which is to re-create the sexes and thus save the human race from certain extinction. (*Myra Breckinridge*: 9)

One wonders whether Myra reveals the influence of Susan Sontag, whose famous essay "Notes on Camp" had appeared a few years earlier. If by "camp" we understand an exaggeration of style and artifice above content, this makes sense of Philip Core's comment that: "*Myra Breckinridge* may not be a camp book, but it is certainly the first bestseller intentionally to use all the elements of camp taste for the specific purpose of describing the society which contains them."[5] The mix of androgyny, worship of old movies, and references to the "new novel" all remind an aware reader of Sontag's essays. The novel is both a tribute to the Hollywood movies of the 1930s and 1940s and, as John Mitzel argues, a move by Gore to liberate himself from his own generation and move with the new mores of the late 1960s, a shift caught in Myra's somewhat embarrassed attendance at a student orgy.⁶ It is also a baroque continuation of the themes of *The City and the Pillar*, with an older and more cynical Vidal using camp irony to undermine the dominant assumptions of sex and gender. In some ways Myra foreshadows the radical gay liberation movement, which emerged the following year, even though Vidal has claimed he only realized Myra was a transsexual halfway into writing the book.

Myra proclaims her mission as: "the destruction of the last vestigal traces of traditional manhood in the race in order to realign the sexes, thus reducing population while increasing human happiness and preparing humanity for its next stage" (*Myra Breckinridge and Myron*: 36). That Myra sets out to "prepare humanity" through the ritual deflowering, with a dildo, of the young and naïve Rusty cloaks a standard homosexual fantasy in the language of gender politics. As Catherine Stimpson puts it: "Myra's rape of Rusty is still ugly, but it is Myra's sadistic shouts of ecstasy as she rides her 'sweating stallion into forbidden country' that revolts us, not her dildo" ("My O My O Myra," in Parini 1992: 195). For Myra, all relationships are battles for power, and the rape, for which she admits some regret, is necessary to destroy male supremacy. A woman who is, in fact, a homosexual man revenges her/himself on a heterosexual man with the aim of symbolically reversing the sex/gender order. Or, more likely, to shock, titillate, and offend in order, ultimately, to instruct.

Myra Breckinridge was part of a major cultural assault on the assumed norms of gender and sexuality which swept the western world in the late 1960s and early 1970s, cousin at least to *Hair*, *The Rocky Horror Show*, David Bowie's *Ziggy Stardust*, and Mick Jagger's character in the film *Performance*. (Brigid Brophy's *In Transit: A Trans-sexual Adventure*, published the following year, might also be read as homage to *Myra*.) Through a whole range of cultural forms artists reflected the larger social questioning of sexual and gender assumptions, symbolized by men growing their hair long while women discarded their make-up and bras, even though the stories of feminist bra-burnings are largely apocryphal. In creating a transsexual as a means of undermining the sexual and gender order Vidal foreshadowed both the political and the cultural events that would see sexuality become the basis for a set of new political and cultural movements. The Stonewall riots in New York City in 1969, often cited as the birth of the gay liberation movement, which followed a police raid on a homosexual bar, were led by a number of drag queens, and the early 1970s were remarkable for a period of deliberate gender and sexual confusion in the arts. Avant-garde American art was particularly rich in exploring these themes through performance groups such as the Cockettes and the film-maker John Waters, and the idea of "genderfuck" lived on for some time in Charles Ludlam's New York Theater of the Ridiculous.[7]

In later years transvestism became tamed as a subject for film, and shows up in such popular movies as *Tootsie* and *Victor/Victoria* (both released in 1982), without the hard edge of the early 1970s. Indeed, *Some Like It Hot*, filmed at a time (1959) when there were still considerable restrictions on what movies could depict, manages to be more radical about gender than most of its descendents. Billy Wilder, who both co-wrote and directed the film, could be said to have anticipated some of Myra's moves. But some of the films of the Spanish director Pedro Almodóvar, and more recently the "nightmare cabaret opera" by Daron Hagen and Paul Muldoon, *Vera of Las Vegas* (1996), show that Myra still lives, in the latter case as an African-American undercover agent.

Vidal continued these themes of destroying sexual and gender norms six years later in *Myron*, a fantasy that revolves around the dissolve between reality and image, as created by Hollywood and television. Myron, now a contented (though incomplete) married man, local Republican, and proprietor of a Chinese takeaway service in San Fernando, falls – or is pushed – into the set of the imaginary movie *Sirens of Babylon*, being filmed in 1948 and starring those two essentially B-grade actors Maria Montez and Bruce Cabot. Both were real figures: Montez was known as "the Caribbean Cyclone," while Cabot had been Fay Wray's savior in the film *King Kong*. A number of "outsiders" live on the backlot of *Sirens*, including a would-be society hairdresser, whom an unkind reader might assume to be Truman Capote, and a bad-tempered cook, whose rants about how a real man violates women to prove his manhood suggest he may be Norman Mailer.

During his time on the set Myron's alter ego, Myra, reasserts herself, setting out to remake both the history of Hollywood, and thus of the world, by saving the fortunes of MGM Studios (to whom Vidal was contracted as a screenwriter for much of the 1950s) but also, in a reprise of *Myra Breckinridge*, by changing the gender of one of the extras, Steve Dude, into the fun-loving Amazon Stefanie Dude, who in time, pace Ronald Reagan, becomes President of these United States, to be challenged by the "Com-symp senator from Massachusetts John F Kennedy . . . [whose] only claim to fame is being the brother-in-law of Marilyn Monroe" (*Myra Breckinridge and Myron*: 438). Whole classes in cultural studies could spend weeks decoding the various levels of gossip, celebrity culture, and malicious revenge caught in this conceit. While *Myron* is generally dismissed as an inferior remake of *Myra*, it is in some ways sharper and more inventive, rather as *Alice through the Looking Glass* is more fun to read than *Alice in Wonderland*.

The smartest commentary on the two books comes from Catherine Stimpson, who is one of the few critics able to appreciate the combination of camp wit, sexual and political satire, and the melancholy lament for an older America represented by the Hollywood movies of the 1940s. "Myra/Myron," she writes "is, then, a series of collisions among sexual codes and rebellious sexual realities, epistemological codes and our heads, sacred codes and profane aspirations to appropriate them, sacred codes that deny sexuality, and sacred codes that enshrine it, 'good taste' and flamboyant sexual performances that defy its criteria" ("My O My O Myra," in Parini 1992: 193). Myra/Myron are Vidal's ultimate revenge on the masculine ethos of Norman Mailer and John Wayne, and the texts of American psychoanalysis, which had abandoned any of Freud's acknowledgment of the polymorphous perverse. As Myra says, "the fluidity which I demand of the sexes is diametrically opposed to Mosaic solidarity" (*Myra Breckinridge and Myron*: 189).

Critics of Vidal would cite *The City and the Pillar* and *Myra Breckinridge* to allege that he is "a pornographer," which may, of course, reveal more about his critics, and what arouses them, than about Vidal himself. If pornography is defined as something intended to sexually arouse, it is difficult to find much in Vidal that would meet the criterion, detailed as are the account of Rusty's rape in *Myra Breckinridge* or Darlene's assaults on Chicano manhood in *Duluth*. In both cases Vidal satirizes the very pornographic scripts that he is accused of writing. Indeed, Vidal presents a view of sex that confronts American mores in ways that are far broader than its particular phobias around homosexuality. He is most radical in his anti-sentimentality, whether expressed through his ideas on love, commercial sex, or fidelity, a dislike of sentimentality already apparent in *Williwaw*. For Gore, love, sex, and companionship are distinct pleasures, not to be found in the same person, an attitude that constantly confounded a culture deeply committed to their being inextricably linked together. As "T" reflects in *The Smithsonian Institution*: "Somehow he had thought that the grown-up world was like the movies, where a good woman loved only one man and if they weren't in a weepie movie with Bette Davis they got married and ended up together once George Brent was dead or in prison" (*The Smithsonian Institution*: 64). Squaw (Mrs Cleveland) is deliberately portrayed as repudiating this view, enjoying intimacies with a number of young men in the various Smithsonian exhibits.

Asked about his relationship with Howard Austen, Vidal's unchanging answer was that it was a relationship without sex, hence one that lasted far better than the average marriage. The critic John Simon, one of many with whom Vidal has enjoyed a long and bitter feud, found this particularly unbelievable: "What sort of companion does one pick up at the Everard Baths, a homosexual meeting and mating place? And why does one go on living with such a person for the rest of one's life?"[8] This is the sort of question only someone with a very narrow view of what constitutes a life partnership could ask, and it reveals a lack of imagination and empathy that demeans Simon rather than Vidal. The year he met Howard, Vidal published one of his unacknowledged novels, *A Star's Progress*, under the name Katherine Everard, possibly a tribute to their meeting.

But the redeeming nature of love is a constant theme of American culture, both high and low, and even apparently cynical views, such the television series *Sex and the City*, always close by asserting the triumph of the romantic ideal. Thus the recent film *Down with Love*, which flirts with a feminist challenge to American sentimentality in the early 1960s, ends, predictably, with the triumph of love and marriage. Few commentators on Vidal have so spectacularly misread him as the unnamed reviewer quoted on the jacket of *In a Yellow Wood*, who claimed: "Vidal sees that love is the single unshakable truth left to us, the only condition in which beauty and decency have a chance of survival."

Vidal has set out his views on sex in a number of essays, which have been collected together by Donald Weise in the volume *Gore Vidal: Sexually Speaking*. Basically Vidal sees sex as a perfectly normal, and pleasurable, part of human experience, which has been confused by a whole series of largely religious doctrines and restrictions. At times he overlays this with comments on the different biological needs of men and women, based on their different roles in reproduction, and almost always he stresses that attraction to one's own sex is a perfectly normal part of human sexual response. Leave aside the Vidalian mix of the stentorian and the satirical, these are views that would be shared by large numbers of secular westerners today. Indeed younger readers might wonder why Vidal found it necessary to argue so strongly for what now seems fairly self-evident, namely that " 'sin', where it does not disturb the public order, is not the concern of the state" ("Sex and the Law," in *United States*: 537, originally published in *Partisan Review* 1965).

Remember that much of Vidal's discussion of sex and the law dates from a period when contraception was hard to obtain, abortion and homosexuality were criminalized, and books now regularly assigned for undergraduate courses were regarded as pornographic. Vidal was particularly scathing of censorship, and in the original version of *Myron* he used the names of current Supreme Court justices to stand in for words widely regarded as obscene, so that his characters "burger" and "rehnquist" in homage to the justices who voted to allow local communities to prohibit certain books and movies from public sale on the grounds of local "community standards."* Vidal has defended pornography, but on the grounds of freedom of speech rather than any romantic view of the genre: "The worst that can be said of pornography," he wrote as long ago as 1965, "is that it leads not to sexual adventure but to the reading of more pornography" ("The Novel in the Age of Science," in *Quarterly Journal of the Library of Congress*, October, 1965, 22: 4: 297).

In the 40 years or so since Vidal wrote some of his key essays on sex the battleground has shifted. On one hand some of Vidal's demands have been achieved, although it was not until 2002 that the United States Supreme Court ruled restrictions on consensual adult homosexual sex were unconstitutional, thus catching up with the rest of the western world. On the other, sexuality has become a major rallying cry for conservatives, who are determined to use the powers of the state to impose a sexual regime that is quickly disintegrating. Since the Reagan Presidency, Republicans have sought to overturn the Supreme Court's rulings on abortion; sex education has been bitterly contested; the battle against "gay marriage" has replaced defense of sodomy laws. The one area on which Vidal has consistently written where little appears to have shifted is commercial sex; while most other rich liberal societies have moved towards various ways of decriminalizing and regulating prostitution, the United States (like Sweden) remains determined to uphold prohibition, against all evidence that this is ineffective. No other issue so starkly shows the clash between the two sides of American ideology, the clash between a belief in individual entrepreneurship and moral regulation.

Writing about Vidal immediately demands a decision as to how to discuss his own sexuality and his attitudes towards sexuality, which are not necessarily the same. Since he published *The City and the Pillar* in 1948 literary critics have pounced on the

---

*Warren Burger was appointed Chief Justice by Richard Nixon in 1969, and served until 1986. He was succeeded by William Rehnquist, who had originally been appointed to the Court by Nixon in 1972. This may be Nixon's most lasting legacy to American politics.

homoerotic elements of Vidal's work to the exclusion of other, more radical, assertions he makes about sex, power, and money. In the *Cambridge History of American Literature*, published in 1999, the literary critic Morris Dickstein centers his not particularly flattering summary of Vidal on that one book and defines Vidal as one of "the daring new gay writers . . . who managed at once to be outlaws and celebrities, media favorites and cultural villains."[9] The opposite approach is that of Edmund Morgan in his review of *Inventing a Nation*, where he writes of Vidal taking on "outsider" status without any consideration of how this status may have been affected by his sexuality. When Kaplan's biography was published in Britain many of the reviews in the press were given headlines such as "He kisses boys and girls" (*Independent*) and "Come on, let's have all the Gorey details" (*Observer Review*), which revealed the adolescent voyeurism all too common in the so-called "quality press."

Neither reducing Vidal to his sexuality nor ignoring its significance will suffice. Sex colors both his hatred of Judeo-Christian religion and his experience of the McCarthy period, when Communism was conflated with homosexuality, despite McCarthy's chief offsider, Roy Cohn, whose homosexuality, like that of J. Edgar Hoover, was widely known but never mentioned. How far McCarthy, whose closeness to his young male aides was striking, was repressing his own homosexual desires is passed over by virtually all commentators on the period. In several throwaway lines, for example in *Washington, D.C.* (260), Vidal has claimed that McCarthy was homosexual,[10] a slightly odd comment given his objection to such categorizations in other contexts, but certainly a common speculation during the 1950s.[11]

For a long time Vidal presented himself as bisexual, while insisting that his was a perfectly normal form of behavior: "Every boy I knew had a similar experience. What we were all up to was a perfectly normal homoeroticism, which sometimes continued for the rest of their lives without lapsing into the physically more complex homosexuality or, for whatever reason, into *serious* heterosexuality, an 'avoidance' that was the one true heresy . . ." (*Palimpsest*: 283). As he grew older he became less concerned to hedge himself in this way, although consistently refusing to identify himself as "gay," even while most of his sexual interests clearly were homoerotic. When Martin Amis interviewed him in 1977 Vidal insisted on being described as "pansexual" rather than "homosexual,"[12] although one assumes he would have accepted the term were it being used adjectivally. While Vidal presents himself as conventionally masculine, and always the dominant partner in sexual encounters, his inventions allow him to play with notions of both gender and sexual fluidity, and Myra is only one of a number of characters who revels in breaking conventional gender expectations. In *The Smithsonian Institution* President Buchanan, "the bachelor President," appears dressed as a respectable widow to convene a ladies' card party.

More than in other western countries, homosexuality provokes great anxiety amongst Americans. James Baldwin, who was doubly stigmatized for his race and his sexuality, once said that American men will kill each other rather than acknowledge a sexual attraction. This theme reappears in much of American culture: one thinks of films such as *Cruising* (1980), *The Sergeant* (1968), or *Reflections in a Golden Eye* (1967), the last based on a novel by Carson McCullers, in all of which fear of the homosexual within leads men to acts of violence. Oscar Wilde's line that we kill the one we love is too often literally true in the American psyche.

Vidal has consistently insisted that homosexuality should be used only to describe behavior and not identity, first arguing this in his early essay on Suetonius' *The Twelve Caesars*, which he tells us could not be published for some years after he wrote it in 1952. Four years earlier, the same year as *The City and the Pillar* appeared, the Kinsey Report, *Sexual Behavior in the Human Male*, was published, and its claim that over a third of adult white men had engaged in "at least one homosexual act to the point of orgasm since the onset of adolescence" was widely disputed. The Kinsey Report – which also showed high rates of adultery and masturbation – was a sensation, denounced by moralists and welcomed by homosexual activists, who would continue to invoke Kinsey for the next half-century (and often misquote him). Vidal wrote of the Report in *The Judgment of Paris* as having "promptly lessened everyone's guilt, and, if only by weight of the numbers given, it made the idea of pederasty much less remote, no longer exclusively associated with managers of flower shops or with a fearful fumbling in the back row of a darkened movie house" (228).

Vidal shares with most western students of sexuality from Freud through to Kinsey the belief that humans have the innate ability to be attracted to both sexes, and are shaped by social and psychological factors towards particular ways of expressing their sexuality, which is potentially far more polymorphous than most will admit. In some ways Vidal was a social constructionist before the term entered academic discourse on sexuality,[13] and many gay activists were to be angered by his refusal (not always consistent) to identify as "gay." (Social constructionists believe that while sexual behaviors are limited only by biology, how sexuality is imagined and acted out is a product of historical and social factors.) As recently as 2004, commenting on C. A. Tripp's claim in his posthumous book *The Intimate World of Abraham Lincoln* that Lincoln was "bisexual," Vidal insisted that: "homosexual and heterosexual behavior are common to all mammals, and that what differs from individual to individual is the balance between these two complementary but not necessarily conflicted drives" ("Was Lincoln Bisexual?" VanityFair. com 2004, no date).

Vidal's analysis is Platonic rather than Freudian: he explained the relationship in *The City and the Pillar* as involving "lovers [who] were athletes, and so drawn to the entirely masculine that in the case of one, Jim Willard, the feminine was simply irrelevant to his passion to unite with his other half . . ." ("A note on *The City and the Pillar* and Thomas Mann," in *Virgin Islands*: 97, first published in *The Threepenny Review*, Summer 1995). Indeed, Jim reflects that "the idea of being in love with a man was both ludicrous and unnatural; at the most a man might find his twin . . ." (*City and the Pillar*, revised edn: 55). The twin motif is central in *Two Sisters*, where Eric and Erika van Damm appear to embody a Platonic longing for unity, and Vidal seemed to echo Jim's words over 40 years later when he mused: ". . . Is it not [the] search for likeness, that desire and pursuit of the whole –

as Plato has Aristophanes remark – that is the basis of all love? As no one has ever actually found wholeness in another human being, no matter of what sex, the twin is the closest that one can ever come towards wholeness with another . . ." (*Screening History*: 24).[14]

Writing about Vidal's sexuality is difficult, because unlike the next generation – and a few earlier exceptions, such as Christopher Isherwood and the writer and composer Ned Rorem – he chose not to assert an identity as the basis of politics. More typical was the novelist John Cheever, born 13 years earlier, whose writings only hinted at the homosexual cravings revealed in his posthumous papers. Vidal's insistence that categories of sexual preference are misleading, and his use of clumsy terms like "homosexualist" or "same-sexer" to demarcate himself from gay activists, appears increasingly odd, but it also makes sense given his history and age. Yet his emphasis on bisexuality was an assertion of a more sophisticated analysis than that of those who insisted they were "born" gay, and in his willingness to take up "gay" issues Vidal was far ahead of most of his generation, apart from a few odd exceptions. Remember that he was a contemporary of Rock Hudson, whose homosexuality was elaborately disguised by his publicists, and older than James Dean, whose sexual ambivalence was equally well hidden.

It is tempting to speculate that Vidal's own unorthodox sexuality pushed him towards a particular sort of libertarian leftwing politics, a connection that is more explicit in the writings of Isherwood and the now largely forgotten social critic and novelist Paul Goodman. Yet his sexuality, whatever he said about it, remains a problem for the establishment, both political and literary, often dealt with by denial. Over his life Vidal has fluctuated between wanting to stand above homosexuality and seeming to flaunt it, an ambiguity that was also apparent in the career of his contemporary Michel Foucault (1926–84). It is only a generation younger than that of both Vidal's and mine who have been able to genuinely live openly as homosexual without being scarred by the deep stigma associated with it, and Vidal's determination to neither deny nor be defined by his sexuality is remarkable for his time.

Vidal's willingness to write about homosexuality, especially in *The City and the Pillar* and his 1956 collection of short stories, *A Thirsty Evil*, was, ironically, a lot braver than some of the more public "coming out" declarations by public figures in a more recent and tolerant society. Although he sometimes denies it, publication of *The City and the Pillar* both identified Vidal with homosexuality and foreclosed realistic chances for a high-profile political career, his Congressional run in 1960 notwithstanding. His second novel took its name from a few lines of the poet Robert Frost, who wrote of two roads diverging in a yellow wood, and the need to choose. Homosexuality was for Vidal the yellow wood, and rereading that novel now, despite its apparently heterosexual protagonist, makes that clear.

This may not have been as obvious to Vidal then as later: the war had created space for homosexual encounters and the beginning of a sense of community among people who met each other in a time that combined great freedom with equal restraints, leading to a small boom in overt references to homosexuality in writing.[15] Had Vidal been ten years younger, and not experienced military service, his attitudes towards sex would almost certainly have been very different. Even so, *The City and the Pillar* predates almost every other attempt in American literature to depict homosexuality in mainstream literature. The so-called "pansy craze" of the 1930s saw a number of novels which were essentially read only by those "in the know," most obviously the joint novel by Parker Tyler and John Henry Ford, *The Young and the Evil*, which was published in 1933 – but in France, and by a publisher known for its erotica.[16] Although John Hope Burns' *The Gallery* (1947), about which Vidal has written generously, was a mainstream work with a major homosexual theme, this was sufficiently disguised so that my rather tattered paperback edition, published in 1960, proclaims on the cover: "The famous novel of American soldiers and the women of Naples . . .," although the flyleaf acknowledges that it also includes "an evening in a homosexuals' hangout." In Britain, E. M. Forster had written his homosexual romance *Maurice* many years earlier, but it was not published until 1971, after the author's death.

Nonetheless the late 1940s are generally regarded as seeing a new openness about homosexuality in the United States, and a breakthrough in homosexual writings with the attention paid to writers such as Vidal, Tennessee Williams, Truman Capote, and Paul Bowles. The first "gay" organizations in the United States such as the Mattachine Society and Society One were founded in the early 1950s, but soon fell foul of the moral crusade that marked the McCarthy period. A Senate committee, chaired by North Carolina Senator Hoey in 1950, concluded that the employment in government of "sex perverts" constituted a major security problem, and the FBI, under J. Edgar Hoover, enthusiastically created a "sex deviates program" to effect the dismissal of homosexual government officials.[17] These attitudes persisted, and in the late 1950s, when Vidal wrote the screenplay for Tennessee Williams' *Suddenly, Last Summer*, Sebastian's liking for young men had to be even less openly named than in the original play, producing, as Vito Russo wrote: "a film with high moral tone that could not, in the end, explore its own subject."[18] It may be memories of these restrictions that led Vidal to defend Oliver Stone's 2004 film *Alexander*, which was strongly criticized for its depiction of Alexander as bisexual.

Vidal has claimed that the literary establishment championed Arthur Miller because they couldn't acknowledge that the best playwright of the time – Williams – was a fag, and certainly there is evidence about a great deal of cultural anxiety around the prominence of homosexual playwrights in the 1950s and 1960s. (Miller, author of plays such as *The Crucible* and *Death of a Salesman*, became a symbol of conventional gender roles when he married Marilyn Monroe in 1956.) In a couple of prominent articles, Williams was linked with Edward Albee, whose *Who's Afraid of Virginia Woolf?* was a hit in 1962, and William Inge, author of *Picnic* and *Bus Stop*, as creating "a two-sex version of the one-sex experience."[19] It was not until the 1960s, with John Rechy's novel *City of Night* (1963) and Mart Crowley's play *Boys in the Band* (1968), that explicit homosexuality became an acceptable theme for mainstream literature, and even those two works still reproduced the stereotypes which linked homosexuality to inevitable promiscuity, loneliness, and suffering. It took the social and cultural upheavals of the late 1960s to create space for the emergence of a gay movement, and its rapid transition into another lifestyle claiming a particularly American right to both individual happiness and group recognition.[20]

One forgets that just as the jet and the computer are products of a world which was unknown to Vidal as a young man, so too is the modern gay man. There is ample historical evidence it is only in the past half-century and in rich western countries that significant numbers of people began to identify themselves publicly as homosexual, and create a movement and a community based on that identity. The novels of John Rechy, starting with his 1963 best-seller *City of Night*, depict a world of diverse sexual identities and practices which are strangely like those asserted as "culturally specific" in, say, Bangladesh or Colombia today. "Gay" and "lesbian" identities were as alien to most Americans and Europeans in the 1940s (indeed the 1960s) as they are in much of the poor world today; indeed more so, because there were no equivalents to the signs of "gayness" from the rich world which are purveyed through mass media and have become part of the new world of global consumerism.[21]

There are some interesting insights into the evolution of modern gayness in Vidal's novels – would a totally heterosexual novelist have noted Harry Lahr, the "lapdog" of society ladies in 1900s Washington, who "on occasion . . . liked to dress up as a smart lady" (*Empire*: 98). Similar figures could be found in ·Washington society, indeed orbiting the then first lady, at the time Vidal was writing *Empire*. His fictions and memoirs, drawing as they do on over 50 years of experience, are a largely neglected resource for the now fashionable topics of gay history and sociology: at his best Vidal was an acute observer. "Bodies *were* different then," Gore wrote of the 1940s. "We were a lean, sinewy, sweaty race, energized by sex and fear of death, the ultimate aphrodisiac . . . I had forgotten what the so-called workingman's body was like – thick-thighed, flat-chested, with muscular arms, not as comely as an aerobics-styled body of today, but solider, uncalculated, earthlike" (*Palimpsest*: 95).

Louis Auchincloss is in part right when he writes that a homosexual encounter is "the trademark of a Vidal novel, like the fox hunt in Trollope or the appearance of Hitchcock as an extra in each of his films" ("Babylon Revisited," in Parini 1992: 242). Yet while homosexuality is a given in much of his writing, there are few characters like Jim in *The City and the Pillar* for whom homosexuality is central. Rather, Vidal seems determined to illustrate his thesis about bisexuality through characters of both sexes, and in *Kalki* it is the women whose sexuality is most prominent. In the historical chronicles the siblings Blaise and Caroline Sanford are bisexual, although their major relationships appear to be heterosexual. Yet given the hysterical fear of homosexuality in America during the early 1950s – when some politicians seriously posited it as a threat to national security greater even than Communism[22] – Vidal's insistence on writing about it in most of his early novels is significant. Indeed, he prefigures later academic writing about the growth of a gay world, to use the title of a book by Martin Hoffman (1968), and *The City and the Pillar* captures the homosexual ambivalences of the late 1940s very well:

> Like jazz musicians and dope addicts, they spoke in code. The words "fairy" and "pansy" were considered to be in bad taste. They preferred to say that a man was "gay", while someone quite effeminate was a "queen". As for those manly youths who offered themselves for seduction while proclaiming their heterosexuality they were known as "trade", since they usually wanted money. Trade was regarded with great suspicion; in fact, it was a part of the homosexual credo that this year's trade is next year's competition. (*The City and the Pillar*, revised edn: 115)

It would be another 15 years before such discussion would re-emerge in popular novels.

Whatever psychoanalytic explanations of his sexuality there might be, there was a strategic importance for Vidal in refusing a gay identity. He was determined to be taken seriously as a mainstream writer, not confined to a particular niche. Had he declared himself a homosexual he would have risked everything he wrote, most of which was not about sex, being viewed as the "special pleading" of an unpopular minority spokesman. Nor was his dislike of psychoanalysis surprising, given that the dominant school of American psychoanalysis had turned homosexuality into a significant psychological problem and created an industry aimed at making homosexuals "mature" and "normal." As Myra notes, this is a shift from Freud's own "tentative conviction that all human beings are attracted to both sexes" (*Myra Breckinridge and Myron*: 90). Consider the experiences of the historian and playwright Martin Duberman, who was born five years later than Vidal, but experienced considerable trauma and guilt around his sexuality, not eased by periods in therapy.[23] Several generations of American homosexuals suffered considerable emotional damage from these attempts, though they were less overtly cruel than the behavioral attempts to eradicate homosexual desire via shock therapy.

For most of his career Vidal rejected a homosexual identity and insisted he was bisexual; he claims that Kinsey, having taken his sexual history at the Astor Hotel, told him he sounded like "a lower-middle-class Jew, with more heterosexual than homosexual interests" (*Palimpsest*: 103). A cynic might observe that Kinsey's observation reflects more on his reliability than it does on Vidal's sexuality. Indeed, despite his protestations Vidal has acknowledged that "I've met very, very few genuine bisexuals,"[24] insisting rather that bisexuality is part of the human sexual potential and sexual labelling is unnecessarily limiting. But despite his consistent refusal to be labelled as gay, he has been claimed as a gay hero by many activists and writers, and is often identified as a "gay writer" by literary critics.[25]

While Vidal's essays have been often picked up by the gay movement, and anthologized as in *The New Gay Liberation Book* (1979), there is less awareness of his sexual politics in a broader sense. Those critics who write of "gay" literature speak only of his works with an overtly homosexual theme, thus missing the opportunity to discuss the more complex ways in which his "gay sensibility" (not a phrase Vidal would use) affects his other writing. Perhaps the worst example of this is Gregory Woods in *A History of Gay Literature*, who does not even acknowledge as crucial a work such as *Myra*, while asserting that Vidal has failed some implicit test: "There are searching questions to be asked of some established gay writers who did not pay significant attention to the epidemic [i.e. AIDS]. Would it be invidious to name

John Ashbery or Allen Ginsberg or Gore Vidal?"[26] This suggests a Soviet-style political agenda for writers, made more offensive by being a throwaway line in the endnotes.

One longs for a more subtle, indeed playful, analysis which might develop the preoccupation running through many of the inventions with racial stereotypes and assumptions about dick size, circumcision, and anal sex. How can we understand Myra's preoccupation with "Negro size" or Mrs Grover Cleveland's reputation as "a chicken hawk" (in *The Smithsonian Institution*) without recognizing that this is a deliberate use of gay male idiom, intended, as Myra's friend, Letitia van Allen, puts it, for "the new American woman who uses men the way they once used women" (*Myra Breckinridge and Myron*: 115). One might argue that Germaine Greer's reclaiming of "the beautiful boy" in her book *The Boy* follows Myra and Squaw in claiming for women the right to objectify the male body. There is in Vidal's writings a consistent critique of American puritanism, and the hypocrisies with which it is enforced, as in the sadistic glee with which *Duluth*'s police lieutenant Darlene Ecks seeks out illegal immigrants and sexually humiliates them, until she is, finally, humiliated herself – and made pregnant – by a black drug dealer.

There were several occasions where Vidal did intervene to support the gay movement. The most remarkable was in 1978, when he appeared at a public meeting in Boston organized by the Boston-Boise Committee to protest mass entrapment of homosexuals by the Boston police. (The name of the organization was a reference to a major police operation in Boise, Idaho, aimed at destroying an alleged pedophile ring.) The mere attendance at this meeting was enough to force a Boston judge from office. Vidal's appearance showed the mixture of ambivalence, defiance, and genuine radicalism that has characterized his approach to sexual politics, and angered conservatives more than it has exasperated some gay radicals. In 1982, when campaigning for the Californian Senate nomination, several gay groups organized fund-raisers for him. But despite such occasional interventions, Vidal largely stood aloof from the next generation of homosexual – now gay – writers, who represented a rather different, and far more confessional, way of writing about sexuality. This makes it difficult to fully assess Vidal's influence on this next generation, as both they and he tend to underestimate the connection.

Certainly Vidal's life laid out a script that the next generation of writers in part followed, whether consciously or not. There are some interesting parallels with Edmund White, the most distinguished gay novelist of the last three decades, who has drawn very strongly from his own life to write books such as *A Boy's Own Story* and *The Farewell Symphony*. In some ways White seemed to follow Vidal's path, attending an elite private school, spending some time as a young man in Rome, and moving later in life to Paris, and both men are charming, erudite, and snobs. Similarities aside, the two are somewhat distant about each other, although Vidal has said he particularly liked White's novel *Nocturnes for the King of Naples* (Weise 1999: 264). White comes from a different generation to Gore's, and was far more influenced by the gay movement and by ideals of romantic love. Unlike Vidal he sees himself as a gay writer, even while recognizing the danger of being "ghettoized" as a consequence.[27] Yet his most recent novel, *Fanny: A Fiction* (2003), the purported recollections of the utopian feminist Fanny Wright, by the writer Frances Trollope, who is best known for her study *Domestic Manners of the Americans* (1832), echoes Vidal's interest in excavating historical characters to better understand the United States, and shares some of Vidal's mordant wit. Some of the historical figures who appear in *Burr*, such as Thomas Jefferson and the author James Fenimore Cooper, also appear in *Fanny*.

This is not to suggest that White is in any way aping Vidal: his preoccupations are different, even if their historical references overlap. Yet White does appear more influenced by Vidal than has been recognized, and he comes close to acknowledging this in his play *Terre Haute*, which is a fictionalized account of Vidal's encounters with Timothy McVeigh. The play, which was adapted for radio and broadcast by the BBC in 2005 with Sir Ian McKellen as the Vidal figure, assumes a face-to-face meeting, which never, in fact, occurred. It clearly relies heavily on Vidal's accounts of his correspondence with McVeigh, and allows White to speculate on Vidal's personality, and to suggest a motive for Vidal's interest in the case, which is dramatically effective though ultimately unconvincing. Certainly the play reinforces the perception that White is now developing an increasing interest in the broader aspects of American politics and history in ways that allow him to move in some of the directions pioneered by Vidal.[28]

Gore Vidal and queer theory

It is tempting to argue that Vidal said more to subvert the dominant rules on sex and gender in *Myra* than is contained in a shelf of queer theory treatises. Even though most of the now-fashionable themes about the fluidity of sex and gender have run through his writings for 50 years, he is ignored in almost all the would-be canonical texts of queer theory. If by "queer theory" we mean an analysis of society and its representations which problematizes all taken-for-granted assumptions about sexuality and gender, then Vidal should be taken somewhat more seriously by contemporary theorists than he is. Thus Eve Sedgwick in her famous book *Epistemology of the Closet* only mentions Vidal to cite his comment on Oscar Wilde;[29] Marjorie Garber in her stimulating study of transgender, *Vested Interests*, mentions *Myra* – but is more interested in the film than the novel; and Annemarie Jagose, in probably the best introduction to "queer theory" available, ignores him altogether. One of the few theorists who does take Vidal seriously is Robert Corber, who points to the ways in which Vidal's writings prefigure those of the gay liberation movement of the early 1970s.[30] Like the Canadian Bert Archer he acknowledges Vidal's prefiguring of the "queer" critique,[31] accurately pointing to the links between Vidal, gay liberation, and the deconstructionist language of 1990s queer theory. And one of the few publications that takes *Myra* seriously as a "queer" text is an archly eccentric publication, *Myra and Gore*, by a group of Boston activists, termed "a book for Vidalophiles."[32]

One of the consistent themes of Vidal's writings is its undermining of stereotypes that insist on confusing male homosexuality with effeminacy, the usual way of depicting homosexuality until the last 20 years or so. His greatest impact on popular perceptions may have come through his contribution to the 1959 epic *Ben-Hur*, where he introduced an unacknowledged boyhood love affair to explain the tension between Ben-Hur and the Roman Messala: "Yes, it was *The City and the Pillar* all over again . . . First, a sort of cryptic love scene; second, the rebuff, ostensibly over politics but actually over unreciprocated love" (*Palimpsest*: 305). The scene in which the two men engage in a private javelin contest, and the glee with which the actor Stephen Boyd, playing Messala, makes advances to the now resolutely uninterested Charlton Heston, is one of the great moments of unacknowledged homosexuality in mainstream film. While Heston always refused to acknowledge a subtext that is obvious to a contemporary audience, the film not only suggests homosexuality but also portrays both men as not only "masculine," but overly laden with muscle and testosterone.

More than homosexuality the real sexual taboo Vidal confronts is sentimentality, where his attitude to sex is very different to, say, James Baldwin's. Baldwin published his own overtly homosexual novel, *Giovanni's Room*, in 1956. Like *The City and the Pillar*, the book was both commercially successful and scandalous; unlike Vidal's novel it was set in Paris with only white characters. Baldwin would be consistently criticized for this choice (he introduced homosexual black characters into later writings, especially *Another Country* and *Tell Me How Long the Train's Been Gone*), but even after his death some African-American critics refused to acknowledge his homosexuality. The two books are often grouped as significant milestones in the development of American gay writing, and *Giovanni's Room* is equally melodramatic, though written in a lusher and more romantic style than *The City and the Pillar*. Unlike Vidal's refusal in his later writings to romanticize love, Baldwin saw it as of central importance, and one of his consistent themes was the ability of personal relationships to override those of power, in some ways a reversal of the increasing cynicism found in Vidal.

The great exception to Vidal's anti-sentimentality is the love for his schoolmate Jimmie Trimble, who was killed in 1945 at Iwo Jima, site of a Japanese airforce base and one of the great battles of World War II. Ironically the battle is now best remembered for John Wayne's character Sergeant Stryker in the 1949 film *Sands of Iwo Jima* and the raising of the American flag over Mount Suribachi. The relationship with "J.T." is described at length in Vidal's memoirs, but he is a presence in a number of his earlier works, appearing in various guises in *The City and the Pillar*, *In a Yellow Wood*, *The Season of Comfort*, and *Two Sisters*. In *Washington, D.C.* there is an adolescent sexual encounter that is very close to the relationship Vidal would describe three decades later in *Palimpsest*: mutual masturbation on a bathroom floor. The clearest homage to Trimble comes in *The Smithsonian Institution*, where he becomes the schoolboy narrator and hero. As the whole plot of the book is the attempt to reverse time to prevent World War II, it is also an unguarded lament for Jimmie. Here Vidal comes close to Isherwood's position that he would not fight in World War II because he might need to kill his former lover, Heinz Neddermeyer, who was unable to leave Germany permanently and was conscripted into the German army.

But the lament for "J.T." remains an unguarded exception to Vidal's stated positions on sex and love. Thus his totally unsentimental attitude towards commercial sex remains confronting for most Americans, gay and straight, and is almost totally ignored in the commentary on his work. Yet there is considerable reference to prostitution in *Williwaw* and *Two Sisters*, while brothels form almost a minor motif through the history series. In *Burr*, Charles Schuyler is a frequent visitor at 41 Thomas Street, whose proprietor, Mrs Townsend, is first seen reading *Pilgrim's Progress*, and David Herold, who joins the conspiracy to murder Lincoln, both works and plays in "Sal Austin's parlors, where the most attractive girls in the city could be found" (*Lincoln*: 17). Other American writers have dealt with commercial sex – one thinks of John Steinbeck's "whorehouses" or the callgirl in John O'Hara's *Butterfield Eight* – but few have so relentlessly demanded that we accept the reality that prostitution exists, and has benefits to both buyers and sellers.

In a 1991 interview Vidal said:

Prostitution is a natural thing, and in a world made more dangerous with AIDS, [we need] legalized prostitution with medical examinations, which is pretty much what they did in the nineteenth century. 1948 was a terrible year. A French Communist senator – a lady – and an Italian Communist senator – a lady – each of them in 1948 passed laws banning prostitution . . . all the women ended up on the street, and they had a huge epidemic of venereal disease, which was a disaster. Misplaced morality.[33]

(The actual situation is somewhat more complex, and is the subject of ongoing debates within the feminist movement in both countries.) In *Palimpsest* he reminisces about visiting a male brothel in Paris which had been patronized by Proust, and later on regrets the decline of prostitution in Rome, now "either very expensive and antiseptic, or, between AIDS and knives, too dangerous to be bothered with" (*Palimpsest*: 389). For Vidal sexual pleasure is a commodity that can be bought and sold exactly as are other pleasures, a position which is, after all, perfectly consistent with the capitalist ideology espoused by such arbiters of contemporary morality as the Rev. Jerry Falwell.

Here his analysis parallels one section of contemporary feminism, which, far from seeing prostitution as inevitably being built on exploitation of women by men (as is argued by writers such as Carole Pateman and Catherine McKinnon), argues for it as a possible choice which can be liberating. There are two problems to Vidal's argument: it appears to be largely built on male homosexual experience, which is arguably somewhat different to heterosexual prostitution, and it ignores legitimate questions of disparities of power which most feminist analysis of prostitution has stressed. Nonetheless there is a refreshing candor in Vidal's willingness to acknowledge the frequent link between money and sex, and the reality that for millions of people trading sexual favors for money and advancement is neither morally nor emotionally more problematic than are many more respectable menial jobs.

Vidal is almost puritanical in his eschewal of actual writings about sex: there is nothing in his works which matches the damp patches in, say, John Updike's or Philip Roth's novels. The famous rape scene in *Myra* is extremely detailed, but also clinical, appropriately, as it is played out in the name of a medical examination. The playfulness that Vidal extols in his essays about sex is rarely present in his actual descriptions. Indeed, I suspect Vidal's reputation for "pornography" is a reflection of his scorn for the language of "relationships." In his historical series he presents a worldly European realism as against American moralism: "Paris was filled with extruded American ladies, paying dearly for adulteries of the sort for which a French lady would have been applauded" (*Empire*: 311). His characters, like him, refuse to fall for myths of love and romance, except where, as in the satirical Mills & Boon references in *Duluth*, they are clearly mocking them.

It would be wrong to assume that Vidal is misogynist, an all-too-common claim about any writer presumed to be homosexual. Much of his historical saga revolves around two remarkable (and imaginary) women, Emma de Traxler Schuyler, daughter of the narrator of *Burr*, and her daughter Caroline, who in *Empire* becomes a successful newspaper proprietor, trumping this in *Hollywood*, where at the age of 40 she proceeds to become a silent movie star, under the name Emma Traxler. Unlikely as this transition is – even more unlikely is the failure of many of her acquaintances to connect the silent movie star with the Washington businesswoman – it does allow Vidal to explore the foundation of the movie industry, and to relish in the sexual scandals and prudery which have fed each other since the first gossip columnists set up shop in the Los Angeles basin. The fictional Caroline lives from 1878 to 1950, thus surviving through to the end of Vidal's historical reimagination of the American republic, and mixing with friends ranging from the writer Henry Adams to her contemporary Eleanor Roosevelt. Her ambition, she reflects at one point, was to be a true "great-grandson" of Aaron Burr, for women in her day were denied access to high office. Indeed most of his women characters are bisexual – and feminists, at least in their relish of sex.

Since the 1960s the United States has seemed increasingly schizophrenic in its attitudes towards sex. On the one hand there is a huge and increasingly mainstream pornography industry, increasing numbers of television programs in which sexual adventure is taken for granted, and a large and very visible gay and lesbian world. On the other the rise of a politicized evangelism since the 1980s has meant increasing political pressures for "traditional values," which are defined as opposition to abortion and homosexuality, and increasing rhetoric about chastity before, and fidelity within, marriage. The scandals around President Clinton can be read either as showing an abiding deep puritanism in American society – he was, after all, impeached by the House of Representatives – or a new tolerance – he left office with remarkably high approval ratings. Equally the decade of George W. Bush has been marked by ongoing tensions between moral puritans, who espouse abstinence outside marriage and denounce homosexuality as responsible for major moral decay, and the reality of a flourishing commercial sex industry, with cable television depicting scenes of sexual behavior that even ten years ago would have been confined to pornographic videos. Vidal's inventions and essays provide ongoing insights into the peculiar foibles, ambivalences, and deep fears surrounding sexuality as it is discussed and understood in the contemporary United States.

———— seven ————

HOLLYWOOD

"Hollywood is the key to just about everything."

Hollywood: 109

"Naturally, Sex and Art always took precedence over the cinema. Unfortunately, neither ever proved to be as dependable as the filtering of present light through the moving strip of celluloid . . ."

Screening History: 1

"In the decade between 1935 and 1945, no irrelevant film was made in the United States."

Myra Breckinridge: 15

"Movies are life, after all, with the point made simple."

Washington, D.C.: 68

In what may be the best book written on "celebrity," the American critic Richard Schickel points out that Hollywood is a state of mind created out of three basic elements: a technique, an economic necessity, and geographic isolation.[1] From this combination came the concentration of America's, and effectively much of the world's, movie production in the western suburbs of Los Angeles, which for 80 years has been the single greatest crucible for global dreams and celebrities: as Myra says, "the entire range of human (which is to say, American) legend was put on film" (*Myra Breckinridge and Myron*: 13). Central to Vidal's career and writings is an appreciation of the significance of movies as the dominant cultural force for most of the twentieth century. He was born in 1925, and was a contemporary of a generation of screen stars who have become American icons: Marilyn Monroe, Marlon Brando, James Dean, and Judy Garland.

Vidal has spoken on a number of occasions of the importance of movies in his life, both as a teenager and during the war, of which he observed: "Maybe one million saw any action. The other ten million of us sat and saw movies. That's all we did on army posts" (Kaplan 1999: 176). When recuperating from hypothermia at the end of the war he chose to be sent to Van Nuys in greater Los Angeles, so as to be near Hollywood. Vidal is, of course, not unique in being influenced as a writer by films: the less highbrow writer Richard Condon (*The Manchurian Candidate, Prizzi's Honor*) estimated he'd seen 10,000 movies in his life,[2] and John Updike's *In the Beauty of the Lilies* makes films central to his picture of twentieth-century America. Indeed one wonders whether Vidal's strong dislike of this particular novel may be partly because Updike has moved into territory – Hollywood, religion, the decline of the United States – that Vidal regards as his own. The writer Roger Angell echoes Myra (without acknowledgment), claiming "the great cresting tide of late-thirties and early-forties Hollywood – an Augustan era when the studios were cranking out five hundred films each year – swept over us and changed us for ever."[3] Like Vidal, Angell locates the crucial era as that between talkies and television, and Vidal links the two forms in his own life.

Vidal began writing for movies in the mid-1950s and has been a minor presence in Hollywood since, as a writer (his best-known scripts are *Ben-Hur* and *Suddenly, Last Summer* – both of which have homosexual subtexts), as an actor (he had already made a cameo appearance in *Fellini's Roma* in 1971, and in the 1990s appeared in *With Honors, Bob Roberts*,[4] and *Gattaca*), and as a close friend of actors, especially Paul Newman and Joanne Woodward. He wrote for the movies partly from a need for money, but also from the same desire to influence the larger world as led him to flirt with a political career. In *With Honors*, the character he plays, the rightwing Harvard Professor Pitkannan, is accused of being a celebrity rather than an intellectual. From being an often uncredited screenwriter in the 1950s, Vidal had become a "name" to be attached to help sell particular sorts of movies, in the case of *Bob Roberts* or *With Honors* those with a political message close to his own.

Vidal has also written at length about movies, sometimes with the resignation of the novelist who knows that his words will never attract the same attention as a summer blockbuster. In his Harvard lectures that form the basis for the book *Screening History*, he observed ruefully that: "Today the public seldom mentions a book, though people will often chatter about the screened version of unread novels" (*Screening History*: 3). But Vidal himself likes to discuss movies, and his knowledge of movie trivia would do him proud in a game of Trivial Pursuit. He reveals his interest in film in surprising places: in his attack on the Podhoretzes, already discussed, he refers to "Mrs. Norman Podhoretz, also known as Midge Decter (like Martha Ivers, *whisper* her name)." Not even the assiduous readers of *The Nation* would necessarily recognize the reference to the ambitious woman, played by Barbara Stanwyck, in the melodrama *The Strange Love of Martha Ivers*, 35 years earlier.

The first references to Hollywood in Vidal's fiction come in *The City and the Pillar*, where Jim is a tennis coach for a time in movieland and has an affair with an actor. References to the movies surface in other early novels, especially *Messiah*, and the critic Robert Kiernan judged *Myra Breckinridge* and *Myron* as the most important novels on Hollywood since Nathaniel West's *Day of the Locust*.[5] (By contrast the film *Myra* is included in one list of the 100 worst films ever made.) The plot of *Myron* revolves around the mythical 1948 film *Siren of Babylon* and is full of references to now-forgotten movies, and a camp delight in a certain sort of movie talk: "I was saddened," says Myron, now Myra, "to find that Victor Mature (whose photograph taken unaware in the altogether during his heroic service in World War II helped defeat Hitler, Mussolini and Tojo) acted not long ago in an *Italian* film, directed by a one-time bad actor and neo-realismo director, with a script by a Broadway jokester. Worse, in the course of this travesty, the *image of Victor Mature was deliberately mocked!*" (*Myron*: 74). Victor Mature was, as David Thomson puts it, "an incredible concoction of beefsteak, husky voice and brilliantine – a barely concealed sexual advertisement for soiled goods,"[6] and thus emblematic of the sort of masculine myth that Myra claims she needs (literally) to emasculate to prevent the race destroying itself.

As Vidal's historical novels move into the twentieth century, they reflect the significance of movies in shaping American life. "Ultimate power," muses Caroline, "is to reinvent the world for everyone by giving them the dreams that you wanted them to dream" (*Empire*: 115). In *Hollywood* Vidal launches the middle-aged Caroline, already a successful Washington newspaper proprietor, into a film career as a means of bringing the film industry into the Chronicles. As Vidal recognized, the movie industry helped make the twentieth the American century, and Hollywood's producers, writers, and directors were the frontline propagandists for "the American way of life": "We are now supplying the world with all sorts of dreams and ideas. Well, why don't we shape these dreams, deliberately?" (*Hollywood*: 447).

It is hardly surprising that William Randolph Hearst should play a major role in the book, linking as he did the worlds of entertainment and of politics. Hearst (1863–1951) looms as a major figure across 50 years of American public life, and is now best remembered as the inspiration for Orson Welles' movie *Citizen Kane* and F. Scott Fitzgerald's novel *The Last Tycoon*. For Vidal, Hearst is the central figure in the invention of the modern media: "[He] alone had discovered . . . [that] if there is no exciting news to report, create some" (*Empire*: 54). His newspapers pioneered "yellow journalism" – the term comes from the cartoon strip "The Yellow Kid" – and played a central role in encouraging the United States to go to war with Spain in 1898, but like Senator Gore he opposed entry into World War I, and during the 1930s was both an isolationist and an ardent anti-Communist. He was one of the early movie producers, and a major figure in New York Democratic politics, fantasizing about winning the party's Presidential nomination in 1920. There are some counterparts in the current United States, most obviously Rupert Murdoch, with his large press, television, and movie interests, but Hearst was arguably the single most important newspaper proprietor in American history.

Hearst straddled the worlds of commerce, media, and politics, and like both Caroline and Vidal himself straddled the old centers of influence on the east coast and the new in southern California. Unlike most of his literary contemporaries, Vidal moved as much in the world of Hollywood as that of the New York literati, and there is a reciprocal influence between his works and the development of Hollywood as the central institution of American culture. Yet of his works only *The Best Man* has been successfully translated to film. *Visit to a Small Planet* became one of Jerry Lewis' more forgettable films, and projects to film *Messiah* and *Kalki* came to naught, despite Mick Jagger's interest in the latter.[7] The notoriety of *Myra Breckinridge* had attracted producers who saw Vidal as representing the sexual libertarianism of the late 1960s, and produced what is universally regarded as a *very* bad film, *Myra Breckinridge* (1970), starring Raquel Welch as Myra, the journalist Rex Reed as Myron, and a sadly aging Mae West as the film agent Letitia van Allen. A few years later there were discussions about a film, to be produced by Bob Guccione of *Penthouse* magazine and written by Vidal, to be called *Gore Vidal's Caligula*, with a cast that included John Gielgud, Peter O'Toole, and Helen Mirren. The final film (1979) was widely regarded as a disaster – "far more Gore than Vidal" commented *Variety* – and Vidal had to sue to remove his name from the title.

Hollywood both reflects changing moods in American politics and helps create them. Before Ronald Reagan so dramatically demonstrated how the celebrity of show business could be translated into a political career, movie actors, writers, and directors had seen their role in politics as one of supporting political movements and particular political candidates. (It is not accidental that *Hollywood* was published the year of Reagan's inauguration.) The movie industry in the 1930s was a center of ideological support for Roosevelt's New Deal policies, and Reagan began his political life as an ardent New Dealer. Orson Welles campaigned across the country for Roosevelt in 1944, and thought of entering politics, but decided against it. As Vidal relates in his homage to Welles, he was approached to run for the Senate in Wisconsin against Joe McCarthy, but: "I let them convince me that I could never win because . . . I was an actor – hence frivolous. And divorced – hence immoral. And now Ronnie Reagan, who is both, is president" ("Remembering Orson Welles," in *United States*: 1,199, originally published in the *New Statesman* 1989).

In 1944 Helen Gahagan, a Broadway actress who made one Hollywood film and married actor Melvyn Douglas, was elected to the House of Representatives, becoming a friend of Eleanor Roosevelt and a strong supporter of progressive policies. In 1950 she was defeated for the Senate by Richard Nixon, who branded her as "the pink lady." In a sense this marked an ideological shift in Hollywood: Reagan campaigned for Gahagan against Nixon, but his politics started to shift dramatically to the right during the 1950s, and his election as Governor of California in 1966 came two years after fellow actor George Murphy was elected to the Senate as a Republican. Their careers marked a new stage in the linking of Hollywood to politics. Indeed the actor Gene Kelly made a television commercial for Reagan's opponent, in which he ridiculed the idea of an actor becoming Governor. The move of actors into politics – the most recent example being Arnold Schwarzenegger's election as Governor of California – may seem a peculiarly American development, although there are many examples from elsewhere (President Estrada in the Philippines, Glenda Jackson in Britain) of movie stardom as the basis for a political career.

More significant is the way in which movies can reflect particular political outlooks, whether this be support for progressive causes in the 1930s (*The Grapes of Wrath, Tobacco Road*); anti-Communism and fear of subversion in the 1950s (*The Fountainhead, Invasion of the Body Snatchers*); or patriotism in the 1980s (*Rambo: First Blood*). The historian Larry May has sought to chart the rise and fall of certain themes through mainstream movies between the 1920s and 1960s, showing a striking rise in "big business villains" in the years leading up to the Great Depression of the 1930s; a peak in patriotism and "savior institutions" during World War II; and a sharp rise in the portrayal of women as wives and "homemakers" in the post-war years.[8]

For the first part of his career Vidal was associated with the artistic avant-garde of New York City, where he spent much of the first decade after the war. In his speculative novel *The Rebel*, in which James Dean survives the car crash of 1955, Jack Dann places Vidal alongside people like Jackson Pollock and Judith Malina and Frank O'Hara as part of the Village set,* "where the junkies, anarchists, Stalinists, poets, painters, visionaries, cynics, intellectuals and queers hung out . . . Everyone who was cool and gone and groovy and with-it."[9] As part of his move from writing for television to film Vidal also moved his American base from New York to Los Angeles, and took a declining part in New York's cultural and social life. This shift is symbolized by his two serious electoral campaigns, the first in New York State in 1960, the second in California in 1982. It mirrors a broader shift in American culture, as more and more television production moved to Los Angeles; in 1972 Johnny Carson's *The Tonight Show*, perhaps the most influential talk show for several decades, was filmed at NBC's studios in suburban Burbank rather than New York City's Rockefeller Center.

Non-Americans often assume that there is no American intellectual or cultural life outside Manhattan – an illusion shared by Manhattanites – but Los Angeles has a far richer history of literary life than is often recognized, as well as several first-class universities and a newspaper, the *Los Angeles Times*, currently of national significance. Indeed Vidal can be seen as part of an often under-appreciated rich literary scene in Los Angeles, partly based on the expatriate writers and musicians working in the film industry. It is odd that the only book by Vidal that Mike Davis discusses in his study of Los Angeles is *Messiah*,[10] though the city is far less central to that book than it is to *Myra Breckinridge*, where Myra reflects on the "sweet miasmic climate in which thoughts become dreams while perceptions blur and

---

*Pollock was a leading abstract impressionist painter, Malina a cofounder of the Living Theater, and O'Hara a poet. None had particularly close links to Vidal.

distinctions are so erased that men are women are men are everything are one" (*Myra Breckinridge and Myron*: 160). Despite conventional stereotypes Los Angeles is arguably the gayest of all American cities, and was a key center in the early history of the American gay and lesbian movement. Myra is the patron saint of a significant body of gay male writing, including Christopher Isherwood's *A Single Man*, John Rechy's *City of Night*, and the detective stories of Joseph Hansen and Michael Nava.

It seems appropriate that Vidal has written much of his most excoriating work about the United States from the twin vantage points of the Amalfi coast and Los Angeles. Had he maintained his American base in New York and Washington one wonders whether he could have mastered the particular sense of American popular phantasmagoria which runs from *Myra* through *Duluth* and even *Live from Golgotha*, in all of which the fantasies of Hollywood movies merge imperceptibly into the lived absurdities, fears, and aspirations of southern California.

—————— eight ——————

RELIGION

"No evil ever entered the world quite so vividly or on such a vast scale as Christianity did."

Julian: 129

"Neither Christianity nor Marxism nor the ugly certainties of the mental therapists had ever engaged my loyalty or suspended my judgment."

Messiah: 74

"The churches were almost always formed as political institutions to frighten people into the obedience of temporal customs."

The Season of Comfort: 71

Vidal is a rationalist who is fascinated by the religious impulse and its history – and by the apparently limitless credulity of believers. In *Messiah* the narrator reflects on "the religious sense which I so clearly lacked . . . I knew that much of what they evidently believed with such passion was wrong. But at the same time I was invigorated by their enthusiasm, by the . . . dignity their passion lent to an enterprise that in Paul's busy hands resembled, more often than not, a cynical commercial venture" (*Messiah*: 143). At the same time, Vidal is very aware that: "If we do not understand Christianity, then we cannot make much sense of the world we live in, because our society, morally and intellectually, for good and ill, is the result of that great force" (*View from a Window*: 99).

He was already musing on questions of belief in his early novels and *The Judgment of Paris* reveals some of the simultaneous curiosity and distrust about religion that would be taken up in later works. The last of his early novels, *Messiah*, is a satire about a twentieth-century cult founded by the messianic undertaker John Cave – note the initials – which declares death as the only possible deliverance, and sweeps the western world. Although the cult claims to transcend Christianity, its belief in suicide as the ultimate salvation is the logical consequence of what Vidal saw as the "death cult" of monotheistic religion. Very much a product of the pieties and hypocrisies of the 1950s, *Messiah* foreshadows both Vidal's later writings on religion and his experimentation with form. *Messiah* suggests that all religion, once codified, becomes authoritarian.

The narrator of the book has Vidal's own baptismal name of Eugene Luther, which both evokes memories of the founder of Protestantism and recalls Christopher Isherwood, who narrated *The Berlin Stories* under his own full name, William Bradshaw. *Messiah* is a satire directed at the new religiosity that seemed to be sweeping the United States. This was symbolized in the early 1950s by the widely followed evangelical tours of Rev. Billy Graham, a strong supporter of Richard Nixon, who was a forerunner of the more aggressive rightwing fundamentalist Protestant Republicans of the 1970s and 1980s. *Messiah* foreshadows both Vidal's interest in the range of religions, with its references to various early Christian sects, and the actual death cults of later decades, most famously the mass suicide at Jonestown at the People's Temple in Guyana, led by American preacher Jim Jones, in 1978, which would enter into fiction through Armistead Maupin's *Tales of the City*.

Vidal's first important historical novel, *Julian*, is an exploration of the Roman Emperor who tried, unsuccessfully, to reverse the hold of Christianity. The novel is foreshadowed explicitly in the first pages of *Messiah*, whose death cult seems to prefigure Julian's (and Vidal's) objections to Christianity, namely that its followers showed a "curious hopelessness about this life, and . . . undue emphasis . . . on the next" (*Julian*: 331–2). The Emperor known as Julian the Apostate ruled for only two years (361–3), but during that time he enjoyed significant military and administrative achievements. He also sought to abrogate all rights which had been granted to Christians, whom he referred to as

"Galileans," but on his death during the war with the Persians allegedly cried: "Thou has conquered, O Galilean." The *Catholic Encyclopedia* called him "passionate, arbitrary, vain and prejudiced, blindly submissive to the rhetoricians and magicians,"[1] meaning, presumably, he failed to listen to their rhetoricians. Julian's failure, and the subsequent triumph of the Christian Church, is arguably the single most significant moment in two millennia of human history.

The ways in which religious beliefs are used to manipulate the credulous, in this case through mass media, is again a central theme in *Kalki*, an "invention" that Vidal uses to create an allegory of environmental disaster. The story describes a messianic prophet, a Vietnam War veteran, who claims to be the last incarnation of the god Vishnu and destroys all human life outside his own immediate circle in order to save the planet, which he would then repopulate with his own progeny. There seems an echo here of the famous comment made by a United States commander in Vietnam about destroying a village in order to save it.

In *Creation* Vidal explores the intersections of Greek, Persian, Confucian, and Buddhist beliefs. *Creation* is included by Anthony Burgess, himself a novelist of note, in his list of the 99 best contemporary novels, although Harold Bloom rates it below many of his others. The book grew out of the realization that in one lifetime, five centuries before the rise of Christianity, it would have been possible to meet Buddha, Confucius, Zoroaster, and Socrates, a premise that makes for one of the most ambitious novels of all time, and one which quite consciously brings together the full range of alternatives to the monotheistic religions which Vidal so loathes. Imagining and writing *Creation* took a number of years in the 1970s (*Kalki* reflects some of the reading involved during the planning of *Creation*) and is written in the form of a travelogue by the half-Greek, half-Persian Cyrus Spitama. Of all Vidal's major works this is least relevant to the theme of this book, but it stands as an important and highly ambitious novel as exploration of history and ideas.

Julian and *Creation* reflect a deep knowledge of most of the world's religions, far deeper than that possessed by most believers. If Vidal was correct when he cited a survey showing that his two most popular books in Britain were *Creation* and *Duluth* ("An Interview with Gore Vidal," in Parini 1992: 285), we might assume many people's knowledge of comparative religion draws heavily on Vidal's interpretation. Writing *Creation* involved a major attempt to understand belief systems quite different to those dominant in the world in which Vidal moves, and reinforced his views of the dangers of the Judeo-Christian tradition. "Monotheism is easily the greatest disaster to befall the human race," he wrote in 1989. "It is time for us in the West to look to more subtle religious and ethical systems, particularly those of China and India" ("Gods and Greens," in *United States*: 1,043, originally published in *The Observer* 1989). Elsewhere he has expressed his admiration for Confucianism, which is an ethical code rather than a religion. His own view that religion is superstition wielded by men of power to preserve that power runs through much of the narrative.

The influence of religion in contemporary American society is rarely absent from Vidal's fiction or essays. He has been consistently willing to tread on a central American taboo by describing himself as an atheist, and, even more outrageous, by making fun of religion. The popularity of *Julian* in the United States is somewhat surprising, given its indictment of Christianity as intolerant, brutal, and ultimately evil: the Athenian philosopher Priscus muses on "the Christian hysteria which vacillates between murder of heretics on the one hand and a cringing rejection of this world on the other" (*Julian*: 85). Priscus' views are not far from those Vidal has consistently expressed. In *Live from Golgotha* he seemed determined to affront both Christians and Jews, as in his portrayal of Jesus as gross and flatulent, and his preoccupation with Jewish rites of circumcision. There are intentional echoes of the Bible in the opening line of *Life from Golgotha*: "In the beginning was the nightmare, and the knife was with Saint Paul, and the circumcision was a Jewish notion and definitely not mine."

Indeed *Live from Golgotha* seems a calculated attempt to skewer religious pieties, by its account of the Crucifixion, which becomes a major media event, as contemporary media moguls and the adorable (but resolutely heterosexual) St Timothy move across time to write and rewrite the events of the New Testament. Vidal had described the creation of a successful cult in *Messiah*; in *Golgotha* Christianity itself becomes such a cult, in which hucksterism is far more important than "truth": "First a hellfire sermon from Saint [Paul]. Then the collection. Then names and addresses for our master Holy Rolodex while the Saint would take appointments for baptisms and so on. Finally, before skipping town, he'd appoint some deacons and deaconesses and lo! and behold the First Pauline Church of Philippi would open its doors for business" (*Live from Golgotha*: 37). As Vidal plays with historical time, and its remaking and erasure, through a late twentieth-century battle to cover the Crucifixion on live television, the book reinforces his view of religion as based on the manipulation of human credulity through spectacle and superstition.

Vidal saw *Live from Golgotha* as similar to *Myra* in its satirical bite, and Baker and Gibson point out that it includes almost all of the dominant themes of the Vidalian inventions: "The present rewrites the past; politics, religion and show business are indistinguishable; sexual preference is fluid, unstable, anything but categorical; as exposed in language, late twentieth century America is dazzling for its amalgam of the pretentious and the banal . . ."[2] Other critics were less kind, seeing it as tasteless, slapstick, and self-indulgent. It is perhaps unfortunate that Vidal never made a religious figure central to his historical novels; it would have been interesting to see Mary Baker Eddy, who founded Christian Science in the post-Civil War years, and who appears briefly in *Golgotha*, as a major character in, say, *Empire*.

Little of the critical discussion of Vidal covers his critique of religion, though it is arguably the arena where the gap between him and most Americans is most apparent. The influence of fundamentalism on the current administration reveals many of the contradictions in American society on which Vidal's work provides a very particular insight. Vidal's writings on religion also provide a particular lens through which to view what some have argued is a growing disjuncture between American and European perceptions of the world. In terms of mainstream politics the current disjuncture goes back to Reagan's Presidency, when fundamentalist Protestants, firm in their belief in the coming Apocalypse, sat in the White House, alongside, one might note, a first lady with apparent faith in astrology. Ironically President Carter, who appeared a far more devout Christian than Reagan, was defeated by Reagan in part because he lost the support of many of the white "born again" Protestants of whom he was one. Neither Bush Sr nor Clinton seemed to believe particularly in apocalyptic Christianity, and one of the major marks of the second Bush Presidency is that the son seems closer to Reagan in his religious views, and their impact on his belief in America's mission, than was the father, Reagan's Vice President.

As Vidal has aged, his hostility to religion has grown, as has his recognition that it dominated and obscured much of American political life. His grandfather, like Jefferson and Lincoln, had not been a believer, and like them had remained quiet about his agnosticism to preserve his political support. In the Lowell Lecture at Harvard in 1992 Vidal called for "an all-out war on the monotheists,"[3] a reflection, perhaps, of the growing influence of the religious right in American political life. Among rich democracies the United States, along with Israel, is the only country where there is a politically significant strand of opinion that challenges the secular division between church and state, although small fundamentalist Christian parties do exist in other western democracies.

The United States remains marked by its original settlement by those fleeing religious persecution, and the creation of religion has always been a major American industry. Consider, for example, the remarkable success of churches like the Mormons, and the role of missionaries in establishing an American presence in parts of the world such as China and the Pacific. The Mormon Church, with its wealth, its missionary zeal, and its shameful history of killings, racism, and sexism, is not only a particularly American creation, it now enjoys a bizarre legitimacy through its influence within the Republican Party. Most remarkable to foreigners is the peculiarly American combination of apocalyptic beliefs with consumer capitalism, symbolized by fundamentalist preachers raising millions of dollars through television and drive-in church services. Indeed the peculiar genius of American religion is its very *Americanness*, the ability to present religion as part of the faith in progress as in the reference to "science" in deeply irrational sects like Christian Science and Scientology. Perhaps there is also a link to the particularly American belief in the right to happiness, an amendment to Locke's original formula of the right to life, liberty, *and property*, which encourages faith in the perfection of both this life and the next.

In most western liberal democracies religiosity does seem to have declined with greater affluence, but the United States remains the great exception, with a degree of religious belief and practices far exceeding that of any other affluent liberal society. Increasingly the largest cultural gap between the United States and Europe is the striking collapse of religion in the latter as compared to the thriving churches of America. At the end of 2002 one set of figures published in *The Economist* (December 21, 2002) suggested that while only 13 percent of Britons believed in the Devil 45 percent of Americans did, which almost exactly matched figures for opposition to the "unlimited right to abortion." The language of faith and prayer, commonly deployed in American political campaigns, would be met by embarrassed titters in most of the rest of the western world.

The United States is unique in that it is both genuinely secular (in terms of not enforcing any particular religious beliefs) and deeply religious. Indeed compared to my own country, Australia, the United States is far more scrupulous in maintaining the forms of separation between church and state. Australia has a far higher percentage of students in (state-subsidized) religious schools, had a former Archbishop as its Governor General, the formal head of state, and, perhaps a more trivial example, produces exclusively Christian images on its annual Christmas stamps, while the US Post Office carefully draws upon both religious and secular symbols. In Great Britain the established status of the Anglican Church means there is government interference in the governance of the church in a way that would not be countenanced in the United States, and yet there is far less emphasis on the role of religion in public life. Neither country has the large number of religious-based colleges which are important in maintaining evangelical Protestantism in America, a few of which, at least, are academically distinguished.

The absence of an established church in the United States made for a constant flourishing of new religious institutions invented to meet changing social and economic conditions. By contrast religion in England, which for most people meant the Anglican Church, was reduced to a purely symbolic presence, associated with the Establishment. The difference is reflected in the literature of the two countries: compare the constant reappearance of the clergyman as a figure of fun, from Jane Austen's Mr Collins and Canon Chasuble in *The Importance of Being Earnest* to the vicars and parsons who populate twentieth-century detective stories, with the ongoing theme of religion as passionate and central in much of American literature. It is not accidental that two of the great American plays from the second half of the twentieth century are Arthur Miller's *The Crucible* and Tony Kushner's *Angels in America*. In more recent times one can see similar shifts in European countries as the Catholic Church has lost its particular institutional status, and religion has declined as the major fault line between political parties in France, Italy, and Spain. Most of southern – though not necessarily eastern – Europe is seeing a rapid move towards the de facto secular status quo of the Protestant north.

A number of commentaries on both the 2000 and 2004 American Presidential elections drew attention to the deep division between the religious sector of the population, more likely, at least if white, to vote for Bush, and the secular population, concentrated in large cities and on the two coasts, more likely to vote for Gore and Kerry. In reality American secularism has meant the absence of any one official church, not of religion itself. When Bush's first Attorney General, John Ashcroft, used the phrase "no king but Jesus," he seemed unaware of the offense caused to non-Christians by the expression of religious beliefs by the man pledged to protect the guarantees of the Constitution.

While the United States shares with the rest of the "western" world a set of secular beliefs connected with the rise of liberal democracy and individualism, the tension between believers and secularists is deep. Horace Mann, who effectively created the American public school system, thought schools should take religious instruction "to the extremist verge to which it can be carried without invading those rights of conscience . . . guaranteed by the constitution of the state." American schizophrenia on the role of religion comes through in the bitterness of debates around prayer in schools or the inclusion of words invoking God in national symbols. Even though priests are common characters in movies – the combination of masculine attractiveness and non-availability, Leslie Halliwell observed, works well at the box office[4] – Hollywood has tended either to ignore or to sanitize religion.

Even under a President like George W. Bush, who constantly refers to the centrality of his faith, the United States remains officially a secular society. Yet there is little doubt that political decisions are constrained by the power of organized religious belief, often through the very successful mobilization of fundamentalists, who have made up a growing proportion of the Republican Party since the political realignments of the 1970s. The rhetoric of anti-Communism and the Cold War was folded into a generalized defense of faith against "godless Communism," and ever since Billy Graham was a regular attender at the White House evangelists have had extraordinary access to Presidents of both parties. The defeat of the Equal Rights Amendment, the constant attacks on abortion rights and homosexuality, moves to outlaw the teaching of evolution and of human sexuality in schools, are all deeply divisive issues in American public life, and are symbols of the divide between those whose belief leads them to wish to impose their view on others and those who are categorized, often as a term of abuse, as "secular humanists." Moreover, as Vidal has consistently argued, the tax-exempt status of many religious institutions has allowed them to accumulate considerable wealth and influence.

From the outside the connection between religiosity and violence is one of the most striking aspects of American culture. Only in South Africa does one see the same juxtaposition of gun shops and churches, and often the same people patronize both.

More secular democracies, such as those of western Europe, Australasia, and Japan, are also far more restrictive in their gun laws, have ended capital punishment, imprison smaller proportions of their population, and have less restrictive mores around sexuality, although here there are odd variations in the United States, given the way the court system has adopted positions on certain issues, such as pornography and abortion, at odds with public opinion.

As Vidal has suggested, a willingness to use military force to intervene in other parts of the world is closely linked to an evangelical view of the world, whereby the imposition of American values and institutions is seen as mandated by God's teachings. The rhetoric of evil, a favored word of both Presidents Bush Jr and Reagan, echoes their religious perception of the world. In Reagan's case this was accompanied by an apparent belief in the reality of the Apocalypse, which seems more muted in the current administration, which seems more determined to impose God's way in this world, rather than await the afterlife. (There were several, presumably intentional, echoes of biblical allusions to the Apocalypse in the speech President Bush made following the attacks of September 11.) Israel has won support from American Christians since its foundation, but this has increased dramatically in recent years, to the point where rightwing Christians are even more effective lobbyists for hardline Israeli governments than is American Jewry.

——— nine ———

GORE VIDAL'S AMERICA

Vidal has been a presence in American literary, political, and media life for over half a century. He first appeared in a newsreel in 1935 when he briefly piloted a plane as part of his father's promotion of the ease of flight; 70 years later he was giving interviews on American politics. In between he published at least 25 novels, wrote several hundred essays, a number of political pamphlets, and scores of plays and television and movie scripts. While several of his most important novels are set in the ancient world, his central preoccupation has been the creation and the destruction of the American Republic. He can claim to have written both the most substantial fictional history of the United States in his time, and, as Harold Bloom suggested in his review of *Lincoln*, to have foreshadowed the future. Through his inventions Vidal has interrogated the workings of mass media, religion, gender, and ecology in the second half of the twentieth century, and he is a pioneering figure in the gay/queer revolution that still reverberates within American political life. Through his writing, his television appearances, his political campaigns, even as the imaginary Senator in the film *Bob Roberts*, or the reactionary Law Professor in *With Honors*, Vidal has managed to lecture Americans about their nation's failings for half a century.

I wrote most of this book during the successful campaign for re-election of President George W. Bush, during which Vidal was revealed to have been remarkably prescient about a number of issues: the growth of the American Empire; the power of money in American politics; environmental degradation; the growth of

religious fanaticism and the simultaneous growth of sexual freedoms. Vidal grew up sheltered from the ravages of the Depression, and through both family connections and hard work has
always mixed with the American elite. But this has made him an
increasingly acerbic critic of what he sees as a country dominated by a ruling class, based on inherited wealth, and a foreign
policy determined on continuous imperial expansion in the
interests of that ruling class. Difficult not to see in the results
of the 2004 elections, where the Republican right gained in both
the White House and the Senate, proof of Vidal's worst fears,
namely that the impact of imperial adventure, big money, and
religious moralism would increasingly imperil the American
Republic.

Vidal sees himself as both creator and gadfly, and has enter-
tained, declaimed, pontificated, and satirized in ways that have
made him a controversial public figure for over half a century.
Perhaps he is right that the contemporary world no longer has
a place for the celebrity writer, who has been replaced by movie
and television stars as arbiters of public opinion. The particular
combination of serious novelist and political pundit, of an intellectual who remains outside the academy, is increasingly rare,
found still among a few writers and columnists for "the quality
press," but less able to grasp the popular imagination than could
Vidal or Mailer in their heyday. Yet in some ways Vidal's writings tell us more about certain aspects of contemporary America
than can more conventional journalism or scholarship, and his
achievement is to yoke imagination to observation and research
to capture certain crucial moments that define both the current
and the past history of the country. Like "T" in *The Smithsonian
Institution*, who travels back in time to remake history at a deci-
sive moment, Vidal moves across the real and imagined history
and geography of the United States to reveal what is and what
might be.

Let the last words come from an interview with Vidal, which
is now over 30 years old. After a series of conversations with
him, Gerald Clarke reflected: "Like [G. B.] Shaw, Vidal has made
a career of outraging his countrymen. Like Shaw, he is irritating,
pugnacious, yet undeniably brilliant, ever ready to share his wit

with those he disdains. And, like Shaw, who lived to the age of ninety-four, Vidal, the arbiter of our immorals [*sic*], will probably be around forever, his denunciations as pungent and as marketable in 2002 as they are in 1972."[1]

PERSONAL NOTE

I have known Gore, if not well, for 30 years, although I have been careful in writing to use only material that is on the public record. We met through chance: returning from the United States to Sydney in 1969, my copy of *Myra Breckinridge* was seized by Australian Customs as pornographic, and became the test case for a Civil Liberties case on censorship. In the subsequent trial the judge found against the book, even though the British edition, freely on sale in Australia, contained many of the passages the Crown alleged were pornographic. In his ruling Justice Levine wrote: "If, in relation to this book, I was [*sic*] to pose the question . . . 'do you think there are passages in it which are plain dirt and nothing else, introduced for the sake of dirtiness and from the sure knowledge that notoriety earned by dirtiness will command for the book a ready sale?', my answer to that question would have to be 'Yes.'"[1] Several years later Australian restrictions on "pornography" were drastically reduced.

When Vidal came to Australia in 1972 I appeared on a television discussion program with him, following which he invited me to dinner. Subsequently I was to spend time with him in both Italy and Los Angeles. This book is neither biographical nor autobiographical, but at the same time I need to acknowledge his importance in my life (which I have discussed in my memoirs, *Defying Gravity*). My first book, *Homosexual: Oppression and Liberation*, and several subsequent books drew on Vidal's writings, as was true of most of the writings of my generation of gay activists. More significant may be that mine is a reading of Vidal by a non-American, who therefore reads his work with somewhat different preconceptions and assumptions. The theme of expatriatism is one of particular interest to Australians, and is a consistent theme among writers from "settler societies"; there are many counterparts to writers such as Henry James, Gertrude Stein and Vidal among Australians, Canadians, and South Africans, although only in the last case was political persecution a genuine reason to expatriate oneself. Before I started this book I had contemplated writing about both Sumner Locke Elliott and then, briefly, the now almost forgotten actor Farley Granger, who for a short time in the late 1940s seemed to be a looming star. (Hitchcock cast him in *Rope* and *Strangers on a Train*; from the mid-1950s he moved between Italy and New York, where he still lives.) In both cases I was fascinated by the ways in which sexuality contributed to the desire to live abroad.

One suspects that Vidal's expatriatism is far more linked to his sexuality than he acknowledges, and reminiscent of several of his contemporaries such as James Baldwin. The desire to flee home for what seem freer and more cultured shores is common to most colonial writers since the eighteenth century, and even more so for those of us who are homosexual. Oscar Wilde and Somerset Maugham left England for France; a generation later Christopher Isherwood and W. H. Auden moved to the United States to avoid the war, but also because of a climate of greater sexual tolerance than that in Britain. By the time Gore was thinking of leaving the United States to settle in Europe, the United States was already becoming a destination for those in more peripheral colonies, just as in time Canada and Australia would become attractive destinations for people from more sexually repressive regimes in Asia and Latin America.

Shortly before Gore Vidal moved to Europe the Australian writer Sumner Locke Elliott went to the States for not dissimilar reasons, although unlike New York, Sydney in the early 1950s seemed at the end of the world. (Like Isherwood – and unlike Vidal – Elliott also changed his nationality.) I went to the States 15 years later, and discovered my homosexuality there, just as some Asians who come to Australia today make the same discovery. The belief that "there" is sexually freer is, often, of course, more a product of being a foreigner than of objective circumstances, and a common theme in gay experience. In 2003 I met an American who had moved to Rome, impelled by the same mix of longing to escape and to find a more civilized home that characterized Gore 50 years earlier.

Unlike Henry James or Sumner Locke Elliott, Gore only partially expatriated himself and never renounced America; he refused to learn Italian properly as he claimed he was still learning English. Vidal is somewhat of a pedant about language; he corrected my use of the term "different from" (rather than "to") in Sydney and reminded me of this ten years later. Of course not all American writers who expatriate themselves are homosexual, as Ernest Hemingway should remind us. (There is an interesting contrast to some of the abstract artists of the 1950s, such as Robert Rauschenberg and Jasper Johns, who stayed in the United States, but never revealed their sexuality.)[2] But the ongoing fascination, the love/hate relationship, with one's native country that one finds in Vidal's writings also can be found in other expatriates. The Australian Barry Humphries has created an internationally recognized alter ego, Dame Edna Everage, who is a heterosexual suburban version of Myra Breckinridge, and as preoccupied with her Australianness as Gore is with the United States.

Vidal is usually depicted as aloof, ambitious, and sardonic. He has a reputation for pugnacity, and even his admirers can find some of his writing "arch, mean, stale," to quote Ned Rorem.[3] Yet Anaïs Nin, in one of her more generous moods, wrote that she had seen his "tenderness, gentleness, the sincerity and the thoughtfulness . . . Gore in the world is another Gore. He is insatiable for power. He needs to conquer, to shine, to dominate."[4] I have always found him charming, a good host, and an entertaining and witty companion, even if determined, as he acknowledges, to control any encounter. As is true of all celebrities he dominates a room, and demands attention and appreciation. Unlike many celebrities he deserves both.

NOTES

Preface: The Writer as Social Critic

1 Kurt Vonnegut: *Playboy* interview 1973, republished in *Wampeters, Foma and Granfalloons*, London, Pan, 1975: 213.
2 "U. S. of Amnesia," interview with Marc Cooper, *L.A.Weekly*, November 5–11, 2004.

Introduction

1 J. Wenke: *Mailer's America*, Hanover, NH, University Press of New England, 1987: 237.
2 *Alladeen* was a co-production of the New York-based Builders Association and the London-based Motiroti. See the webpage www.alladeen.com.
3 Peter Bradshaw writing in *Mail and Guardian* (Johannesburg), August 15, 2003.
4 E. Fawcett and T. Thomas: *America and the Americans*, London, Collins, 1982.
5 James Michener: *The World is My Home*, London, Secker and Warburg, 1992: 412.
6 See Samuel Hines: "Political Change in America: Perspectives from the Popular Historical Novels of Michener and Vidal," in E. Yanarella and L. Sigelman: *Political Mythology and Popular Fiction*, Westport, Greenwood Press, 1988: 81–99.
7 Christopher Isherwood: *Diaries*, vol. 1, edited by Katherine Bucknell, London, Methuen, 1996: 777.

Chapter 1   Vidal's Life

1   Robin Maugham's *The Wrong People* (originally published in 1967 under a *nom de plume*) captures something of the appeal of Tangier to "bohemian" visitors from Europe and the United States.
2   John Aldridge: *After the Lost Generation*, New York, McGraw Hill, 1951: 183.
3   Sharon Clarke: *Sumner Locke Elliott: A Writing Life*, Sydney, Allen and Unwin, 1996: 212.
4   Martin Walker: *Makers of the American Century*, London, Chatto and Windus, 2000: 203.
5   Garry Wills: *John Wayne's America*, New York, Simon and Schuster, 1997: 29. Wayne continues to be discussed as a model of traditional masculinity, especially in film studies. See Steven Cohan: *Masked Men*, Bloomington, Indiana University Press, 1997: ch. 6: "Why Boys Are not Men"; John Clum: *"He's All Man,"* New York, Palgrave, 2002.
6   Tina Brown: "Tough Time for Democrats," in the *Washington Post*, December 18, 2003: C1.

Chapter 2   Celebrity

1   Peter Messant: *Ernest Hemingway*, New York, St Martin's Press, 1992: 1.
2   Diane Johnson: "Star," in the *New York Review of Books*, April 18, 1993: 25.
3   D. Porter and D. Prince: *Frommer's Italy 2004*, New York, Wiley, 2003: 657.
4   C. Wright Mills: *The Power Elite*, New York, Oxford University Press, 1956: 71–2.
5   D. Boorstin: *The Image*, New York, Atheneum, 1962.
6   Of which this series is an example. See also Chris Rojek: *Celebrity*, London, Reaktion Books, 2001; Joshua Gamson: *Claims to Fame*, Berkeley, University of California Press, 1994. On Vidal's use of television see Marcie Frank: *How to Be an Intellectual in the Age of TV*, Durham, NC, Duke University Press, 2005.
7   See C. Mallory: "Mailer and Vidal: The Big Schmooze," in *Esquire*, May, 1991.
8   Norman Mailer: *The Presidential Papers*, London, André Deutsch, 1964: 228–9.

9 Loren Glass: *Authors Inc.* New York University Press, 2004: 228.
10 Richard Posner: *Public Intellectuals*, Cambridge, MA, Harvard University Press, 2001: ch. 5, 167–220.
11 On Sontag's career see Carl Rollyson and Lisa Paddock: *Susan Sontag: The Making of an Idol*, New York, Norton, 2000.
12 Quoted by David Malouf: "Fifteen Minutes," in *Griffith Review* (Brisbane), 5, 2004: 16.
13 E.g. Loren Glass: op. cit.: 155.
14 Gerald Clarke: "Petronius Americanus," in *The Atlantic Monthly*, March 1972: 44–51.

Chapter 3   America and its History

1 Paul Johnson: *A History of the American People*, London, Weidenfeld and Nicolson, 1997: 827, 834.
2 For various accounts of the incident see George Plimpton: *Truman Capote*, New York, Doubleday, 1997: 378–83.
3 See Chris Rojek: *Frank Sinatra*, Cambridge, Polity, 2004.
4 In Gore Vidal, V. S. Pritchett, David Caute, Bruce Chatwin, Peter Conrad, and Edward Jay Epstein: *Great American Families*, New York, Norton, 1977 (first published in the *Sunday Times* magazine, London).
5 Edmund Morgan: "A Tract for the Times," in the *New York Review of Books*, December 18, 2003: 26.
6 Owen Dudley Edwards: "Fiction as History," in *Encounter*, 1985, 64: 1: 42.
7 Harry Barnard: "Essay Review: Gore Vidal: *1876*," in *Hayes Historical Journal*, 1977, 1(3): 218–19.
8 Richard Current: "Fiction as History," in *Journal of Southern History*, 1, February 1986: 52, 81.
9 There is at least one book which compares Vidal and Doctorow as historical novelists, Stephen Harris: *The Fiction of Gore Vidal and E. L. Doctorow*, Bern, Peter Lang, 2002.
10 Thomas Keneally: "Bore Vidal," in *New Republic*, July 2, 1984: 32.
11 Edmund Morris: *Dutch*, New York, Random House, 1999.
12 Susan Baker and Curtis Gibson: *Gore Vidal: A Critical Companion*, Westport, Greenwood, 1997: 136–7, 133.
13 Samuel Eliot Morrison: *The Oxford History of the American People*, New York, Oxford University Press, 1965: 356.

14 Buckner Melton: *Aaron Burr: Conspiracy to Treason*, New York, Wiley, 2001: 152. See the bibliography in this book for further reading.

15 Vidal: "A Conversation with Myself," a promotional pamphlet issued in conjunction with the paperback release of *Burr*, New York, Bantam, 1974.

16 Quoted by Jonathan Dee: "Ragtime—Review," in *Harper's*, June 1999.

17 This is quoted by Barbara Tuchman, herself a distinguished and popular non-academic historian, in *Practicing History*, New York, Knopf, 1981: 46.

18 Jane Austen: *Northanger Abbey* (1818), London, Pan, 1968: 106.

19 John Dean, who as Nixon's counsel helped bring down his Presidency over Watergate, has written a book intended to re-establish Harding's reputation: *Warren G. Harding*, New York, Times Books, 2004.

20 See "The Agreed-Upon Facts," in W. Zinsser (ed.): *Paths of Resistance: The Art and Craft of the Political Novel*, Boston, Houghton Mifflin, 1989: 146.

21 Thomas Disch: *The Dreams our Stuff is Made of*, New York, Free Press, 1998: 15.

22 Todd Gitlin: "Heroes, Fools and the Mirth of a Nation," in the *Los Angeles Times Book Review*, August 29, 2004: 6.

23 "The Agreed-Upon Facts," in William Zinsser: op. cit.: 150.

24 Ronald Steel: "The Missionary," in the *New York Review of Books*, November 20, 2003: 27.

25 Vidal: "Foreword" to Bill Kauffman: *America First! Its History, Culture and Politics*, Amherst, NY, Prometheus, 1995: 11.

26 John Walker (ed.): *Halliwell's Film and Video Guide 2003*, London, Harper Collins, 2002: 289.

27 Gore Vidal and Ian Buruma: "Pearl Harbor: An Exchange," in the *New York Review of Books*, May 17, 2001: 67.

28 Jon Gaddis: *We Now Know: Rethinking Cold War History*, Oxford, Clarendon, 1997: 35; see also James Chace: "The Winning Hand," in *New York Review of Books*, March 11, 2004: 19.

29 Thomas Fleming: *The New Dealers' War*, New York, Basic, 2001: 24.

30 David Malouf: *Made in England*, Quarterly Essay 12, Melbourne, Black, 2003: 53.

31 Christopher Hitchens: *Unacknowledged Legislation*, London, Verso, 2000: 70.

32 Interview with Katrina Heron: "Original Spin," in *Da Wired* (www.fazieditore.it), July, 1998.

33 Martin Walker: op. cit.: xii.

34 Like many Hollywood movies *Ben-Hur* had multiple writers. Credit is given in the film to the original writer, Karl Tunberg, but most of his script was rewritten by a number of authors, including Vidal and the British playwright Christopher Fry.

35 Bernard Dick: *The Apostate Angel*, New York, Random House, 1974: 60–4.

36 Garry Wills, op. cit.: 149.

37 See, for an exaggerated example, Cynthia Weber: "Something's Missing: Male Hysteria and the U.S. Invasion of Panama," in M. Zalewski and J. Parpart: *The "Man" Question in International Relations*, Boulder, Westview, 1998.

Chapter 4   Politics

1 E.g. "Gore Vidal speaks out against American Imperialism," interview with Amy Goodman (www.democracynow.org/article: pl ?sid=04/06/04).

2 "Surrealism and Patriotism: the Education of an American Novelist," in *New Left Review*, 1985, 149: 101 (interviewers identified as TA and RB). The campaign is documented in Gary Conklin's film *Gore Vidal: The Man who Said No.*

3 Jon Wiener: "The Scholar Squirrels and the National Security State: An Interview with Gore Vidal," in *Radical History Review*, 1989: 44.

4 On the famous incident at the White House see Sally B. Smith: *Grace and Power*, New York, Random House, 2004: 238–9.

5 The most vivid account of the two conventions remains Mailer's *Miami and the Siege of Chicago*, New York, Signet, 1968. Vidal's account of the Republican Convention at Miami is contained in his essays *United States.*

6 For accounts of the exchange see the long essays by Buckley ("On Experiencing Gore Vidal") and Vidal ("A Distasteful Encounter with William F. Buckley Jr.") in *Esquire*, republished in H. Hayes (ed.): *Smiling through the Apocalypse: Esquire's History of the Sixties*, New York, Crown, 1969.

7   In an interview with Hubert Juin, *Le Monde*, March 10, 1978, quoted in Nicole Broussard: *Gore Vidal l'iconoclaste*, Nanterre, Publidix, 1997: 117.

8   Gerald Clarke: "Petronivs Americanus, op. cit.: 50.

9   "Surrealism and Patriotism," op. cit.: 100.

10 Calvin Trillin: "Gadfly," in the *New Yorker*, May 10, 2004: 81.

11 Anders   Lewis: "The   Inventions   of   Gore   Vidal," FrontPageMagazine.com, January 13, 2004.

12 Bill Kauffman: op. cit.

13 Martin Amis: "Mr. Vidal: Unpatriotic Gore," in *The Moronic Inferno*, London, Jonathan Cape, 1986: 106–7 (originally published in the London *Observer*).

14 Daniel Lazare: "Skeletons in the Closet," in *The Nation*, January 5, 2004: 3.

15 Todd Gitlin: "A View from the Patriotic Left," in *Globe and Mail* (Toronto), September 10, 2002.

16 Richard Clarke: *Against All Enemies*, New York, Free Press, 2004.

17 He repeated this claim in an interview with Emily Udell: "Imperial Amnesia," in *In These Times*, November 2, 2004.

18 See David McCullough: *Truman*, New York, Simon and Schuster, 1992: 266–7.

19 Introduction to Gore Vidal et al.: *Great American Families*: 7.

20 Emily Udell: op. cit.

21 "Sullivan's Travels," in T. Mico, J. Miller-Monzon, and D. Rubel (eds.): *Past Imperfect*, New York, Holt: 219.

22 Kevin Phillips: *American Dynasty*, New York, Viking, 2004.

23 There is a copious literature on the siege of Waco. For an overview see Stuart Wright (ed.): *Armageddon in Waco*, University of Chicago Press, 1995.

24 Fiachra Gibbons: "Vidal Praises Oklahoma Bomber for Heroic Aims," in *The Guardian*, August 17, 2001.

25 Gordon Wood: "Slaves in the Family," in the *New York Times Book Review*, December 14, 2003: 10.

26 Larry Kramer: "The Sadness of Gore Vidal," in Weise 1999: 252.

27 Andrew Bacevich: *American Empire*, Cambridge, MA, Harvard University Press, 2002: 3.

28 Chalmers Johnson: *The Sorrows of Empire*, London/New York, Verso, 2004: 285.

29 Niall Ferguson: *Colossus: The Rise and Fall of the American Empire*, New York, Penguin, 2004: 4.

30 Henry Bromell: *Little America*, New York, Vintage, 2001: 23.

31 Christopher Hitchens: op. cit.: 81.
32 One example of a critique which does this is George Packer: "Paved with Good Intentions," in *Mother Jones*, July/August 2003.
33 Quoted by John Cassidy: "Goodbye to All That," in the *New Yorker*, September 15, 2003: 93.
34 Bruce Cummings: "Boundary Displacement: Area Studies and International Studies during and after the Cold War," in *Bulletin of Concerned Asian Scholars*, 1, January–March, 1997.
35 Buckley: op. cit.: 562.
36 Vidal read and reviewed several books by Domhoff, a disciple of C. Wright Mills, in 1972. See "Homage to Daniel Shays," in *United States*: 906–18, originally published in the *New York Review of Books* 1972.
37 Introduction to D. Donnelly, J. Fine, and E. Miller: *Money and Politics*, Boston, Beacon Press, 1999: xii.
38 Luke Mitchell: "Blood for Oil," in *Harper's Magazine*, July 2004: 77.
39 Gore Vidal interviewed by Amy Goodman: "The Most Un-American Speech I've Ever Heard," in *Democracy Now*, January 25, 2005 (www.democracynow.org).
40 Review, *Publisher's Weekly*, April 19, 2004.
41 C. Wright Mills: *The Sociological Imagination*, New York, Oxford University Press, 1959: 5, 7.
42 Martin Gidron: *The Severed Wing*, Livingston, AL, Livingston Press, 2000.
43 Leslie Fiedler: *Waiting for the End*, London, Cape, 1965: 97.
44 Norman Podhoretz: *My Love Affair with America*, New York, Free Press, 2000: 51 footnote.
45 Edward Alexander: "Gore Vidal's Anti-Jewish Nationalism," in *Society*, 1988, 25: 3: 77.
46 Arthur Schlesinger Jr: "The Making of a Mess," in the *New York Review*, September 23, 2004: 40–3.
47 D. Reuben: *Everything You Always Wanted to Know about Sex (but Were Afraid to Ask)*, New York, D. McKay, 1969. Reuben has also written self-help books on love, dieting, and "mental first aid."
48 Joseph Epstein: "Homo/Hetero: The Struggle for Sexual Identity," in *Harper's Magazine*, September, 1970. The demonstration at the magazine is discussed in Peter Fisher: *The Gay Mystique*, New York, Stein and Day, 1972.
49 Russell Jacoby: *The Last Intellectuals*, New York, Basic, 1987: 90.
50 "Surrealism and Patriotism", op. cit.: 96.

51 See Stimpson in Parini 1992: 197.

52 On the book and others of its time see Philip Klinker: "The 'Racial Realism' Hoax," in *The Nation*, December 14, 1998.

53 Vidal made the suggestion on the Australian Broadcasting Commission's *Four Corners* program, December 9, 1974.

54 Transcript of interview with Mark Davis, *Dateline*, SBS Television (Australia), March 14, 2003.

Chapter 5   Vidal as Writer

1 Ron Hogan: "Interview with Fred Kaplan," the Beatrice Interview 1999 (www.beatrice.com/interviews).

2 Introduction to Mark Twain: *Following the Equator and Anti-imperialist Essays*, New York, Oxford University Press, 1996: xxxiii–xxxiv.

3 Fred Kaplan: Introduction, *The Essential Gore Vidal*, New York, Random House, 1999: x–xi.

4 Quoted in the definition of "ludic," *American Heritage Dictionary*, 4th edition, New York, Houghton Mifflin, 2000.

5 Quoted in M. Mewshaw: "Inventing Calvino," in the *Los Angeles Times*, April 20, 2000.

6 Joseph O'Neill: "The Best Novelists, the Worst Movie Adaptations," in the *New York Times*, November 9, 2003.

7 Tom Wolfe: *Hooking up*, New York, Farrar, and Giroux Straus 2000: 145–71.

8 Colm Tóibín: *The Master*, New York, Scribners, 2004: 336.

9 Daniel Aaron: "What Can You Learn from a Historical Novel?" in *American Heritage*, October 1992, 43: 6: 56.

10 David Laskin: *Partisans*, University of Chicago Press, 2000: 234.

11 Quoted by Robert Kiernan: *Gore Vidal*, New York, Frederick Ungar: 137.

12 Kiernan, op. cit.: 143.

13 Walter Clemons: "Gore Vidal's 'Chronicles of America,'" in *Newsweek*, June 11, 1984.

14 Fred Kaplan: op. cit.: ix.

15 Tim Page (ed.): *The Diaries of Dawn Powell 1931–65*, South Royalton, VT, Steerforth Press, 1995: 338.

16 Spender in Parini 1992; Norman Mailer: *Advertisements for Myself*, New York, Putnam, 1959: 405.

17 Martin Amis: op. cit.: 106.

18 Harold Bloom: *The Western Canon*, New York, Harcourt Brace, 1994: 21.
19 John Lahr: "Way of the World," in the *New Yorker*, October 2, 2000: 140.
20 Christopher Hitchens: op. cit.
21 Tim Page: *Dawn Powell*, New York, Henry Holt, 1998.

Chapter 6 Sex

1 Georges-Michel Sarotte: *Like a Brother, Like a Lover*, New York, Anchor Press, 1978: 302 (originally published in French in 1976). There is a less interesting reading of the novel in Roger Austen: *Playing the Game*, Indianapolis, Bobbs Merrill, 1977: 118–25.
2 Nicole Bensoussan: op. cit. Part 1 is entitled "A Decadent Society."
3 Leslie Fiedler: "Come Back to the Raft Ag'in, Huck Honey!" in his *Collected Essays*, vol. 1, New York, Stein and Day, 1971: 149.
4 See Peter Parker: *Isherwood: A Life*, London, Picador, 2004: 572–3.
5 Philip Core: *Camp: The Lie that Tells the Truth*, New York, Delilah Books, 1984: 185.
6 See John Mitzel with Steven Abbott: *Myra and Gore*, Dorchester, MA, Manifest Destiny, 1974.
7 See David Kaufman: *Ridiculous! The Theatrical Life and Times of Charles Ludlam*, New York, Applause Books, 2002.
8 John Simon: "What Gore Remembers," in *The New Criterion on line*, December 14, 1995 (www.newcriterion.com/archive/14/dec95/simon.htm).
9 M. Dickstein: "The New Fiction," in S. Bercovitch: *The Cambridge History of American Literature* 5: 7: *1940–90*, Cambridge University Press, 1999: 147; 148–52.
10 See e.g. his comments as quoted in Charles Kaiser: *The Gay Metropolis*, Boston, Houghton Mifflin, 1997: 77.
11 See e.g. Ted Morgan: *Reds*, New York, Random House, 2003: 457.
12 Martin Amis: op. cit.: 105.
13 For an explanation of constructionist versus essentialist views of sexuality see Jeffrey Weeks: *Sexuality*, London, Routledge, 2003.
14 See the discussion in Jorg Behrendt: *Homosexuality in the Work of Gore Vidal*, Hamburg, Lit Verlag, 2002: 62–6, and Nikolai Endres: "The Pillaged Pillar: Hubris and Polis in Gore Vidal's *The City and the Pillar*," *Classical and Modern Literature*, Fall 2004, 24: 2: 47–78.

15 See the overview of male homosexual fiction 1940–69 in Michael Bronski: *Pulp Friction*, New York, St Martin's Press, 2003: 339–68.

16 David Bergman: "Fiction," in George Haggerty: *Gay Histories and Cultures: An Encyclopedia*, New York and London, Garland, 2000: 313.

17 See e.g. Athan Theoharis: *J. Edgar Hoover, Sex and Crime*, Chicago, Ivan Dee, 1995: 103–8. Interestingly Theoharis queries the widely held belief that Hoover was homosexual, although his book reveals little understanding of the complexity of the description.

18 Vito Russo: *The Celluloid Closet*, New York, Harper and Row, 1987 (rev. edn): 117.

19 Stanley Kaufmann: "Homosexual Drama and Its Disguises," in the *New York Times*, January 23, 1966. See the discussion in Fintan O'Toole: "These Illusions Are Real," in the *New York Review of Books*, September 23, 2004: 44.

20 See Dennis Altman: *The Homosexualization of America*, New York, St Martin's Press, 1981.

21 For the recent development of modern western forms of homo-sexual identity see George Chauncey: *Gay New York*, New York, Basic, 1994. On the "globalization" of such identities see Dennis Altman: *Global Sex*, University of Chicago Press, 2001.

22 See David Johnson: *The Lavender Scare*, University of Chicago Press, 2004.

23 See for example Martin Duberman: *Cures: A Gay Man's Odyssey*, New York, Dutton, 1991.

24 W. I. Scobie: Interview with Vidal, *The Advocate* (1977), republished in Mark Thompson (ed.): *Long Road to Freedom*, New York, St Martin's Press, 1994: 151.

25 E.g. D. Bergman (ed.): *The Violet Quill Reader*, New York, St Martin's Press, 1994: xiv.

26 Gregory Woods: *A History of Gay Literature*, New Haven, CT, Yale University Press, 1998: 418: n.29.

27 "Edmund White speaks to Edmund White," in *Review of Contemporary Fiction*, Fall 1996, 16: 3.

28 See Edmund White's essay "More History, Less Nature," in the *Times Literary Supplement*, July 25, 2003, in which he writes of the role of the historical novel in ways that are not dissimilar to those of Vidal (who is not mentioned).

29 Eve Kosofsky Sedgwick: *Epistemology of the Closet*, Berkeley, University of California Press, 1990: 146.

30 Robert Corber: *Homosexuality in Cold War America*, Durham, N.C., Duke University Press, 1997, esp. ch. 5.
31 Bert Archer: *The End of Gay*, London, Fusion, 2002: 23.
32 John Mitzel with Steven Abbott: op. cit.
33 "An Interview with Gore Vidal" by Harry Kloman, *The Gore Vidal Index* (www.pitt.edu/~kloman/vidal.html).

Chapter 7   Hollywood

1 Richard Schickel: *Intimate Strangers*, New York, Forum, 1986: 46.
2 Louis Menand: "Brainwashed," in the *New Yorker*, September 15, 2003: 88.
3 Roger Angell: "Movie Struck," in the *New Yorker*, October 20, 2003: 66.
4 See discussion of *Bob Roberts* in P. J. Davies: "Hollywood in Elections and Elections in Hollywood," in P. Davies and P. Wells: *American Film and Politics from Reagan to Bush Jr*, Manchester University Press, 2002: 58–9.
5 Robert Kiernan: op. cit.: 94.
6 David Thomson: *The New Biographical Dictionary of Film*, New York, Knopf, 2002: 576.
7 See Vidal: "Introduction" to *Kalki*, London, Abacus, 1993: viii–ix.
8 Larry May: *The Big Tomorrow*, University of Chicago Press, 2000: 273–81.
9 Jack Dann: *The Rebel*, New York, Harper Collins, 2004: 58.
10 Mike Davis: *Ecology of Fear* New York, Metropolitan Press: 310–11. There is a similar omission of Vidal in the otherwise good book by David Fine: *Imagining Los Angeles*, University of New Mexico Press, 2000.

Chapter 8   Religion

1 "Julian the Apostate," *Catholic Encyclopedia*, vol. 8, online edition, 2003 (www.newadvent.org/cathen).
2 Baker and Gibson: op. cit.: 183.
3 Vidal: "America First? America Last? America at Last?" Lowell Lecture, Harvard University, April 20, 1992.

4 Leslie Halliwell: *Halliwell's Filmgoers Companion*, 8th edn, London, Granada, 1984: 502.

Chapter 9   Gore Vidal's America

1 Gerald Clarke: op. cit.: 51.

Personal Note

1 Judgment of His Honor Judge Levine in the NSW District Court Sydney, April 16, 1970.
2 See Jonathan Katz: "The Silent Camp: Queer Resistance and the Rise of Pop Art," in *Visions of a Future: Art and Art History in Changing Contexts*, edited by Hans-Jorg Heusser and Kornelia Imesch, Zurich, Swiss Institute for Art Research, 2004: 147–58.
3 Ned Rorem: *Lies: A Diary 1986–99*, Washington, DC, Counterpoint, 2002: 142.
4 G. Stuhlmann (ed.): *The Journals of Anaïs Nin 1944–7*, London, Peter Owen, 1972: 140, 142.

REFERENCES

Along with a few key works about him, Vidal's own works are referred to in the text and I have used the following editions. As many of his novels have been reissued, sometimes with editorial changes – a recent edition of *Creation*, for example, restores five chapters cut from the original manuscript and one edition of *Williwaw* retitled it *Dangerous Voyage* – this can be somewhat confusing. The original British edition of *Myra Breckinridge* included cuts to satisfy the censors, restored in later editions. A number of his essays appear in more than one collection, and his most recent political books have tended to be largely reprints of earlier articles. Where I have cited a collection I have also provided the original date and place of the essay.

Vidal's works cited

The City and the Pillar (originally published 1948), New York, Signet, 1950; revised edition, New York, Signet, 1965.

The Season of Comfort (first published 1949), London, Abacus, 1997.

The Judgment of Paris (first published 1952), published as *The Judgement of Paris*, London, Panther, 1974.

Death before Bedtime (as Edgar Box) (first published 1953), New York, Signet, 1954.

Messiah (first published 1954), London, Panther, 1973.

Visit to a Small Planet and Other Television Plays, Boston, Little, Brown, 1956.

The Best Man (1959, first produced 1960), New York, Signet, 1964.

Romulus (1961, first produced 1962), Dramatists Play Service, 1962.

Julian (first published 1964), London, Panther, 1972.

Washington, D.C. (originally published 1967), New York, Signet, 1968.

Myra Breckinridge (first published 1968): quotes are taken from *Myra Breckinridge and Myron*, London, Abacus, 1993.

Two Sisters (first published 1970), London, Panther, 1972.

An Evening with Richard Nixon (first produced 1971), New York, Random House, 1972.

Burr (first published 1973), London, Panther, 1974.

Myron (first published 1974), London, Panther, 1975.

1876, New York, Random House, 1976.

Matters of Fact and of Fiction: Essays 1973–6, London, Heinemann, 1977.

Kalki (first published 1978), London, Abacus, 1993.

Duluth, New York, Random House, 1983.

Lincoln, New York, Random House, 1984.

Empire (first published 1987), London, Abacus, 1994.

Hollywood, London, André Deutsch, 1989.

A View from the Diners Club, London, André Deutsch, 1991.

Screening History, London, André Deutsch, 1992.

Live from Golgotha (first published 1992), London, Abacus, 1993.

United States: Essays 1952–92 (first published 1993), London, Abacus, 1994.

Palimpsest: A Memoir, New York, Random House, 1995.

Virgin Islands: A Dependency of the United States: Essays 1992–7 (first published 1997), London, Abacus, 1998.

The Smithsonian Institution, New York, Random House, 1998.

The American Presidency, Monroe, ME, Odonian Press, 1998.

The Golden Age, New York, Random House, 2000.

The Last Empire: Essays 1992–2001 (first published 2001), London, Abacus, 2002.

Perpetual War for Perpetual Peace: How We Got to Be So Hated, New York, Thunder's Mouth Press, 2002.

Dreaming War: Blood for Oil and the Cheney-Bush Junta, New York, Thunder's Mouth Press, 2002.

Inventing a Nation, New Haven, Yale University Press, 2003.

Imperial America, New York, Nation Books, 2004.

Key works about Vidal cited

Fred Kaplan: *Gore Vidal: A Biography*, New York, Random House, 1999.

Jay Parini (ed.): *Gore Vidal: Writer against the Grain*, New York, Columbia University Press, 1992.

References

Robert Stanton and Gore Vidal (eds.): *Views from a Window: Conversations with Gore Vidal*, Secaucus, NJ, Lyle Stuart, 1980.

Donald Weise (ed.): *Gore Vidal: Sexually Speaking*, San Francisco, Cleis, 1999.

There is an excellent website, maintained by Harry Kloman: *The Gore Vidal Index* (www.pitt.edu/~kloman/vidalframe.html), from which a certain amount of factual information has been obtained. Vidal's papers are held at the Houghton Library at Harvard, and are currently being sorted and catalogued.

CHRONOLOGY

Year	US President	Gore Vidal's publications[1]	Other publications, plays, and films
1946	Truman	Williwaw	The Member of the Wedding (Carson McCullers)
			All the King's Men (Robert Penn Warren)
1947		In a Yellow Wood	A Streetcar Named Desire (Tennessee Williams)
1948		The City and the Pillar	The Naked and the Dead (Norman Mailer)
			Other Voices, Other Rooms (Truman Capote)
			The Lady from Shanghai (*dir.* Orson Welles)
1949		The Season of Comfort	The Man with the Golden Arm (Nelson Algren)
		A Search for the King	
1950		Dark Green, Bright Red	
1951			Catcher in the Rye (J. D. Salinger)
1952		The Judgment of Paris	From Here to Eternity (James Jones)
		Death in the Fifth Position*	
1953	Eisenhower	Death before Bedtime*	Invisible Man (Ralph Ellison)
			The Crucible (Arthur Miller)

Year	US President	Gore Vidal's publications[1]	Other publications, plays, and films
1954	Eisenhower	Messiah	The Old Man and the Sea (Ernest Hemingway)
		Death Likes It Hot*	The Ponder Heart (Eudora Welty)
			Rear Window (*dir.* Alfred Hitchcock)
			On the Waterfront (*dir.* Elia Kazan)
1955			Lolita (Vladimir Nabokov)
			The Man in the Grey Flannel Suit (Sloan Wilson)
			Cat on a Hot Tin Roof (Tennessee Williams)
			The Talented Mr Ripley (Patricia Highsmith)
			Rebel Without a Cause (*dir.* Nicholas Ray)
			The Seven Year Itch (*dir.* William Wilder)
1956		Visit to a Small Planet and Other Television Plays	Giovanni's Room (James Baldwin)
		A Thirsty Evil (stories)	
		The Catered Affair (screenplay)	
1957		Visit to a Small Planet (play)	On the Road (Jack Kerouac)
			Catch-22 (Joseph Heller)
			Atlas Shrugged (Ayn Rand)
			West Side Story (Leonard Bernstein/Stephen Sondheim)
			Jailhouse Rock (*dir.* Richard Thorpe)
1959		The Best Man (play)	Advertisements for Myself (Norman Mailer)

Year	US President	Gore Vidal's publications[1]	Other publications, plays, and films
	Eisenhower	Ben-Hur (screenplay)	The Naked Lunch (William Burroughs)
		Suddenly, Last Summer (screenplay)	Some Like It Hot (*dir.* Billy Wilder)
1960			Psycho (*dir.* Alfred Hitchcock)
1961	Kennedy	Romulus (play/ adaptation)	Stranger in a Strange Land (Robert Heinlein)
			The Hustler (*dir.* Robert Rossen)
1962		Rocking the Boat (essays)	Another Country (James Baldwin)
			Who's Afraid of Virginia Woolf? (Edward Albee)
			One Flew over the Cuckoo's Nest (Ken Kesey)
1963			The Group (Mary McCarthy)
			City of Night (John Rechy)
			Dr Strangelove (*dir.* Stanley Kubrick)
1964	Johnson	Julian	Herzog (Saul Bellow)
			The Feminine Mystique (Betty Friedan)
1965			In Cold Blood (Truman Capote)
1966		Is Paris Burning? (screenplay)	The Confessions of Nat Turner (William Styron)
			Against Interpretation (Susan Sontag)
			Bonnie and Clyde (*dir.* Arthur Penn)
1967		Washington, D.C.	

Year	US president	Gore Vidal's publications[1]	Other publications, plays, and films
1968	Johnson	Myra Breckinridge	Couples (John Updike) Armies of the Night (Norman Mailer) Expensive People (Joyce Carol Oates)
1969	Nixon	Reflections upon a Sinking Ship (essays)	Portnoy's Complaint (Philip Roth) Hair: a Musical (Gerome Ragni, James Rado, and Galt MacDermot)
1970		Two Sisters	Sexual Politics (Kate Millett) M*A*S*H (*dir.* Robert Altman) The Godfather (*dir.* Francis Ford Coppola)
1971		An Evening with Richard Nixon (play) Homage to Daniel Shays (essays)	
1973		Burr	Fear of Flying (Erica Jong) Breakfast of Champions (Kurt Vonnegut)
1974	Ford	Myron	Gravity's Rainbow (Thomas Pynchon)
1975			Nashville (*dir.* Robert Altman)
1976		1876	Ragtime (E. L. Doctorow) Interview with the Vampire (Anne Rice) All the President's Men (*dir.* Alan J. Pakula)
1977	Carter	Matters of Fact and Fiction (essays)	Song of Solomon (Toni Morrison) Falconer (John Cheever) Star Wars (*dir.* George Lucas)

Year	US President	Gore Vidal's publications[1]	Other publications, plays, and films
	Carter		Close Encounters of the Third Kind (*dir*. Steven Spielberg)
			Annie Hall (*dir*. Woody Allen)
1978		Kalki	Tales of the City (Armistead Maupin)
			The World According to Garp (John Irving)
1979			Sweeney Todd (Stephen Sondheim)
			Apocalypse Now (*dir*. Francis Ford Coppola)
1980			Sophie's Choice (William Styron)
			A Boy's Own Story (Edmund White)
1981	Reagan	Creation	
1982		The Second American Revolution (essays)	Rabbit is Rich (John Updike)
1983		Duluth	The Color Purple (Alice Walker)
1984		Lincoln	
1985		Vidal in Venice (with George Armstrong)	
1986			World's Fair (E. L. Doctorow)
			Neuromancer (William Gibson)
1987		Empire	The Bonfire of the Vanities (Tom Wolfe)
			Less Than Zero (Brett Easton Ellis)
1988		At Home (essays)	Born on the Fourth of July (*dir*. Oliver Stone)

Year	US President	Gore Vidal's publications[1]	Other publications, plays, and films
1989	Bush Sr	Hollywood	Angels in America (Tony Kushner)
1991		A View from the Diners Club (essays)	Harlot's Ghost (Norman Mailer)
1992		Screening History (essays)	The Secret History (Donna Tartt)
		Live from Golgotha	The Shipping News (E. Annie Proulx)
1993	Clinton		
1994			Forrest Gump (*dir*. Robert Zemeckis)
			Pulp Fiction (*dir*. Quentin Tarantino)
1995		Palimpsest (memoirs)	Fargo (*dir*. Joel Coen)
1996		The American Presidency (1996–8; pamphlet, originally a television series)	In the Beauty of the Lilies (John Updike)
1998		The Smithsonian Institution	
1999			Dutch (Edmund Morris)
			Fight Club (*dir*. David Fincher)
			American Beauty (*dir*. Sam Mendes)
2000		The Golden Age	
2001	Bush Jr	The Last Empire (essays)	The Corrections (Jonathan Franzen)
2002		Dreaming War (pamphlet)	
		Perpetual War for Perpetual Peace (pamphlet)	

Year	US President	Gore Vidal's publications[1]	Other publications, plays, and films
2003	Bush Jr	Inventing a Nation (essay)	Fanny: A Fiction (Edmund White)
2004		Imperial America (essay)	The Plot against America (Philip Roth)

[1] This list does not include reissues, even where there may have been significant modifications to the text, the many television plays and adaptations, or the several books of interviews with Vidal that exist.
* As Edward Box.

GENERAL INDEX

Sondheim, Stephen 43
Sontag, Susan 19, 24, 25, 48, 105, 120, 131
Sorrows of Empire, The (Johnson) 91
Sousa, John Philip 43
South Africa 92–3, 171
Soviet Union 56, 57–8, 77
Spanish-American War 43, 158
Spartan, The (Snedeker) 114
Spender, Stephen 123
Spock, Benjamin 75
Sprague, William (Governor) 86
Stallone, Sylvester 63
Stanwyck, Barbara 157
Star's Progress, A (Vidal as Everard) 135
Star Wars (film) 47
Steel, Ronald 50
Stein, Gertrude 177
Steinbeck, John 151
Stepford Wives, The (film) 68
Stephenson, Neal 125
Stevenson, Adlai 13, 97
Stimpson, Catherine 132, 134
Stinnett, Robert 52, 53
Stone, Oliver 87, 143
Stonewall Riots 133
Stoppard, Tom 55
Strange Love of Martha Ivers, The (film) 157
Strangers on a Train (film) 36, 177
Students for Democratic Society 73
Sturges, Preston 85
Styron, William 119
Suddenly Last Summer (film) 12, 143, 156
Suetonius 14, 139
Sullivan's Travels (film) 85–6

Supreme Court 43, 88, 137
Susskind, David 67
Sweden 137

Take Me Out (Greenberg) 130
Talented Mr Ripley, The (film) 1
Tales of the City (Maupin) 164
Tangier 10–11, 180 n. 1
Tatum, James 117
Tell Me How Long the Train's Been Gone (Baldwin) 150
Terre Haute (White) 148
That Hamilton Woman (film) 52
Theater of the Ridiculous 133
Thernstrom, Stephen and Abigail 107
Thirsty Evil, A (Vidal) 142
Thomson, David 157
Tilden, Bill 128
Time (magazine) 18, 26
Time's Arrow (Amis) 55
Tobacco Road (film) 160
Tóibín, Colm 119
Tolson, Clyde 31
Tom Sawyer (Twain) 113
Tonight Show, The 161
Tootsie (film) 133
Trevelyan, George 41
Trilateral Commission 87
Trimble, Jimmie 8, 54, 114, 151
Tripp, C. A. 140
Trollope, Frances 148
Truman, Harry (President) 29, 30, 56, 57–8, 62, 65, 69, 83, 86, 92, 94
Truman, Margaret 54, 70
Tuchman, Barbara 182 n. 17
Tunberg, Karl 182 n. 34
Twain, Mark 17, 112–13
Twelve Caesars, The (Suetonius) 139

INDEX OF FICTIONAL CHARACTERS

[Note: some of these are real people, who might also appear above. They are listed as fictional where they are mentioned predominantly as literary rather than historical figures; e.g., the picture of Lincoln in the novel of that name is meant to be historically accurate, whereas the Lincoln in *The Smithsonian Institution* is clearly an invention.]